®

MW00719761

References for the Rest of Us! ®

COMPUTER BOOK SERIES FROM IDG

Are you intimidated and confused by computers? Do you find that traditional manuals are overloaded with technical details you'll never use? Do your friends and family always call you to fix simple problems on their PCs? Then the *...For Dummies®* computer book series from IDG Books Worldwide is for you.

...For Dummies books are written for those frustrated computer users who know they aren't really dumb but find that PC hardware, software, and indeed the unique vocabulary of computing make them feel helpless. *...For Dummies* books use a lighthearted approach, a down-to-earth style, and even cartoons and humorous icons to diffuse computer novices' fears and build their confidence. Lighthearted but not lightweight, these books are a perfect survival guide for anyone forced to use a computer.

> *"I like my copy so much I told friends; now they bought copies."*
>
> **Irene C., Orwell, Ohio**

> *"Quick, concise, nontechnical, and humorous."*
>
> **Jay A., Elburn, Illinois**

> *"Thanks, I needed this book. Now I can sleep at night."*
>
> **Robin F., British Columbia, Canada**

Already, hundreds of thousands of satisfied readers agree. They have made *...For Dummies* books the #1 introductory level computer book series and have written asking for more. So, if you're looking for the most fun and easy way to learn about computers, look to *...For Dummies* books to give you a helping hand.

™

IDG BOOKS
WORLDWIDE

7/96r

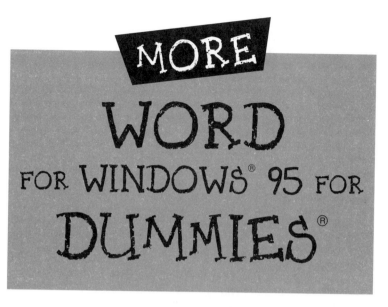

MORE

WORD
FOR WINDOWS® 95 FOR
DUMMIES®

by Doug Lowe

IDG
BOOKS
WORLDWIDE

IDG Books Worldwide, Inc.
An International Data Group Company

Foster City, CA ♦ Chicago, IL ♦ Indianapolis, IN ♦ Southlake, TX

MORE Word For Windows® 95 For Dummies®

Published by
IDG Books Worldwide, Inc.
An International Data Group Company
919 E. Hillsdale Blvd.
Suite 400
Foster City, CA 94404
www.idgbooks.com (IDG Books Worldwide Web Site)
http://www.dummies.com (Dummies Press Web Site)

Library of Congress Catalog Card No.: 96-76363

ISBN: 1-56884-608-8

Printed in the United States of America

10 9 8 7 6 5 4 3 2

1A/RY/QZ/ZW/IN

Distributed in the United States by IDG Books Worldwide, Inc.

Distributed by Macmillan Canada for Canada; by Contemporanea de Ediciones for Venezuela; by Distribuidora Cuspide for Argentina; by CITEC for Brazil; by Ediciones ZETA S.C.R. Ltda. for Peru; by Editorial Limusa SA for Mexico; by Transworld Publishers Limited in the United Kingdom and Europe; by Academic Bookshop for Egypt; by Levant Distributors S.A.R.L. for Lebanon; by Al Jassim for Saudi Arabia; by Simron Pty. Ltd. for South Africa; by Pustak Mahal for India; by The Computer Bookshop for India; by Toppan Company Ltd. for Japan; by Addison Wesley Publishing Company for Korea; by Longman Singapore Publishers Ltd. for Singapore, Malaysia, Thailand, and Indonesia; by Unalis Corporation for Taiwan; by WS Computer Publishing Company, Inc. for the Philippines; by WoodsLane Pty. Ltd. for Australia; by WoodsLane Enterprises Ltd. for New Zealand. Authorized Sales Agent: Anthony Rudkin Associates for the Middle East and North Africa.

For general information on IDG Books Worldwide's books in the U.S., please call our Consumer Customer Service department at 800-762-2974. For reseller information, including discounts and premium sales, please call our Reseller Customer Service department at 800-434-3422.

For information on where to purchase IDG Books Worldwide's books outside the U.S., please contact our International Sales department at 415-655-3172 or fax 415-655-3295.

For information on foreign language translations, please contact our Foreign & Subsidiary Rights department at 415-655-3021 or fax 415-655-3281.

For sales inquiries and special prices for bulk quantities, please contact our Sales department at 415-655-3200 or write to the address above.

For information on using IDG Books Worldwide's books in the classroom or for ordering examination copies, please contact our Educational Sales department at 800-434-2086 or fax 817-251-8174.

For authorization to photocopy items for corporate, personal, or educational use, please contact Copyright Clearance Center, 222 Rosewood Drive, Danvers, MA 01923, or fax 508-750-4470.

is a trademark under exclusive license to IDG Books Worldwide, Inc., from International Data Group, Inc.

About the Author

Doug Lowe has written more than 20 computer books, including *PowerPoint For Windows 95 For Dummies* and *Word For Windows 95 Secrets*. Doug enjoys presenting boring technostuff in a style that is both entertaining and enlightening. He is a contributing editor for the magazine *DOS Resource Guide*.

Welcome to the world of IDG Books Worldwide.

IDG Books Worldwide, Inc., is a subsidiary of International Data Group, the world's largest publisher of computer-related information and the leading global provider of information services on information technology. IDG was founded more than 25 years ago and now employs more than 8,500 people worldwide. IDG publishes more than 270 computer publications in over 75 countries (see listing below). More than 90 million people read one or more IDG publications each month.

Launched in 1990, IDG Books Worldwide is today the #1 publisher of best-selling computer books in the United States. We are proud to have received eight awards from the Computer Press Association in recognition of editorial excellence and three from *Computer Currents'* First Annual Readers' Choice Awards. Our best-selling ...*For Dummies*® series has more than 25 million copies in print with translations in 30 languages. IDG Books Worldwide, through a joint venture with IDG's Hi-Tech Beijing, became the first U.S. publisher to publish a computer book in the People's Republic of China. In record time, IDG Books Worldwide has become the first choice for millions of readers around the world who want to learn how to better manage their businesses.

Our mission is simple: Every one of our books is designed to bring extra value and skill-building instructions to the reader. Our books are written by experts who understand and care about our readers. The knowledge base of our editorial staff comes from years of experience in publishing, education, and journalism — experience which we use to produce books for the '90s. In short, we care about books, so we attract the best people. We devote special attention to details such as audience, interior design, use of icons, and illustrations. And because we use an efficient process of authoring, editing, and desktop publishing our books electronically, we can spend more time ensuring superior content and spend less time on the technicalities of making books.

You can count on our commitment to deliver high-quality books at competitive prices on topics you want to read about. At IDG Books Worldwide, we continue in the IDG tradition of delivering quality for more than 25 years. You'll find no better book on a subject than one from IDG Books Worldwide.

John J. Kilcullen

John Kilcullen
President and CEO
IDG Books Worldwide, Inc.

Author's Acknowledgments

I'd like to thank project editor Tim Gallan for keeping things on track throughout this project, and Leah Cameron, Mary Goodwin, and Jim McCarter for the technical and editorial prowess. I'd also like to thank Kezia Endsley, Kristin Cocks, Becky Whitney, Michael Partington, and Michael Simsic for their help with the first edition.

Oh, and thanks to Margie Nunez, Linda Wilson, and Jason Simmons for various and sundry contributions. And thanks also to Dan Gookin for authoring the most excellent *Word For Windows 95 For Dummies,* without which this sequel would not be possible.

Dedication

To Bethany

Publisher's Acknowledgments

We're proud of this book; please send us your comments about it by using the Reader Response Card at the back of the book or by e-mailing us at `feedback/dummies@idgbooks.com`. Some of the people who helped bring this book to market include the following:

Acquisitions, Development, & Editorial

Project Editor: Tim Gallan

Acquisitions Editor: Tammy Goldfeld

Copy Editors: Leah P. Cameron, Mary Goodwin

Technical Reviewer: Jim McCarter

Editorial Manager: Kristin A. Cocks

Editorial Assistant: Constance Carlisle

Production

Project Coordinator: Debbie Sharpe

Layout and Graphics:
Brett Black, Cheryl Denski, Elizabeth Cárdenas-Nelson, Maridee V. Ennis, Jane Martin, Theresa Sánchez-Baker, Gina Scott, Michael Sullivan

Proofreaders: Nancy L. Reinhardt, Robert Springer, Carrie Voorhis, Karen York

Indexer: Sherry Massey

General & Administrative

IDG Books Worldwide, Inc.: John Kilcullen, President & CEO; Steven Berkowitz, COO & Publisher

Dummies, Inc.: Milissa Koloski, Executive Vice President & Publisher

Dummies Technology Press & Dummies Editorial: Diane Graves Steele, Associate Publisher; Judith A. Taylor, Brand Manager

Dummies Trade Press: Kathleen A. Welton, Vice President & Publisher; Stacy S. Collins, Brand Manager

IDG Books Production for Dummies Press: Beth Jenkins, Production Director; Cindy L. Phipps, Supervisor of Project Coordination; Kathie Schutte, Supervisor of Page Layout; Shelley Lea, Supervisor of Graphics and Design

Dummies Packaging & Book Design: Patti Sandez, Packaging Assistant; Kavish+Kavish, Cover Design

◆

The publisher would like to give special thanks to Patrick J. McGovern, without whom this book would not have been possible.

◆

Contents at a Glance

Cartoons at a Glance

By Rich Tennant • Fax: 508-546-7747 • E-mail: the5wave@tiac.net

page 7

page 255

page 331

page 141

page 1

page 213

Table of Contents

Introduction

Welcome to *MORE Word For Windows 95 For Dummies*, the book for people who lie awake at night pondering questions of cosmic significance, such as "What if my head explodes?" and "How do you do footnotes in Word?"

This book won't help you with the first question, but it surely will help with the second, and dozens of other questions like it. What the heck are styles? How do you make an outline? Is there happiness to be found in the Mail Merge feature?

If such questions boil your blood, this book is just what you need. It lets you catch your breath and count to ten before putting your fist through the monitor. After it calms you down, it shows you how to use the so-called "advanced features." When you're done, you'll say, "Geez Louise, that wasn't so bad. Why was I so upset?"

The 5th Wave
By Rich Tennant

"WE SHOULD HAVE THIS FIXED IN VERSION 2."

This book talks about "advanced" Word for Windows features in everyday —
and often irreverent — terms. No lofty prose here. I have no Pulitzer Prize
expectations for this book, although I was kind of hoping it would be made into
a major motion picture starring Harrison Ford so that maybe I could retire.
Other than that, my goal is to make an otherwise dull and lifeless subject at
least tolerable, if not kind of fun.

About This Book

This isn't the kind of book you pick up and read from start to finish, as if it were
a cheap novel. If I ever see you reading it at the beach, I'll kick sand in your face.
This book is more like a reference; it's the kind of book that you can pick up,
turn to just about any page, and start reading. I've included 33 chapters, each
one covering a specific aspect of using Word for Windows — like using styles,
drawing pictures, creating macros, or making an index. Just turn to the chapter
you're interested in and start reading.

Each chapter is divided into self-contained chunks, all related to the major
theme of the chapter.

For example, the chapter on creating an index contains nuggets like these:

 ✔ Marking index entries

 ✔ Creating an index

 ✔ Marking a range of pages

 ✔ Building an index from a list of words

 ✔ Creating subentries

 ✔ Creating cross-references

 ✔ Updating an index

You don't have to memorize anything in this book. It's a "need-to-know" book:
you pick it up when you need to know something. Need to know how to create a
three-column layout? Pick up the book. Need to know how to generate a Table
of Contents? Pick up the book. Otherwise, put it down and get on with your life.

What about Word For Windows 95 For Dummies?

Ah . . . now we're getting somewhere. This book is actually the sequel to *Word For Windows 95 For Dummies* by Dan Gookin. It picks up where Dan's book leaves off. If you're totally new to Word for Windows, you should probably check out Dan's book first. (Well, actually, you should get *both* books!)

As a special bonus and at no extra charge, you'll find references to mail merge topics covered not only in this book, but in *Word For Windows 95 For Dummies* as well.

How to Use This Book

This book works like a reference. Start with the topic you want to learn about; look for it in the table of contents or in the index to get going. The table of contents is detailed enough so that you should be able to find most of the topics you're looking for. If not, turn to the index where you'll find even more detail.

Once you've found your topic in the table of contents or the index, turn to the area of interest and read as much or as little as you need or want. Then close the book and get on with it.

On occasion, this book directs you to use specific keyboard shortcuts to get things done. When you see something like this,

Ctrl+Z

it means hold down the Ctrl key while pressing the *Z* key, and then release both together. Don't type the plus sign.

Sometimes I'll tell you to use a menu command, like this:

File⇨Open

This line means use the keyboard or mouse to open the File menu; then select the Open command. (The underlined letters are the keyboard *hot keys* for the command. To use them, first press the Alt key. In the preceding example, you would press and release the Alt key, press and release the *F* key, and then press and release the *O* key.)

Whenever I describe a message or any other information that you see on the screen, it will look like this:

```
Are we having fun yet?
```

Anything you are instructed to type appears in bold, like this: Type **b:setup** in the Run dialog box. Type exactly what you see, with or without spaces.

Another little nicety about this book is that when you are directed to click one of the many little buttons that litter the Word for Windows screen, a picture of the button appears in the margin. This way, you can see what the button looks like to help you find it on the screen.

This book rarely directs you elsewhere for information — just about everything you need to know about using Word for Windows is right here. On occasion, I'll suggest you turn to *Windows 95 For Dummies* (by Andy Rathbone) for more specific information about global warming and Klingon relaxation techniques — oops — I mean Windows 95. I may also refer you to *Word For Windows 95 For Dummies* on occasion. These books are published by IDG Books Worldwide.

Oh, I almost forgot. In the interest of saving trees, I will frequently abbreviate *Word for Windows 95* to simply *WinWord* or sometimes *Word 95* or even *Word 7*.

Foolish Assumptions

I'm going to make only three assumptions about you:

1. You use a computer.
2. You use Windows 95.
3. You use Word for Windows 95.

Nothing else. I don't assume that you're a computer guru who knows how to change a controller card or configure memory for optimal usage. Such computer chores are best handled by people who *like* computers. Hopefully you are on speaking terms with such a person. Do your best to keep it that way.

How This Book Is Organized

Inside this book, you find five parts arranged into chapters. Each chapter is broken down into sections that cover various aspects of the chapter's main subject. The chapters are arranged in a logical sequence, so it makes sense to read them in order if you want. But you don't have to read it that way. You can flip the book open to any page and start reading.

Here's the lowdown on what's in each of the five parts:

Part I: Wait! There's More!

The chapters in this part dive head-first into the subtle nuances of WinWord features that you thought you already knew all about: character and paragraph formatting, styles, templates, and so on. You'll be so excited about the new things you discover in these chapters that you'll want to write home, or maybe even call.

Part II: WinWord's Gee-Whiz Desktop Publishing Features

WinWord is a surprisingly good desktop publishing program — good enough so that you can create pretty fancy newsletters, brochures, and other documents without the need for a separate desktop publishing program. The chapters in this part show you how.

Part III: Making WinWord Work the Way You Do

This part shows you how to customize WinWord by setting its many options, controlling the various button bars that appear on-screen, and creating simple macros to automate routine chores.

Part IV: I Always Wondered How to Do That

This part shows you how to use those features you've heard about but never had the nerve to try.

Part V: Shortcuts and Tips Galore

When it comes to WinWord, you can always learn more shortcuts. Some of them are even kind of fun.

Icons Used in This Book

This is my favorite icon because it means that a step-by-step explanation of how to do something is coming up.

Watch out! Some technical drivel is just around the corner. Read only if your pocket protector is firmly attached.

Pay special attention to this icon — it lets you know that some particularly useful tidbit is at hand, perhaps a shortcut or a way of using a command you might not have considered.

Danger! Danger! Danger! Stand back, Will Robinson!

Did I tell you about the memory course I took?

Pay attention; something interesting lurks nearby.

Word For Windows 95 For Dummies has a whole part devoted to lists of tens: "Ten Commandments of WinWord," "Ten Weird Things You Probably Don't Know About," and so on. These Tens lists have become sort of a tradition in the . . . *For Dummies* books. The *MORE . . . For Dummies* books don't have these chapters, but this book has the next best thing: Tens lists right in the chapters. For example, the chapter on formatting characters and paragraphs has "Ten Commandments of Formatting." The chapter on styles has "Ten Points to Remember about Styles." These Tens lists are set off by this tell-tale icon.

Where to Go from Here

Yes, you can get there from here. With this book in hand, you're ready to charge full speed into the strange and wonderful world of WinWord. Browse through the table of contents and decide where you want to start. Be bold! Be courageous! Be adventurous! Above all else, have fun!

Part I

Wait! There's More!

The 5th Wave — **By Rich Tennant**

"GENTLEMEN, I SAY RATHER THAN FIX THE 'BUGS', WE CHANGE THE DOCUMENTATION AND CALL THEM 'FEATURES'."

In this part . . .

This part of the book is an ever-so-gentle introduction to the most basic features in Word for Windows. I don't go hog-wild into desktop publishing and other fancy stuff until later in this book. For now, I lay a solid foundation for formatting characters and paragraphs by using styles and templates and some other good-habit-forming Word for Windows features.

Some of the chapters in this part may seem like a review, but as you know, you never know what you don't know until you know that you don't know it. Or something like that. So bear with me as you tackle more WinWord features.

Chapter 1
More about Editing

*E*diting is what you hate most about Word for Windows. Word processing is made up of basically two chores: editing and formatting. *Formatting* is *fun* because you get to ditz around with fonts and sizes and alignments until your one page memo about office lockup procedures is suitable for framing. *Editing*, on the other hand, is *work*, because instead of fooling around with appearances, editing requires that you focus on actual words. Bother.

This chapter is a quick review of the basics of editing your fine prose. You probably already know most of the basics of editing documents — such as deleting unwanted text, inserting a word here or there, and rearranging sentences. Otherwise, you'd be reading *Word For Windows 95 For Dummies* (by Dan Gookin, published by IDG Books Worldwide, Inc.) instead of *MORE Word For Windows 95 For Dummies*. Still, a little review never hurts now and then, especially on a topic as important as editing. After all, editing is probably how you spend most of your time with Word.

Getting Around

Other than actual typing, the most basic editing skill is moving the insertion point around within a document. You undoubtedly know how to do that by using the arrow keys and the PgUp (PageUp) and PgDn (PageDown) keys. However, Word provides plenty of keyboard shortcuts that enable you to move around your document even more quickly. The most useful of these keyboard shortcuts are summarized in Table 1-1.

Table 1-1 Keyboard Shortcuts for Navigating through Documents

Keyboard Shortcut	What It Does
Up/Down Arrows	
Up	Previous line
Down	Next line
Ctrl+Up	Previous paragraph
Ctrl+Down	Next paragraph
Alt+Up	Previous object
Alt+Down	Next object
Left/Right Arrows	
Left-arrow	Left one character
Right-arrow	Right one character
Ctrl+Left-arrow	Left one word
Ctrl+Right-arrow	Right one word
Alt+Left-arrow	Left one word (same as Ctrl+Left-arrow)
Alt+Right-arrow	Right one word (same as Ctrl+Right-arrow)
Page Up/Page Down	
PgUp	Previous screen
PgDn	Next screen
Ctrl+PgUp	Top of window
Ctrl+PgDn	Bottom of window
Ctrl+Alt+PgUp	Previous page
Ctrl+Alt+PgDn	Next page
Alt+PgUp	Top of column
Alt+PgDn	Bottom of column
Home/End	
Home	Beginning of line
End	End of line
Ctrl+Home	Beginning of document
Ctrl+End	End of document

Keyboard Shortcut	What It Does
Other	
Alt+F1	Next field
Shift+F1	Previous field
F11	Next field (Same as Alt+F1)
Shift+F11	Previous field (Same as Shift+F1)
Ctrl+F6	Next document window
Shift+Ctrl+F6	Previous document window
F5	Go to; calls up the Go To dialog box
Shift+F5	Go back to the previous insertion point

Going Places with Edit⇨Go To

The Go To command is the Word equivalent of the "Go Directly To Jail" card in Monopoly. This command enables you to jet over to any of several specific locations in your document, without passing Go or collecting $200.

You can call up the Go To command from the Edit menu (Edit⇨Go To) by pressing F5 or by double-clicking on the page number portion of the status bar at the bottom of the Word window. Whichever way you choose, the Go To dialog box appears, as shown in Figure 1-1.

Figure 1-1:
The Go To
dialog box.

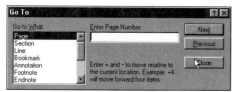

The Go To dialog box is used most often to go to a specific page number. To do that, simply type the page number into the Enter Page Number field, click Go To (the Next button changes to a Go To button the moment you type a page number) and click Close or press the Esc key to dismiss the Go To dialog box.

Besides going to a specific page, you can also go forward or backwards a certain number of pages. To go forward, type a plus sign followed by the number of pages you want to skip. For example, to go 3 pages forward, type **+3.** To go backwards, type a minus sign instead of a plus sign. For example, type **-20** to go backwards 20 pages.

In addition, besides going to a specific page, the Go To command enables you to go to a particular section or line, or any of several types of goodies that may reside in your document, such as bookmarks, annotations, footnotes, and so on. To go to something other than a page, just change the setting of the Go To <u>W</u>hat drop-down list box.

One of the most annoying bugs to be found in Word is right here in the Go To dialog box. The problem is that the Go To dialog box stays on the screen after Word has found the page and taken you to it. If you Go To Page 11, you have to press the Esc key to dismiss the Go To dialog box before you can begin working on page 11. Microsoft would probably tell you that it designed the feature that way; that is, most users, after going to page 11, don't want to do anything to page 11 but want instead to go to page 23 (and making them press F5 again would be a nuisance). Nonsense! The Go To dialog box should disappear after taking you to wherever you want to go. It shouldn't stick around like an unwanted houseguest.

Yes, You Can Go Back

A funny thing about Word is that it has more than a few useful commands that aren't accessible from the menus or toolbars. One such command is the Go Back command. Most Word users don't know about the Go Back command because they can only access it via its keyboard shortcut, Shift+F5, and if they didn't read the manual, they'd probably never stumble across it on their own. Yet the Go Back command can be very useful. Word remembers the last five locations at which you've edited your document, and each press of Shift+F5 returns you to one of those previous editing locations.

Selecting Text with Mouse and Keyboard

After typing and moving the insertion point around your document, the next most basic editing skill is selecting text. In Word, you must always select text before you can apply any formatting or editing to the text. For example, to make text boldface, you must first select the text and then use a formatting command to apply the boldface formatting.

The easiest way to select text is by dragging the mouse over the text you want to select. You can also use the following mouse actions to select text:

> ✔ Another way to select a block of text with the mouse is to click at the start of the block, hold down Shift, and click at the end of the block. This action selects all text in-between the clicks.

✔ To select a single word, double-click the mouse anywhere on the word.

✔ To select an entire paragraph, triple-click the mouse anywhere on the paragraph.

✔ To select an entire sentence, hold down Ctrl and click the mouse anywhere in the sentence.

✔ To select a column of text, hold down Alt, press and hold the left mouse button, and drag. Drag the mouse left or right to increase or decrease the width of the column selected, and drag the mouse up or down to extend the column up or down. (This technique is most useful after you've arranged text into columns by using tabs and you want to rearrange the columns.)

Some mouse selection techniques require you to click the *selection bar*, that invisible but ever-present narrow band to the left of the text. (By the way, your mouse pointer turns into a right-pointing arrow when it's in the selection bar.)

✔ Click the selection bar once to select an entire line of text.

✔ Double-click the selection bar to select an entire paragraph.

✔ Triple-click the selection bar to select the entire document.

✔ To select several paragraphs, double-click the selection bar to select the first paragraph, hold the mouse button down after the second click, and drag the mouse up or down the selection bar to select additional paragraphs.

If you are allergic to the mouse, you can use the keyboard shortcuts summarized in Table 1-2 to select text.

Table 1-2   Keyboard Shortcuts for Selecting Text

Keyboard Shortcut	What It Does
Ctrl+A	Select entire document.
Ctrl+NumPad5	Select entire document.
Alt+NumPad5	Select entire table.
F8	Extend the selection, similar to holding down the Shift key or dragging the mouse. After pressing F8, the selection is extended as you move the insertion pointer.
Ctrl+Shift+F8	Extend a column selection.

Copy, Cut, and Paste

Table 1-3 summarizes the three most important keyboard shortcuts in all of Windows.

Table 1-3 The Three Most Important Word Keyboard Shortcuts	
Keyboard Shortcut	*What It Does*
Ctrl+C	Copies the selected text to the Clipboard.
Ctrl+X	Cuts the selected text to the Clipboard. The original text is removed from the document.
Ctrl+V	Pastes the contents of the Clipboard at the insertion point.

The standard toolbar in Word has buttons for the copy, cut, and paste functions, and you can access them via the <u>E</u>dit menu. But memorizing and using the keyboard shortcuts is far more convenient. As a plus, you discover that just about all Windows programs — including Windows itself — honor these keyboard shortcuts.

If you have trouble remembering these shortcuts, consider first that they are positioned adjacent to one another on the bottom row of the keyboard. Then consider the following memory aids:

- ✔ **Ctrl+X:** The X is reminiscent of the X drawn to cross out something you want removed.

- ✔ **Ctrl+C:** The C is short for Copy.

- ✔ **Ctrl+V:** The V is reminiscent of a proofreading mark (a caret, ^) that indicates where something should be inserted.

If the preceding memory aids don't help, have these shortcuts tattooed on the back of your hand. That way, you can see them as you type.

Dragging and Dropping

Drag-and-drop editing (or *dragon dropping*) helps you to move text from one location in a document to another by using only the mouse, without using the Clipboard. You simply highlight the text you want to move and use the mouse to drag the text to a new location. When you release the mouse button, the text is cut from its original location and pasted to the new location.

If you hold down the Ctrl key while dragging text, you can copy the text, instead of moving it, to the new location. In other words, the text is not deleted from its original location.

You can drag and drop text between two open documents, but both documents must be visible on the screen. To ensure that both documents are visible, use the Window⇨Arrange All command.

The Magic of Undo and Repeat

The Undo command is one of the best ways to become a Word guru. Without the Undo command, you would be afraid of experimenting with Word for fear of losing your document. But with this command at hand, you can try anything you want, knowing that the worst that can happen is that you may have to use the Undo command to undo your mistake.

You can access the Undo command from the Edit menu (Edit⇨Undo), but Undo is used frequently enough that you should simply memorize its keyboard shortcut: Ctrl+Z. While you're at it, go ahead and memorize the keyboard shortcut (Ctrl+Y) for an almost equally useful command: Repeat. The Repeat command, as its name implies, repeats the last action. If you just used the Format⇨Font command to make a bevy of formatting changes all at once, select some other text that you want similarly formatted and then press Ctrl+Y. By using this Repeat command, you can apply the same formats to the other text.

The Repeat command repeats just about any action you can do in Word, including Undo. When the most recent command is Undo, the Repeat command becomes the Redo command: It redoes the action undone by the Undo command. Undo and Redo are a perfect combination for people who can't decide whether they like something or not.

Unlike most word processors, Word keeps track of more than one recent action. In fact, you can undo up to 100 recent actions. To undo more than one action at a time, click on the down-arrow in the standard toolbar's Undo button to reveal a list of the 100 recent undoable actions. Drag the mouse to select the actions you want to undo and release the mouse to undo them all in one fell swoop. See Figure 1-2.

The Redo button in the standard toolbar has a similar capability to redo up to 100 recently undone actions.

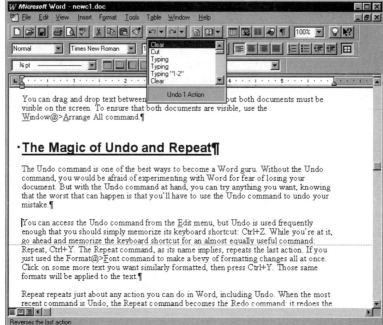

Figure 1-2:
Undoing
more than
one
command.

Working with Bookmarks

A *bookmark* is a name you assign to a location in a document or to a selection of text so that you can easily return to that location at a later time. Using a bookmark is a safer and more effective method than attempting to fold down the corner of your monitor to mark a page.

To create a bookmark, position the insertion point where you want to place the bookmark and press Ctrl+Shift+F5. This key combination brings up the Bookmark dialog box, as shown in Figure 1-3. Type the name of the bookmark and click the Add button.

The bookmark name can be a maximum of 20 characters in length and can include letters and numbers, but no spaces, punctuation, or special symbols except the underscore character (_). The bookmark name must begin with a letter. Notice that the Add button doesn't become active until you start typing a valid bookmark name, and if you type an incorrect bookmark name (for example, if you include a space or any special character except the underscore), the Add button is deactivated.

You can create a bookmark for a selection of text rather than for a specific insertion point location, but you usually have little reason to bother selecting the text. If the only reason you are creating the bookmark is to go to it later, don't bother selecting a range of text; just place the insertion point at the location you want to return to and create a bookmark.

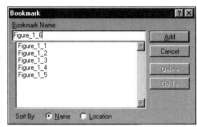

Figure 1-3:
Adding a
bookmark.

After you've created a bookmark, you can go to it at any time by pressing Ctrl+Shift+F5 to call up the Bookmark dialog box, clicking on the bookmark you want to go to, and clicking the Go To button.

You can also go to a bookmark by calling up the Edit⇨Go To command, selecting Bookmark in the Go To What list, selecting the bookmark in the Enter Bookmark Name drop-down list, and clicking Go To. Going to the bookmark using Ctrl+Shift+F5 is a lot easier, though.

 Actually, you don't have to select Bookmark in the Go To What list if you remember the bookmark name. Simply type the bookmark name in the Enter Page Number field and press the Enter key. Word is smart enough to figure out that what you entered was a bookmark, not a page number.

To delete a bookmark, press Ctrl+Shift+F5 to call up the Bookmark dialog box, select the bookmark you want to delete, and click Delete.

Using the Find Command

The Edit⇨Find command enables you to search for text anywhere in your document. The command also lets you search for specific formats, such as a particular font or style, and for special symbols such as paragraph marks or annotations.

You summon the Find command by choosing Edit⇨Find from the menu or by pressing Ctrl+F. Unfortunately, the Find command has no toolbar button, but you can add one if you're willing to customize your toolbars. Word even supplies a predefined toolbar button image that looks like a set of binoculars.

However you invoke it, the Find command displays the Find dialog box, as shown in Figure 1-4. The following sections explain how to use this dialog box for various searches.

Figure 1-4:
The Find
dialog box.

Finding missing text

You can use the Edit⇨Find command to find text anywhere in a document. Just follow these steps:

1. **Choose Edit⇨Find or press Ctrl+F to summon the Find dialog box.**

   Refer to Figure 1-4 for a glimpse of this dialog box.

2. **Type the text you want to find in the Find What field.**

   For example, "Bandersnatch."

3. **Click the Find Next button.**

4. **Wait a second while Word searches your document.**

   When Word finds the text, it highlights that text on-screen. The Find dialog box remains on-screen so you can click Find Next to find yet another occurrence of the text.

5. **Stop when you see the message indicating that no more occurrences of the text could be found.**

You can bail out of the Find dialog box at any time by clicking Cancel or pressing the Esc key.

You can change the direction of Word's search by changing the setting in the Search drop-down box. Three choices are available:

- ✔ **Down:** Starts the search at the position of the insertion point and searches forward toward the end of the document.

- ✔ **Up:** Searches backward from the insertion point, toward the beginning of the document.

   Both the Down and Up options search until they reach the bottom or top of the document; then they ask whether you want to continue searching the rest of the document.

- ✔ **All:** Searches the entire document without regard to the position of the insertion point.

Check the Match Case check box before beginning the search if it matters whether the text appears in uppercase or lowercase letters. This option is handy when you have, for example, a document about Mr. Smith the blacksmith.

Speaking of Mr. Smith the blacksmith, use the Find Whole Words Only option to find your text only when it appears as a whole word. If you want to find the text where you talk about Mr. Smith the blacksmith's mit, for example, type **mit** in the Find What text box and check the Find Whole Words Only check box. That way, the Find command looks for *mit* as a separate word and doesn't show you all the *mit*s in *Smith* and *blacksmith*.

Check the Use Pattern Matching check box if you want to include wildcard characters or other search operators in the Find What field. Table 1-4 summarizes the search operators that you can use if you select this option.

Table 1-4 Advanced Search Operators for the Find Command

Operator	*What It Does*
?	Finds a single occurrence of any character. For example, **f?t** finds *fat* or *fit.*
*	Finds any combination of characters. For example, **b*t** finds any combination of characters that begins with *b* and ends with *t,* such as *bat, bait, ballast,* or *bacteriologist.*
#	Any numerical digit.
[*abc*]	Finds any one of the characters enclosed in the brackets. For example, **b[ai]t** finds *bat* or *bit,* but not *bet* or *but.*
[*a-c*]	Finds any character in the range of characters enclosed in the brackets. For example, **b[a-e]t** finds *bat* or *bet,* but not *bit* or *but.*
[!*abc*]	Finds any character except the ones enclosed in the brackets. For example, **b[!ai]t** finds *bet* or *but,* but not *bat* or *bit.*
@	Finds one or more occurrences of the preceding character. For example, **10@** finds *10, 100,* or *1000.*
{*n*}	Specifies that the preceding character must be repeated exactly *n* times. For example, **10{2}** finds *100,* but not *10* or *1000.*
{*n,*}	Specifies that the preceding character must be repeated at least *n* times. For example, **10{2,}** finds *100* or *1000,* but not *10.*

(continued)

Table 1-4 *(continued)*

Operator	What It Does
{n,m}	Specifies that the preceding character must be repeated from *n* to *m* times. For example, **10{2,3}** finds *100* or *1000,* but not *10* or *10000.*
<	Finds the following text only if it appears at the beginning of a word. For example, **<pre** finds *predestined* and *prefabricated,* but not *appreciate* or *apprehend.*
>	Finds the preceding text only if it appears at the end of a word. For example, **ing>** finds *interesting* and *domineering,* but not *ingenious* or *ingest.*

Check the Sounds Like check box if you're not sure exactly how to spell the text for which you're searching. Word can search for words that are pronounced the same as the word you're searching for. For example, if you search for **your** with the Sounds Like option on, Word stops when it finds *you're.* Don't expect too much from this option, however. For example, if you typed **low** in the Find What field, you'd expect the option to find *Lowe* (well, *I* would anyway). But it doesn't.

With Word 7, a new option, Find All Word Forms, was added to the Find command. If you select this option, Word looks for alternate forms of most verbs. For example, if you search for **run**, Word finds *runs, running,* and *ran.* And the program is smart enough to know about certain oddball words such as go: If you search for **go**, Word finds not only *goes, going,* and *gone,* but also *went.* Searching for **be** finds *is, was, am, were, being,* and *been.*

Don't expect miracles, however. Find All Word Forms doesn't pick up every imaginable word form, especially where nouns are concerned. For example, a search for **introduction** doesn't pick up *introductory,* and **religion** doesn't catch *religious.* Find All Word Forms is more adept at finding alternate word forms for verbs than for nouns.

Finding formats

To find specific types of formatting, choose the Edit⇨Find command. The keyboard shortcut is Ctrl+F. Either way, the Find dialog box appears. (Refer to Figure 1-4.) Click the Format button and choose the type of format you want to search for from the pop-up menu. The following options are available:

> ✔ **Font:** Enables you to search for specific font formatting. You can search for specific fonts or for font formatting such as bold, italics, font size, and so on.

✔ **Paragraph:** Enables you to search for specific paragraph formatting, such as indentation and alignment.

✔ **Tabs:** Enables you to search for paragraphs with specific tab settings.

✔ **Language:** Enables you to search for paragraphs formatted for a particular language.

✔ **Frame:** Enables you to search for specific frame formatting.

✔ **Style:** Enables you to search for paragraphs formatted with a particular style.

✔ **Highlight:** Enables you to search for highlighted text.

Make sure that the Find What field itself is blank; otherwise, the Find command searches for specific text that's formatted with the style you specify.

Finding special characters

You can also use the Find command to search for special characters such as em dashes or annotation marks. Call up the Find command (Edit➪Find or Ctrl+F) and click the Special button to reveal a list of special characters that you can search for, as shown in Figure 1-5. Select the character you want to search for and click Find Next to begin the search.

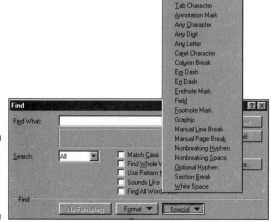

Figure 1-5: Searching for special characters.

When you select a special character, Word inserts a code into the Find What text box. If you know the code, you can bypass the Special button and its huge menu by typing the code directly into the Find What field. Table 1-5 summarizes the codes.

Table 1-5	Search Codes for Special Characters
Character	*Code*
Paragraph mark	^p
Tab character	^t
Annotation mark	^a
Any character	^?
Any digit	^#
Any letter	^$
Caret character	^^
Column break	^n
Em dash	^+
En dash	^=
Endnote mark	^e
Field	^d
Footnote mark	^f
Graphic	^g
Manual line break	^l
Manual page break	^m
Nonbreaking hyphen	^~
Nonbreaking space	^s
Optional hyphen	^-
Section break	^b
White space	^w

Replacing Text

You can use the Edit⇨Replace command to replace all occurrences of one bit of text with other text. The following steps show you the procedure:

1. Choose Edit⇨Replace or press Ctrl+H.

   The Replace dialog box appears, as shown in Figure 1-6.

Figure 1-6:
The Replace
dialog box.

2. **Type the text you want to find in the Fi̱nd What text box.**

3. **Type the text you want to substitute for the Fi̱nd What text in the Replace With text box.**

4. **Click the F̱ind Next button.**

   When Word finds the text, it highlights that text on-screen.

5. **Click the Ṟeplace button to replace the text.**

6. **Repeat the F̱ind Next and Ṟeplace sequence until you're finished.**

As for the F̱ind command, you can use the Match C̱ase, Find W̱hole Words Only, Use Pattern M̱atching, Sounds Ḻike, and Fiṉd All Word Forms options. The last option is even smart enough to properly replace alternate word forms with the correct version of the replacement text. For example, if you replace **run** with **walk**, Word replaces *running* with *walking* and *ran* with *walked.*

If you're absolutely positive that you want to replace all occurrences of your Fi̱nd What text with the Repḻace With text, click the Replace A̱ll button. Taking this step automatically replaces all remaining occurrences of the text. The only problem is that you're bound to encounter at least one spot where you didn't want the replacement to occur. Replacing the word **mit** with **glove**, for example, changes *Smith* to *Sgloveh* (and no, *Sgloveh* is not the Czechoslovakian form of the name *Smith*).

Because Word is not 100-percent confident in its capability to properly replace all alternate word forms, you get a warning message if you select the Fiṉd All Word Forms option and click Replace A̱ll. Fiṉd All Word forms is tricky enough that you should verify each replacement.

Creating Desktop Scraps

In Word 7, you can now drag text completely away from Word into another application. The target application for this type of drag-and-drop edit is usually Windows 95 itself, or more precisely, the Windows 95 desktop. When you drag text out of Word 7 onto the Windows 95 desktop, the text is placed in a *document scrap* and given its own icon, as shown in Figure 1-7. You can then drag the text back into a Word 95 document at a later time: a few minutes later or a few days later. The scrap can sit on the desktop indefinitely. You can also double-click the scrap icon to open the scrap as a document.

Document scraps are a great way to move bits and pieces out of one or several documents for use later in another document. In essence, scraps enable your desktop to double as a super-clipboard, capable of holding not just one, but many text snippets that you can paste together later. (Just be careful that your Windows 95 desktop doesn't become cluttered with scraps just like your real desk!)

If you need to create more than a few scraps and you don't want your desktop to become cluttered, create a folder called *Scrapbook* (or whatever name suits your fancy) and drag the scraps into the folder instead of to the desktop. Then, you can close or minimize the Scrapbook folder to hide the scraps.

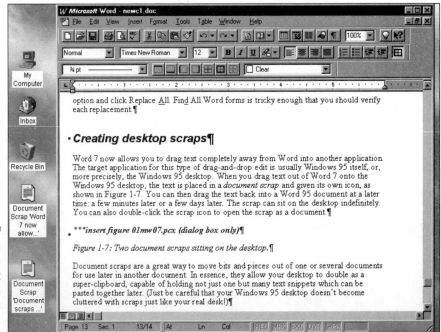

Figure 1-7:
Two document scraps sitting on the desktop.

Chapter 2
More about Formatting

*H*ow I loved my first computer. It had one of those daisy-wheel printers that created pages that looked like they had been typed on an actual typewriter. And my word processing software was so advanced that I could actually underline individual words and even set tab stops. And it could print out an entire page of letter-quality text faster than Congress can give itself a pay raise!

Those were the good old days. Back then, you didn't worry too much about what your text looked like, because you didn't really have that much control over appearances. So instead, you had to focus on — brace yourself — your actual words. Your document's words were actually more important than your document's appearance.

Nowadays, it seems as if appearance is everything! Who cares what your document says, as long as it looks great. The most brilliantly conceived proposal can go unread unless it looks like it was produced by a Madison Avenue ad agency. Sigh.

If you need a refresher in the basics of formatting text with Word 7 for Windows, you've landed in the right chapter. The formatting stuff in this chapter is pretty basic, so much of it may be review if you've been using WinWord for awhile. But heck, a little review never hurt, and you may find a few juicy formatting tidbits in here that you didn't know you didn't know.

I hate this stuff as much as you do. Because I'm a writer, I like to concentrate on what my words *say* rather than how they look. If you agree, I highly recommend that you plow straight on to the next chapter as soon as you finish this one. Chapter 3 thrusts you into the world of *styles,* which are the secret to freedom from the bondage of all the formatting nonsense presented in this chapter.

Understanding Formatting in WinWord

Before getting into the details of applying specific formats to your document, you should review the *gestalt* of how Word for Windows formats your text. In WinWord, there are three basic types of formats: characters, paragraphs, and sections.

Characters: Characters are the smallest element that you can format in WinWord. You can make characters bold, italic, or underlined, change their font size, and more! If you're deranged enough, you can format every character of your document differently. Doing so gives your documents a ransom-note appearance, which is something you probably want to avoid.

Paragraphs: The next biggest element you can format in WinWord is a paragraph. You can format each paragraph so that it has its own tab stops, line spacing, extra space before or after the paragraph, indentation, alignment (left, right, centered, or justified), and more. Paragraphs also have default character formats. So the only time you need to apply a character format is when you want your characters to vary from the paragraph's default character format, such as when you want to italicize a word or make it boldface.

Sections: WinWord also enables you to control the layout of pages. You can format each page by setting the top, bottom, left, and right margins, setting the number of columns and the size of each column, setting the paper size, controlling the placement of headers and footers, and more. You can format your document so that all pages have the same layout, or you can divide your document into *sections,* each with a different page layout. That's why WinWord refers to these formats as *section formats.*

✔ Unlike some other word processors who shall remain nameless but whose initials are *W-O-R-D-P-E-R-F-E-C-T,* WinWord does not depend on codes that have been handed down from medieval chambers of formatting torture. If you're an experienced WordPerfect user, you'll be constantly looking for the Reveal Codes command until you figure this out. In WinWord, formats are applied to portions of your document — characters, paragraphs, and pages — and are not controlled by codes that are embedded within the text that you can see and edit.

✔ Paragraph formatting information is contained within the paragraph mark at the end of the paragraph, which looks like this:

| ¶ |

If you can't see these marks on the screen, call up the Tools⇨Options command and click the View tab. Then check the Paragraph Marks command. You can also refer to Chapter 15 for nauseating detail on setting various WinWord options.

✔ If you delete that paragraph mark, the paragraph is merged with the following paragraph. Any formatting that was applied to the paragraph mark you deleted is lost — the text assumes the formatting of the following paragraph.

✔ If you use more than one page layout in a document, the document is divided into two or more sections. Each section except the last one ends with a *section break*, which looks like this:

| ⸺⸺⸺⸺⸺⸺⸺⸺⸺⸺⸺⸺End of Section⸺⸺⸺⸺⸺⸺⸺⸺⸺⸺⸺⸺ |

Section marks work much like paragraph marks: if you delete one, the text before the section mark assumes the page layout of the section following the mark.

✔ Every document has at least one section, but you see section marks only if you divide the document into two or more sections. Where's the section mark for the last section of a document? There is none. The formatting information for the last section of a document is stored in the last paragraph mark in the document.

Formatting Characters

The sections that follow show you how to apply various formats to characters. Like most things in WinWord, you discover that there's more than one way to apply these formats. The easiest way is to use keyboard shortcuts (if you can remember them) or the various buttons and gizmos on the Formatting toolbar. Otherwise, you can use the Format⇨Font command if you like to play with dialog boxes.

Applying character formats the easy way

You can apply character formats before or after you type the text you want to format. To apply a character format to text as you type it, follow these steps:

1. **Type text up to the point where you want to apply a format.**

2. **Turn on the special character formatting by using one of the keyboard shortcuts or toolbar buttons listed in Table 2-1.**

   Nothing happens at first, but wait. . . .

3. **Type away.**

   Anything you type assumes the format you applied in Step 2.

4. **Turn off the special character formatting by using the keyboard shortcut again.**

   Or, if you clicked one of the buttons on the Formatting toolbar, click it again. Either way, WinWord discontinues the special formatting. Any text you subsequently type is formatted as usual.

To apply a character format to text you've already typed, follow these steps:

1. **Highlight the text you want to format.**

   To highlight a single word, double-click anywhere in the word. To highlight an entire paragraph, triple-click anywhere in the paragraph. Otherwise, highlight the text that you want formatted by dragging the mouse over it while holding down the left mouse button or by using the arrow keys to move the cursor while holding down the Shift key.

   If WinWord's Automatic Word Selection option is enabled, you don't have to double-click to select an entire word; WinWord automatically selects the entire word if the insertion point is anywhere in the word. To activate this option (or to deactivate it if it is already activated), use the Tools⇨Options command, click the Edit tab, and then click the Automatic Word Selection button. Click the OK button or press Enter to close the Options dialog box.

2. **Apply the format using one of the keyboard shortcuts or toolbar buttons listed in Table 2-1.**

   The effects of your formatting should be immediately apparent.

3. **Move on.**

   Disperse. There's nothing more to see here. Return to your homes.

Table 2-1	Character Formatting the Easy Way	
Toolbar Button	**Keyboard Shortcut**	**What It Does**
B	Ctrl+B	Bold
I	Ctrl+I	*Italic*
U	Ctrl+U	Underline (continuous)

Toolbar Button	Keyboard Shortcut	What It Does
	Ctrl+Shift+W	Word <u>underline</u>
	Ctrl+Shift+D	<u>Double underline</u>
	Ctrl+Shift+A	ALL CAPS
	Ctrl+Shift+K	SMALL CAPS
	Shift+F3	Change case
	Ctrl+=	Subscript
	Ctrl+Shift+=	Superscript
Times New Roman	Ctrl+Shift+F	Change font
10	Ctrl+Shift+P	Change point size
	Ctrl+]	Increase size one point
	Ctrl+[	Decrease size one point
	Ctrl+Shift+>	Increase size to next available size
	Ctrl+Shift+<	Decrease size to previous available size
	Ctrl+Shift+Q	Switch to Symbol font (Γρεεκ Τραγεδψ)
	Ctrl+Shift+Z	Remove character formatting
	Ctrl+spacebar	Remove character formatting

Some other tidbits on character formatting:

- ✔ You can gang tackle text with formats, if you want. For example, you can format text as ***bold italic double-underlined*** if you're really desperate for attention.

- ✔ To remove *all* character formatting, highlight the text that you want to return to normal; then press Ctrl+spacebar or Ctrl+Shift+Z.

- ✔ To remove a specific character format, such as bold or italic, but leave other character formats intact, highlight the text and type the keyboard shortcut or click the toolbar button for the format you want to remove.

- ✔ Ordinarily, you can remove a text format, such as bold or italic, for an entire word by placing the insertion point anywhere within the word and pressing the keyboard shortcut for the format. However, there's a subtle bug in Word 7: You can't remove a format for an entire word if the insertion point is immediately before the last letter of the word. For example, suppose you type the word *bold* and then press the left arrow key so the insertion point rests between the *l* and the *d*. If you then press Ctrl+B, the entire word is formatted in bold. But if you press Ctrl+B again, nothing happens. Further proof that the programmers at Microsoft are human after all.

✔ To paraphrase Chuck Yeager, there are old WinWord users, and there are bold WinWord users, but there are no old bold WinWord users.

Using the Format⇨Font command

The character formatting options you're likely to use most — bold, italics, underlining, font, and point size — are all readily accessible from the Formatting toolbar or easy-to-remember keyboard shortcuts. Most of the other character formatting options don't dare show their faces on the Formatting toolbar, and you probably won't use them enough to learn their keyboard shortcuts. Bother.

If you find yourself in the unenviable position of needing to apply a character format that's not on the toolbar and you can't remember the shortcut, you have three alternatives. First, you can try to talk yourself out of it. Who needs double-underlining, anyway? If that doesn't work, you can flip open this book, turn to Table 2-1, and look up the keyboard shortcut.

As a last resort, you can use the Format⇨Font command. Yes, I know it pops up a dialog box that looks like it was designed by Bill Z. Bub himself, but it does give you one-stop shopping for all of WinWord's character formatting options.

The Format⇨Font command is the only way to apply the following formats to characters:

✔ Dashed underline

✔ Color

✔ Strikethrough

✔ Character spacing

These formats do not appear on any of the standard toolbars, and they have no keyboard shortcuts. So if you want to apply them, you have to use the Format⇨Font command. (If you use any of these weird formats regularly, consult Chapter 16 to learn how to assign a keyboard shortcut to them.)

Here's the procedure for applying mystifying, strange formatting:

1. **Highlight the text you want to mangle with oddball formatting.**

2. **Conjure up the Format⇨Font command.**

   Press Alt+O and then *F* to activate the command. Or use its convenient and easy-to-remember mnemonic keyboard shortcut, Ctrl+D. (Just remember that the *D* stands for *those demonic character formats*. Works for me.)

3. **Tremble before the Font dialog box.**

   After all, it was designed by Bill Z. Bub himself. Figure 2-1 shows its ghastly appearance.

4. **Play with the controls.**

   Fiddle with the various controls to set the Font, the Font Style (bold, italic, and so on), and the Size. Click the Effects you want (Strikethrough, Superscript, and so on). Use the drop-down list boxes to set the Underline and Color. Have a ball.

5. **Click OK when you've had enough.**

   The dialog box vanishes, and your text is magically transformed with the formats you selected.

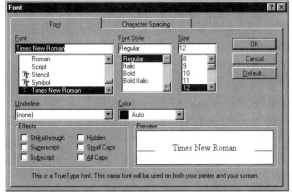

Figure 2-1:
The Font
dialog box.

Some notes about using the Font dialog box:

> ✔ If you haven't yet typed the text you want to mangle, use the Format⇨Font command, choose the formats you want, click OK, and then start typing. When you're done, press Ctrl+spacebar or Ctrl+Shift+Z to resume normal type.

✔ To remove oddball formats that you've applied with the Format⇨Font command, select the text and press Ctrl+spacebar or Ctrl+Shift+Z. Or conjure up the Format⇨Font command once again and uncheck the formats you want to get rid of.

✔ Notice the tabs across the top of the Font dialog box? They enable you to switch between basic font formatting controls and character spacing controls. If you click the Character Spacing tab, you see options to control the spacing between characters, raise or lower characters from the baseline, and apply a spiffy desktop publishing feature called *kerning*. These options are in the realm of desktop publishing, so ignore them for now. If you can't wait, skip ahead to Chapter 10 for information about using these options.

Formatting Paragraphs

The following sections show you how to apply various formats to a paragraph. Once again, there's more than one way to apply these formats. The easy way is to use keyboard shortcuts or toolbar buttons, but if you must, you can resort to the Format⇨Paragraph, Format⇨Tabs, or Format⇨Borders and Shading commands.

Applying paragraph formats the easy way

To apply a paragraph format, follow this painless procedure:

1. Click anywhere in the paragraph that you want to format.

It matters not where in the paragraph, so long as the cursor is somewhere in the paragraph.

2. Use one of the keyboard shortcuts or toolbar buttons summarized in Table 2-2.

The effect of your formatting should be obvious.

3. There is no third step. You're done.

Made you look!

Fun with fonts

Ever notice the little icons that appear next to font names in WinWord's font lists? These icons identify the various types of fonts you can use with WinWord.

Printer fonts | These are fonts designed for specific printers. For some reason known only by Windows moguls, they may not appear on the screen exactly as they appear on the printed page.

TrueType fonts | These are Windows fonts in which the font is displayed on the screen exactly as it is on the printed page. Any printer that works with Windows can print TrueType fonts. Stick to TrueType for best results.

PostScript fonts | These are fonts designed to work with PostScript-compatible laser printers, which are more expensive, but are the first choice of desktop publishing fanatics. Use these only if you have a PostScript laser printer.

If you make the wise decision to stick to TrueType fonts, follow this simple procedure to remove the non-TrueType font clutter from WinWord's font lists (and the font lists for all other Windows programs, for that matter):

1. **Click the Start button in the Windows 95 task bar.**

2. **Choose Settings and then click Control Panel.**

   The Control Panel appears.

3. **Double-click the Fonts icon.**

   A window listing all of the fonts installed on your computer appears.

4. **Choose the View⇨Options command.**

   The Options dialog box appears.

5. **Click the TrueType tab at the top of the Options dialog box.**

6. **Check the Show only TrueType fonts in the programs on my computer checkbox.**

7. **Click OK and then click the Close button in the Fonts window.**

Now you don't have to worry about non-TrueType fonts; only TrueType fonts show up in WinWord.

Table 2-2	Paragraph Formatting the Easy Way	
Toolbar Button	**Keyboard Shortcut**	**What It Does**
	Ctrl+L	Left-aligns a paragraph
	Ctrl+R	Right-aligns a paragraph
	Ctrl+J	Justifies a paragraph
	Ctrl+E	Centers a paragraph
	Ctrl+M	Increases left indent
	Ctrl+Shift+M	Reduces left indent
	Ctrl+T	Creates hanging indent
	Ctrl+Shift+T	Reduces hanging indent
	Ctrl+1	Single-spaces paragraph
	Ctrl+2	Double-spaces paragraph
	Ctrl+5	Sets line space to 1.5
	Ctrl+0 (zero)	Removes space before or sets space before to 1 line
	Ctrl+Q	Removes paragraph formatting

Keep these notes in mind when formatting your paragraphs:

✔ As with character formats, you can heap paragraph formats atop one another. Just keep typing keyboard shortcuts or clicking toolbar buttons until the paragraph is formatted just right.

✔ To remove paragraph formatting, use the easy-to-remember Ctrl+Q keyboard shortcut (the *Q* stands for *quit using those diabolical paragraph formats*).

✔ Paragraph formats are stored in the paragraph marker at the end of the paragraph. Don't make the mistake of spending hours polishing a paragraph's appearance and then deleting the paragraph marker to merge the text into the following paragraph. If you do, all the formatting you so carefully applied is lost. (If that happens, quickly press Ctrl+Z to undo the deletion.)

Using the Format⇨Paragraph command

If you find yourself in the unenviable pickle of needing to use a formatting option that's not on the Formatting toolbar and you can't remember its keyboard shortcut, you can always conjure up the Format⇨Paragraph command and pick and choose your paragraph formats from a palette of delightful formatting treasures.

Here's the procedure for using the Format⇨Paragraph command:

1. **Click anywhere in the paragraph that you want to format.**

   It doesn't matter where in the paragraph, just so the cursor is somewhere in the paragraph.

2. **Summon the Format⇨Paragraph command.**

   Press Alt+O and then *P*. The Paragraph dialog box appears, shown in Figure 2-2.

3. **Play with the controls.**

   You can increase the Left or Right indentation, or you can choose a First Line or Hanging indent from the Special drop-down list box. You can also increase or decrease the amount of spacing Before and After the paragraph and set the Line Spacing. Notice also the Alignment drop-down list box hiding in the corner.

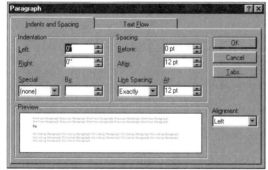

Figure 2-2:
The
Paragraph
dialog box.

As you play with the controls, keep an eye on the Preview box to see the effect of your changes.

4. **Click OK when you're done.**

   Presto change-o! You're done.

You can set left and right indentation as well as first line and hanging indents by playing with the ruler. See the section "Setting tabs with the ruler" later in this chapter for details.

Additional info on using paragraph formatting options:

- You can change the unit of measure that's used for setting indentation by using the Tools⇨Options command, clicking the General tab, and setting the Measurement Units field to the unit of measure you want to use. See the sidebar "Measuring up" for more information about units of measure.

- Notice the Text Flow tab at the top of the Paragraph dialog box. Click it and you see options for controlling how paragraphs are positioned on the page. More information on these options is in the section "Text flow," coming up in a jiffy.

- Oh, and the Paragraph dialog box has a Tabs button that zaps you over to the Tabs dialog box so that you can set tab stops. This too is covered later, in the section "All about Tabs."

Text flow

When you conjure up the Format⇨Paragraph command, you can click the Text Flow tab to awaken a different set of paragraph formatting options. Figure 2-3 shows the Paragraph dialog box, Text Flow options.

Measuring up

The way Word for Windows measures things, such as line spacing and indentations, is confusing if you don't understand the terminology. Here are the units of measure WinWord accepts:

in   Inches. You know what they are.

cm Centimeters. You should know by now, but in case you're not sure, there are 2.54 centimeters in an inch.

pt   Points, a term used by typographers to measure type. There are 72 points in an inch and 12 points in a pica.

pi   Pica, another wacky term used by typographers. There are roughly 6 picas in an inch and 12 points in a pica.

li   Line — the same as a pica.

cb Cubit, 17.5 inches. There are 105 picas in a cubit, and 1,260 points in a cubit. (Just kidding. WinWord doesn't really accept cubits as a valid measurement unless the filename extension for the document you're working on is ARC.)

Figure 2-3:
The
Paragraph
dialog box
with the
Text
Flow tab
selected.

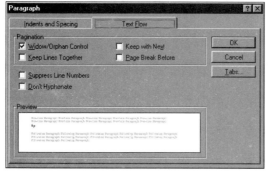

Here's what each of these options does:

Widow/Orphan Control: If a paragraph falls at the bottom of the page, Widow/Orphan Control prevents WinWord from splitting the paragraph if it means that one line would be left stranded at the bottom of one page or the top of the next page. Instead, the entire paragraph is bumped to the next page. Widow/Orphan Control is on by default; you should leave it on.

Keep Lines Together: Sometimes you have a paragraph that you don't want split up across pages. For example, suppose you want to quote a work of fine literature, such as a classic poem from Winnie-the-Pooh:

> Cottleston, Cottleston, Cottleston Pie,
> A fly can't bird, but a bird can fly.
> Ask me a riddle and I reply:
> *"Cottleston, Cottleston, Cottleston Pie."*

Obviously, you would lose the stunning emotional impact of this powerful poem if you allowed WinWord to split it across two pages. Give it the Keep Lines Together option so WinWord moves the whole thing to the next page if it doesn't fit in its entirety on the current page.

Keep with Next: This option prevents WinWord from inserting a page break between a paragraph and the one that follows it. You use it mostly for headings, to prevent a heading from being stranded at the bottom of a page.

Page Break Before: This option forces WinWord to place the paragraph at the top of the next page. Use it for chapter or section headings when you want each chapter or section to start on a new page.

Suppress Line Numbers: If you use WinWord's line numbering feature, this option tells WinWord to skip the paragraph when numbering lines.

Don't Hyphenate: If you use WinWord's hyphenation feature, this option tells WinWord to not hyphenate any words in the paragraph. Hyphenation is explained ad nauseam in Chapter 10.

All about Tabs

You can set tab stops in one of two ways: by dropping them directly on the ruler or by ditzing around with the Format⇨Tabs command. Dropping tabs directly on the ruler is far and away the easier method of the two. You should get involved with the Format⇨Tabs command only when you want to use *leaders* (little rows of dots that run across the page).

Setting tabs with the ruler

Here's the procedure for setting tabs with the ruler:

1. **If the ruler isn't visible, use the View⇨Ruler command to make it visible.**

2. **Type some text that you want to line up with tab stops.**

   Type several paragraphs if you want. Hit the Tab key once and only once between each column of information that you want lined up. Don't worry if everything doesn't line up at first. You'll fix it later.

3. **Select the paragraph or paragraphs whose tabs you want to set.**

   If you're setting tabs for just one paragraph, click the mouse anywhere in the paragraph. If you're setting tabs for more than one paragraph, drag the mouse to select at least some text in each paragraph.

4. **Click the mouse on the ruler at each spot where you want a new tab stop.**

   Watch as the text you selected in Step 2 lines up under the tabs you create. Add one tab stop to the ruler for each column of information you want aligned.

5. **Adjust.**

   Nothing works quite right the first time. If you dropped a tab at 1½ inches and want to move it to 1¾ inches, just click and drag the tab marker with the mouse and slide it to the new location. When you release the mouse button, text in the currently selected paragraphs is adjusted in the new tab position.

Here's more fascinating information about tabs:

- Default tab stops are placed every half an inch. However, each time you create a new tab stop, any default tab stops to the left of the new tab stops are deleted. In other words, default tab stops exist only to the right of tab stops you create.

- WinWord enables you to create four types of tab alignments: left, center, right, and decimal. To change the type of tab that's created when you click the ruler, click the Tab Alignment button at the far left edge of the ruler. Each time you click the button, the picture on the button changes to indicate the alignment type:

⊡ Left tab; text is left aligned at the tab stop.

⊡ Center tab; text is centered over the tab stop.

⊡ Right tab; text is right aligned at the tab stop.

⊡ Decimal tab; numbers are aligned at the decimal point over the tab stop.

✔ Rush Limbaugh fans often refuse to use left tab stops.

✔ You can quickly summon the Tabs dialog box by double-clicking the lower-half of the ruler. Watch where you double-click, though, because the first click adds a tab stop.

✔ If you want to add a leader to a tab, first create the tab stop by dropping it on the ruler. Then conjure up the Format⇨Tabs command, select the tab stop you want the leader added to, and select a leader type (dots, dashes, or solid line). Then click OK and check the results.

✔ To remove a tab stop from the ruler, click the tab stop you want to remove and drag it straight down, off the ruler. When you release the mouse, the tab stop is deleted.

✔ To quickly remove all tab stops, issue the Format⇨Tabs command or double-click in the bottom half of the ruler to summon the Tabs dialog box. Click the Clear All button to remove the tabs and then click OK to return to the document.

Running a bar tab

You must be 21 to use this feature in most states.

One of the more unusual things you can do with tabs is create vertical bars between columns of information, like this:

Star Trek	Happy Days	All In The Family
Star Trek: The Next Generation	Laverne and Shirley	The Jeffersons
Star Trek: Deep Space Nine	Mork and Mindy	Archie's Place

Here, the vertical bars between the columns are actually special deviant versions of tab stops. To create them, here's what you do:

1. Create some tab stops on the ruler.

Create *two* tab stops for each column of information you need, about ⅛ inch apart.

2. Conjure up the Format⇨Tabs command.

The Tabs dialog box, shown in Figure 2-4, appears.

3. Yell, "Norm!"

4. Convert every other tab stop to a bar tab.

Click the first tab stop; then select Bar as the alignment type. Click the Set button to make the change permanent; then click the third tab stop and make it a bar tab, too. Repeat for every other tab stop.

You must click the Set button after changing each tab stop to a bar tab. Otherwise, WinWord doesn't run your bar tab.

5. Click OK.

When the Tabs dialog box vanishes, check out the vertical bars between text columns. Notice that the tab marker in the ruler appears as a small vertical line.

6. Adjust.

If you don't like the way the tab stops are positioned, move 'em in the ruler by clicking them and dragging them.

Figure 2-4: The Tabs dialog box.

All you ever wanted to know about bar tabs is found in these three small bullets:

✓ Bar tabs aren't like regular tab stops in that the Tab key doesn't stop at them. Try it. Create a bar tab; then press the Tab key. The cursor zooms right past the bar tab to the next available tab stop.

✔ If the bar tab extends above or below the line, it's because the paragraph format calls for extra space above or below the paragraph. Use the Format⇨Paragraph command to remove the Above or Below space. (If you need the extra space, add it to the adjoining paragraphs instead.)

✔ Bar tabs are a crude way of making tables. WinWord has a special feature just for making tables, called — believe it or not — the Table Feature. Use it instead. It's covered in Chapter 9.

Formatting Pages

To control the layout of text on the page, use the File⇨Page Setup command. This command displays the dialog box shown in Figure 2-5.

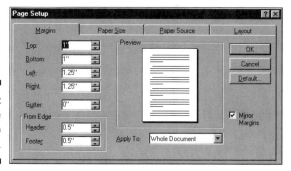

Figure 2-5:
The Page
Setup
dialog box.

As you can see, the Page Setup dialog box has four tabs, which control the following options:

Margins: The options on this tab enable you to set the margins. Normally, this tab contains options to set the Top, Bottom, Left, and Right margins. However, if you click the Mirror Margins button, as I did in Figure 2-5, the Left and Right options change to Inside and Outside. Then the margins for each page alternate: on odd numbered pages, the inside margin is on the left; on even-numbered pages, the inside margin is on the right. The Margins tab also enables you to set the position of headers and footers.

Paper Size: The options on the Paper Size tab enable you to specify the size of the paper (for example, 8½ × 11 inches, 8½ × 14 inches, and so on) and the orientation — whether the page is printed normally (*portrait*) or sideways (*landscape*).

Paper Source: The Paper Source options enable you specify that the first page of the document is to be printed on paper drawn from a different source than the paper used for the rest of the document. For example, you may specify that the first page be printed on paper manually fed to the printer, and the rest of the document printed on paper drawn from the paper tray. This is used mostly for two-page letters, where the first page is printed on manually fed letterhead, and subsequent pages are printed on plain paper in the printer's paper tray.

Layout: This oddball tab enables you to set up different headers for the even and odd-numbered pages, control how text is aligned between the top and bottom page margin, suppress endnotes (more on this in Chapter 8), and number the lines on the page. Hmph.

The Apply To option in the Page Setup dialog box can be set to Whole Document or This Point Forward. If you select This Point Forward, a new section is created at the current cursor location.

The Ten Commandments of Formatting

When Bill Gates came down from the mountain, he originally had 15 formatting commandments. But he dropped one of the three tablets, shattering it to pieces, so now I have but ten.

I. Thou shalt remember thy keyboard shortcuts to speed thy way

Don't bother memorizing the keyboard shortcuts for formats you rarely or never use. But do memorize the shortcuts for the formats you use frequently. It's much faster to press Ctrl+B than it is to click the mouse button or contend with menus and dialog boxes. Make a short list of the shortcuts you want to learn and tape them to your computer or somewhere within eyesight.

II. Thou shalt not press Enter at the end of each line

You defeat the whole purpose of word processing if you press the Enter key at the end of each line you type. Let WinWord figure out where to break each line.

III. Thou shalt not create empty paragraphs

Don't press the Enter key twice to leave extra space between paragraphs. Instead, format the paragraph with 1½ or 2 blank lines before the first line.

IV. Thou shalt not use extraneous spaces

On a typewriter, you're supposed to hit the spacebar twice between sentences. With proportional fonts, you should use only one space following the period at the end of a sentence. Also, don't use spaces to align text in columns. Use tabs instead.

V. Thou shalt not use extraneous tabs

Don't hit the Tab key two or three times to move text across the page. Instead, hit the tab key once and then set a tab stop where you want the text aligned.

VI. Thou shalt not underline when italics will do

Underlining is for typewriters. Italics is for computers. You paid lots of hard-earned money for your computer, so you may as well get your money's worth.

VII. Thou shalt not use more than three fonts on a page

Avoid the ransom note look at all costs. Use one font for your text, a second font for headings, and maybe a third font for emphasis. But no more than three fonts altogether, please.

VIII. Thou shalt not use Exact Line Spacing

The Exact Line Spacing option is a source of much trouble. Use Single, 1.5 lines, or Double instead.

IX. Thou shalt use the AutoCorrect feature

The AutoCorrect feature can correct typos on the fly, as well as help with simple formatting chores such as making sure sentences start with capital letters and using "curly quotes" properly.

To activate this feature, use the Tools⇨AutoCorrect command. When the AutoCorrect dialog box appears, check the things you want WinWord to automatically correct; then click OK.

X. Thou shalt use styles

The best way to deal with all this formatting nonsense is to put all the formatting you'll ever need into styles. Then you don't have to worry about line spacing, hanging indents, fonts and font sizes, or anything else. Just apply the correct style and everything is taken care of. (Styles are discussed in detail in the next chapter. Aren't you lucky?)

Chapter 3

More about Styles

Styles are what Tigger likes best. They are the secret to freeing yourself from the tyranny of Word's Format menu. With styles, you toil at a paragraph's formatting until you get the paragraph just right; then you type a name by which Word remembers all of the formatting you've applied to the paragraph. From then on, you can apply the same formatting to other paragraphs simply by calling up the style. No more hunting and pecking your way through the Format menu commands, trying to recall how you got the paragraph to look so good.

I like Microsoft's styles so much, I *almost* bought the company. If you're not yet using styles, I suggest you learn how to use them right away. Although the concept of styles may be confusing at first, they aren't really that hard to learn. An hour or so invested in learning how styles work pays off in many saved hours of unnecessary formatting time later.

Understanding Styles

The basic idea behind styles is to store all of the formatting information for a paragraph under a single name. That way, you can quickly apply the saved formats to other paragraphs simply by referring to the style's name. For example, suppose you want to format headings using 16-point Arial Bold, with 18 points of space above the heading and 6 points below, and with a line drawn beneath the paragraph. You'd have to bounce the mouse all over the place to format a heading like this manually. But if you've stored the formats in a style, you can apply all of them with a single mouse click or a keyboard shortcut.

Styles contain all of the formatting information specified with the following WinWord commands:

Format⇨Font: Includes the font name, style (regular, bold, italic, or bold italic), and special character attributes such as small caps or superscripts, as well as character spacing and kerning.

Format⇨Paragraph: Includes left and right indentation, first line indentation and hanging indents, line spacing, before and after spacing, and text flow (widow/orphan control, keep with next, and so on).

Format⇨Tabs: Includes tab stop positions, tab types, leader tabs, and bar tabs.

Format⇨Borders and Shading: Includes borders and line styles as well as fill shades.

Tools⇨Language: Enables you to use an alternate dictionary for spelling and hyphenation.

Format⇨Frame: Enables you to place text in a frame and wrap text around it. (See Chapter 12 for more information about frames.)

Format⇨Bullets and Numbering: Enables you to set up numbered or bulleted lists. (See Chapter 5 for more information about bullets and numbers.)

With all these formats stored together under one name, you can imagine how much time styles can save you. Styles are an integral part of the way WinWord works. Even if you think you don't use styles, you do: WinWord documents start off with several predefined styles, including the ubiquitous Normal style. The Normal style governs the default appearance of paragraphs in your document.

Here are some other benefits of using styles:

✔ Suppose you don't know how to drop a line three points beneath the paragraph, and you don't want to learn how. No problemo. Just bribe your friendly WinWord guru into creating the style for you. Once the style is created, you don't have to know how to use the formatting instructions contained in the style. All you have to know is how to apply the style, and that's as easy as clicking the mouse.

✔ The real beauty of styles comes when you decide that the headings are too small — can't you make them 18 point instead of 16 point? Without styles, you'd have to adjust the size of each heading separately. With styles, you simply change the style and — *voilà!* — all the paragraphs assigned to that style are automatically adjusted.

✔ Styles are stored along with your text in the document file. Thus, each document can have its own collection of styles, and styles with the same name can have different formatting characteristics in different documents. For example, a style named *Bullet List* may have ordinary round bullets in one document but check marks or pointy index fingers in another.

✔ You can also store styles in special types of documents called *templates*. This method makes it easier to set up styles and use them over and over again. You find everything you ever wanted to know about templates in the next chapter.

✔ WinWord comes with 28 templates already set up to format various types of documents, such as letters, reports, proposals, memos, and so on. If one of these templates suits your fancy, you may not need to create your own styles. Just apply the template you like to your document and then use the styles it contains. See Chapter 4 for more information about templates.

✔ Oops, 18 point is too big for the headings. How about 14 point? Once again, no need to change each heading paragraph individually. Just change the style, and each heading paragraph is changed automatically.

✔ Another benefit of using styles is that some WinWord features, most notably Table of Contents and Outline view, work best when you use styles for your headings and body text. Don't even attempt to use these features if you don't use styles. (Outlines are covered in Chapter 6; tables of contents are covered in Chapter 21.)

Basic Style Stuff

The basics of working with styles are not difficult to master. The following sections detail the various procedures you need to get comfortable working with styles.

Creating a new style

To create a new style, follow these steps:

1. Tweak a paragraph until it is formatted just the way you want it.

Select the entire paragraph and set the font. Then use the Format⇨Paragraph command to set the line spacing, before and after spacing, and indentation for the paragraph. If you use tabs for the paragraph, set them using the ruler or the Format⇨Tabs command. Add any other formatting you need, such as bullets, numbering, shading, borders, and so on.

2. Press Ctrl+Shift+S.

Or click the style list box on the Formatting toolbar (the style list box is the left-most box on the Formatting toolbar).

3. Type a name for the style.

Be descriptive. You can use more than one word, but avoid typing a name that's so long it doesn't fit in the style list box.

4. Press Enter.

The style is added to WinWord's list of styles for the document so that you can reuse it.

Keep these points in mind when creating styles:

✔ When thinking up a name, try to come up with a name that describes the function of the paragraph in the document (for example, *Salutation* or *Vogon Poetry*) or that describes the type of formatting the style contains (like *Dbl Indent* or *Bullet List*).

✔ You can access the style you create only in the current document. To make the style accessible in other documents, you need to put it in a template. Templates are covered in Chapter 4.

✔ So far, I've avoided the Format⇨Style command. I'm trying to avoid it as long as possible.

Applying a style

To apply a style to a paragraph, follow these steps:

1. Put the cursor in the paragraph that you want to format.

You don't have to select the entire paragraph; just move the cursor anywhere in it.

2. Choose the style you want from the style list box.

Click the down arrow next to the style list box or press Ctrl+Shift+S; then scroll through the list of styles until you find the one you want. Then click it. The formatting contained in the style is applied to the paragraph.

You can use the preceding procedure to change the style assigned to a paragraph. When you do that, all the formatting drawn from the original style is replaced with formatting from the new style.

To apply a style to two or more adjacent paragraphs, simply select a range of text that includes all the paragraphs you want formatted. Then choose the style. When you press the Enter key to create a new paragraph, the new paragraph normally assumes the same style as the preceding paragraph. See the section "Setting the style of the next paragraph" later in this chapter for an important — and useful — exception.

Every paragraph in a document is assigned to a style. The default style for the first paragraph in a new document is called *Normal*.

You can tell which style is assigned to a paragraph by clicking anywhere in the paragraph and looking at the style list box. It shows the name of the style assigned to the paragraph. Or, if the style area is revealed, you can see the name of each paragraph's style to the left of the paragraph. Use the Tools⇨Options, View command to reveal the style area.

Here are some helpful hints to using styles effectively:

- ✔ If the style that you are looking for doesn't appear in the style list, hold down the Shift key and click the down arrow next to the style list box. Sometimes WinWord doesn't list all the available styles unless you do this.
- ✔ To quickly return a paragraph to Normal style, press Ctrl+Shift+N.
- ✔ To assign the built-in Heading 1, Heading 2, or Heading 3 styles, press Ctrl+Alt+1, Ctrl+Alt+2, or Ctrl+Alt+3.
- ✔ You can create keyboard shortcuts for any style that you create. See the section "Assigning shortcut keys to styles" later in this chapter.

Overriding style formatting

Ordinarily, all the formatting you need for a paragraph should come from the paragraph's style. However, there are occasions when you want to add additional formatting to a paragraph or change some aspect of a paragraph's formatting. The most common example of this is applying character formats such as bold or italics to characters within the paragraph. However, you can also apply paragraph formats to a paragraph that is formatted with a style. Any formats you apply simply augment or replace formats specified in the style.

Here are some guidelines:

- ✔ Formats that you apply to a paragraph directly rather than via a style are called, naturally enough, *direct formats.*

- ✔ Any direct paragraph formatting you apply is lost if you later decide to apply a different style to the paragraph. For example, if you apply the Normal style to a paragraph and then add 12 points of space above the paragraph, the extra 12 points of space above is lost if you apply a different style to the paragraph.

- ✔ Character formats are a little different. In most cases, WinWord preserves character formatting that you've applied directly even when you change the paragraph's style. For example, if you create a paragraph formatted with the Normal style, italicize a few words in the paragraph, and then apply another style to the paragraph, the italic words remain italicized.

- ✔ Sometimes, however, WinWord negates direct character formatting that you've applied. This happens when you select a block of text in the paragraph and change the style. WinWord examines the text you selected, and if more than half the text has had direct formatting applied, all the direct formatting in the paragraph is removed. This is a strange rule which makes no sense to me, so I just ignore it. (This strategy works for many of life's little problems, doesn't it?)

- ✔ Notice how I still haven't touched the Format⇨Style command?

Changing a style

There are two ways to change the formatting of an existing style: with or without the Format⇨Style command. Because the Format⇨Style command is a cumbersome beast, I recommend the first procedure.

Here's the procedure for changing a style without using the Format⇨Style command:

1. **Find a paragraph that is formatted with the style you want to change.**

2. **Change its formatting.**

   Use keyboard shortcuts, toolbar buttons, or commands on the Format menu if you must. To change the character format for a style, first select the entire paragraph by triple-clicking it; then apply the character format.

   Besides triple-clicking, there are other ways to select an entire paragraph. You can double-click in the selection area just to the left of the paragraph. If the style area is revealed, you can click the paragraph's style name in the style area.

3. **Reapply the style to the paragraph.**

   Click the down arrow next to the style list box, or press Ctrl+Shift+S; then click the name of the style.

4. **When the Reapply Style dialog box appears, click OK.**

   Figure 3-1 shows the Reapply Style dialog box. It presents you with two options: you can either update the style with the changes you've made to the paragraph, or you can discard the changes and reapply the style as it was. Assuming you want to update the style to reflect the changes you've made (that's the default choice), just click OK or press Enter.

Figure 3-1:
The Reapply
Style
dialog box.

5. **Notice how other paragraphs formatted with the same style are changed automatically.**

   Aren't styles great?

If you fiddle with a paragraph a bit and then decide you liked it the way it was, reapply the style, but pick the second choice in the Reapply Style dialog box (Return the formatting of the selection to the style).

Giving in to the Format⇨Style Command

So far, I've conveniently avoided the Format⇨Style command. I could only put off the inevitable for a short time, however. Now it's time to pay the piper. The following procedure describes how you can use the Format⇨Style command to change a style.

1. **Summon the Format⇨Style command.**

   Remember how to do this? Simply click the menu commands or press Alt+O and then *S*. The Style dialog box appears, as shown in Figure 3-2.

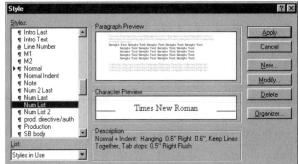

Figure 3-2:
The Style
dialog box.

2. Rummage through the Styles list until you find your style and then click it.

If you selected a paragraph formatted with the style you want to change before calling up Format⇨Style, that style appears in the Style dialog box. (To find styles quickly, type the first letter of the style you want to find. The style list jumps to the first style that starts with that letter.)

3. Click Modify.

The Modify Style dialog box appears, as shown in Figure 3-3.

Figure 3-3:
The Modify
Style
dialog box.

4. Change the format of the style.

Click the Format button to reveal the mini-Format menu, shown in Figure 3-4. Choose any of these menu commands to summon an appropriate formatting dialog box. (The dialog boxes that appear when you choose one of these commands are identical to the ones that appear when you choose the corresponding command from the main Format menu.)

Figure 3-4:
The Modify
Style dialog
box's
Format
menu.

5. After you have made your formatting changes, click OK.

Doing so returns you to the Style dialog box. The Cancel button changes to a Close button.

6. Click Close.

The style is updated and any paragraphs formatted with that style are updated to reflect the new style.

If you don't like the results of your style changes, press Ctrl+Z to undo them.

Deleting a style

Styles can be very useful, so useful in fact that you may soon start creating them at the drop of a hat. Pretty soon, your documents are filled with styles you no longer use. When that happens, it's time to prune your style garden back, deleting styles you no longer use.

Fortunately, deleting styles is easy. Just follow these simple steps:

1. Conjure up the Format⇨Style command.

2. When the Style dialog box appears, choose the style that you want to delete from the Styles list box.

3. Click the Delete button.

4. That's all!

When you delete a style, any paragraphs formatted with the style return to Normal style.

Styles go in and out of fashion all the time, so don't feel bad about deleting them.

Neat Things to Do with Styles

There's much more to using styles than creating and applying them. The sections that follow chronicle some of the more interesting things you can do with styles.

Assigning shortcut keys to styles

WinWord enables you to assign keyboard shortcuts to your favorite styles. Then you can apply those styles by simply pressing the keyboard shortcut. There are two ways to assign keyboard shortcuts: with and without the Format⇨Style command.

To create a keyboard shortcut using the Format⇨Style command, follow these steps:

1. **Conjure up the Format⇨Style command.**

2. **Choose the style that you want to create a shortcut for.**

3. **Click the Modify button.**

4. **When the Modify Style dialog appears, click the Shortcut Key button.**

   The Customize dialog box appears, ready for you to assign a keyboard shortcut for the style. (See Figure 3-5.)

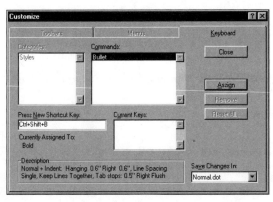

Figure 3-5: Assigning a keyboard shortcut to a style.

5. **Type the keyboard shortcut you want to assign to the style.**

   For example, Ctrl+Shift+B.

6. **Click Assign to assign the keyboard shortcut.**

7. **Click Close; then click OK and then Close again to get all the way out of there.**

To assign a keyboard shortcut without using the Format⇨Style command, follow these steps:

1. **Press Ctrl+Alt+gray plus.**

   That's the gray plus sign key on the numeric keypad, way over at the far right side of the keyboard.

2. **Check out the mouse pointer that looks like a pretzel.**

   Avoid the temptation to douse it with mustard.

3. **Choose the style from the style list box on the Formatting toolbar.**

   Click the down arrow next to the style list box; then click the style you want to assign a shortcut to. WinWord displays the Customize dialog box, ready for you to type a shortcut.

4. **Type the keyboard shortcut that you want to use.**

   Like Ctrl+Alt+R.

5. **Click Assign to assign the shortcut to the style.**

6. **Click Close; click OK; then click Close.**

   You're done.

Keep these tidbits in mind when using keyboard shortcuts:

✔ You can assign more than one keyboard shortcut to a style if you want.

✔ To remove a keyboard assignment you previously assigned, click it in the Current Keys list in the Customize dialog box; then click the Remove button.

✔ The four predefined paragraph styles already have keyboard shortcuts associated with them:

Ctrl+N	Normal
Ctrl+Alt+1	Heading 1
Ctrl+Alt+2	Heading 2
Ctrl+Alt+3	Heading 3

✔ You can create keyboard shortcuts using virtually any combination of keys on the keyboard. The shortcuts can utilize the Shift, Ctrl, and Alt keys, either alone or in combination. For example, you could assign Ctrl+K, Alt+K, Ctrl+Shift+K, Ctrl+Alt+K, or even Ctrl+Alt+Shift+K.

✔ You also can create complex keyboard shortcuts such as Ctrl+Shift+I, 1. To activate this shortcut, the user must press Ctrl+Shift+I; then release those keys and press the 1 key.

- ✔ When you type a keyboard shortcut in the Customize dialog box, WinWord displays the current command assigned to the keyboard shortcut you press. Take note of this assignment to make sure that you aren't stepping on some other useful function's toes. In the case of Figure 3-5, I pressed Ctrl+Shift+B, which is already assigned to the Bold command. I decided to assign the shortcut anyway, though, because Ctrl+B is an easier and more commonly used shortcut for bold.

- ✔ You can also assign styles to toolbar buttons or custom menus. See Chapters 17 and 18 for details.

Basing one style on another

Suppose you create 20 different styles for various types of paragraphs in a complicated document, only to discover that your boss wants the entire document to use Palatino rather than Times New Roman as the base font. Do you have to change all 20 styles to reflect the new font? Not if you set your styles up using *base styles*.

A base style is a style that provides formatting information for other styles. For example, suppose you have a style named Bullet List, and you want to create a similar style named Bullet List Last that you use for the last paragraph of a series of bulleted paragraphs. The only difference between Bullet List and Bullet List Last is that Bullet List Last has additional space after the paragraph. Otherwise, the styles are identical. Base styles enable you to do this. In this case, Bullet List Last consists of all the formatting from its base style, Bullet List, plus 6 points of space after.

A style *inherits* all the formats that are specified in its base style. If the base style changes, the changes are inherited, too. However, a style can override the formats that it inherits from the base style. For example, if a style does not specify a point size, any paragraphs formatted with the style inherits the point size from the base style. However, if a style specifies a point size, then the point size of the base style is ignored.

Here's the procedure for creating a style that's based on another style:

1. **Choose the paragraph you want to format.**

2. **Apply the style that you want to use as the base style to the paragraph you selected.**

3. **Change the formatting of the paragraph.**

   Add whatever extra formats you want to be applied to the new style. These formats are added to the base style's formats.

4. Create the new style.

See the earlier section "Creating a new style" for help with this step. The new style is based on the style that was originally applied to the paragraph.

You can also set the base style by using the Format➪Style command. Click Modify on the Style dialog box; then choose the base style in the Based On text box of the Modify Style dialog box.

Any changes you make to a style are automatically reflected in any styles that are based on the style you change. Thus, if all 20 of your paragraph styles are based on the Normal style, you can change the font for all 20 styles simply by changing the font for the Normal style. (Except for any styles that are based on Normal, but then specify their own font to override the font picked up from the Normal style. In that case, those styles retain their own fonts.)

You can quickly tell what a style's base style is and what additional formats are added to the base style by looking at the style's description displayed at the bottom of the various style dialog boxes. Look at Figures 3-2, 3-3, or 3-5 to see what I mean. In these figures, the description for the Num List dialog box is as follows:

```
Normal + Indent: Hanging 0.6" Right 0.6", Keep Lines
Together, Tab stops 0.5" Right Flush
```

Here, you can tell that the Num List style is based on the Normal style, but adds a hanging indent, Keep Lines Together, and a right tab stop.

A style does not have to be based on another style. If you don't want a style to be based on another style, use the Format➪Style command, choose the style you want to modify, and click the Modify button. Then change the Based On drop-down list box to "(no style)."

A style that serves as a base style may itself have a base style. For example, Bullet List Last may be based on Bullet List, which in turn may be based on Normal. In that case, the formats from Normal, Bullet List, and Bullet List Last are merged together whenever you apply the style.

Setting the style of the next paragraph

When you press the Enter key to create a new paragraph, the new paragraph normally assumes the same style as the previous paragraph. In some cases, that's exactly what you want it to do. However, for some styles, the style of the following paragraph is almost always a different style. For example, a paragraph formatted with the Heading 1 style is rarely followed by another Heading 1 paragraph. Instead, a Heading 1 paragraph is usually followed by a Normal paragraph.

Instead of always changing the style assigned to a new paragraph in situations like this, you can specify the style to be assigned to the next paragraph with the Format⇨Style command. Then, when you press the Enter key, the new paragraph is assigned the style you specified. This little trick can almost completely automate the chore of formatting your documents.

To set the style for a following paragraph, follow these steps:

1. **Conjure up the Format⇨Style command.**

   The Style dialog box appears.

2. **Choose the style you want to modify.**

   Scroll through the list of styles until you find the one you want. For example, Heading 1.

3. **Click the Modify button.**

   The Modify Style dialog box appears.

4. **Choose the style for the next paragraph in the Style for Following Paragraph text box.**

   Click the arrow to reveal a drop-down list of all available styles in the document. Click the one that should ordinarily follow paragraphs formatted with the style you're modifying. For example, Normal.

5. **Click OK.**

   You return to the Style dialog box.

6. **Click Close.**

   You're done.

✔ Examine the Style for Following Paragraph setting for each of your styles to see whether you can save yourself some work. Heading styles should specify Normal for the following paragraph, as should any other type of paragraph that usually occurs in singles. You may find other styles that should have this field set, too. For example, I have a Chapter Number style that specifies Chapter Title as Style for Following Paragraph.

✔ This is such a great time-saver that I wish I had about eight more things to add to this short bullet list to make it look more important. But the only thing of note to say here is — just do it!

Viewing style assignments by enabling the style area

If you want to have a bird's eye view of the styles applied to each paragraph, open up the style area — a narrow band on the left-hand edge of the document window. Figure 3-6 shows what WinWord looks like with the style area activated.

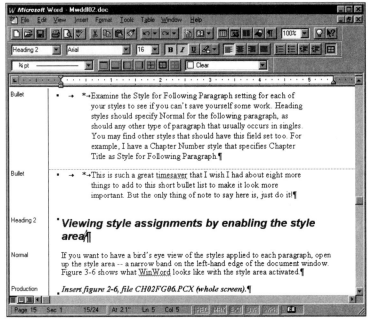

Figure 3-6: The style area.

Follow these simple steps to enable the style area:

1. Choose the Tools⇨Options command.

The Options dialog box appears.

2. Find the View tab and click it.

The Options dialog box has 12 tabs, so you may have to hunt for a moment to find the View tab.

3. Set the Style Area Width text box to 0.6 inch.

The Style Area Width text box is located at the bottom left of the dialog box. You can set it to any width you want, but 0.6 inch is just about wide enough to accommodate most style names.

4. Click OK.

The style area should appear.

Here are some helpful hints:

✔ You can adjust the width of the style area by dragging the line that separates it from the rest of the document window. Just position the mouse over the line and press the mouse button when the pointer changes shape. Drag the line to increase or decrease the width of the style area.

✔ To remove the style area altogether, drag the line all the way to the left of the window or invoke the Tools⇨Options command and set the Style Area Width text box to 0.

✔ You can select an entire paragraph by clicking the paragraph's style name in the style area.

✔ The problem with the style area is that it restricts the width of the document window. If you can't see the entire width of your text with the style area enabled, you may want to leave it off.

✔ The style area is visible only in Normal and Outline View. If WinWord is in Page Layout View when you call up the Tools⇨Options command, you won't see the Style Area Width field. Use the View⇨Normal or View⇨Outline commands to switch to Normal or Outline View.

Viewing formatting using the Help button

Unsure about the formatting you've applied to a paragraph or character? Fear not. You can use the Help button, located at the far right edge of the Standard toolbar, to find out what formats have been applied and whether those formats came from a style or were directly applied.

Here's the procedure for examining formats using the Help button:

1. Click the Help button.

The mouse pointer picks up a question mark riding piggyback.

2. Click the character whose format you want to examine.

If you're interested in the paragraph formatting, click any character in the paragraph. For the formatting applied to a specific character, you must click directly on that character.

3. Check it out.

A big cartoon bubble appears, showing the formats applied to the paragraph and character (see Figure 3-7).

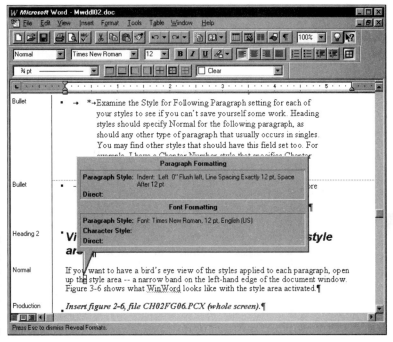

Figure 3-7:
Using the
Help button
to examine
formats.

4. Click the Help button again or press Esc when you're done.

The formatting bubble shows paragraph and character formatting separately. The top part of the bubble shows the formatting applied to the paragraph from the paragraph style and applied directly. The bottom part shows the character formatting taken from the paragraph style, the character style (if any), and direct character formatting.

To see formatting information for another character, click again. The Help function remains active until you dismiss it by clicking the Help button again or pressing the Esc key.

Character style? He never said anything about character styles. What's he talking about? (See the next section.)

Creating and using character styles

The vast majority of WinWord styles are *paragraph styles*, which affect formatting for an entire paragraph. WinWord has a little-known and seldom-used feature called *character styles*, which enables you to create styles applied to specified characters rather than entire paragraphs.

Here's the blow-by-blow account of how you create a character style:

1. **Summon the Format⇨Style command.**

   The Style dialog box appears.

2. **Click the New button.**

   The New Style dialog box appears, as shown in Figure 3-8.

3. **Change the Style Type text box to Character.**

4. **Type a name for the new character style in the Name text box.**

   In Figure 3-8, I typed **Shady** in the Name text box.

5. **Use the Format button to specify the character formats you want for the style.**

   In Figure 3-8, I specified Lt. Gray for the character color.

6. **If you want to assign a keyboard shortcut to the style, use the Shortcut Key button.**

   When the Customize dialog box appears, type your shortcut key, click the Assign button, and then click the Close button.

7. **Click OK; then click Close.**

Figure 3-8:
Creating a
character
style.

To apply a character style, select the range of characters you want to apply the style to and then apply the style using the style list box on the Formatting toolbar or by typing the style's keyboard shortcut.

Like paragraph styles, character styles can be based on other styles. You can use a special style name, *Default Paragraph Font*, to make the character style inherit the font formats of the underlying paragraph style.

The shady character style is best used in documents written by shady characters.

Don't let me tell you the difference between direct character formats and character styles

The difference between a character style and direct character formatting is subtle. When you assign a new style to a paragraph, any formatting applied by character styles is preserved. Formatting applied by direct character formats (bold, italic, and so on) is usually preserved, but not if you selected a block of characters before applying the new paragraph style, and more than half the characters in the block were directly formatted. In that case, all direct formatting for the paragraph is removed.

If you frequently assign paragraph styles by marking a block of text in the paragraph, and you're annoyed when you lose direct character formatting, consider using character styles instead of direct formatting. Create the following character styles:

Bold text: Default Paragraph Font + Bold, keyboard shortcut Ctrl+B.

Italic text: Default Paragraph Font + Italic, keyboard shortcut Ctrl+I.

Bold Italic text: Default Paragraph Font + Bold Italic, keyboard short cut Ctrl+Shift+B.

By specifying Ctrl+B and Ctrl+I as keyboard short-cuts for bold text and italic text, you apply them in exactly the same way that you apply direct bold and italic formatting.

However, the need for a separate bold italic text style points out another difference between character styles and direct character formats. You cannot gang-tackle text with character styles. If you type Ctrl+B to apply the bold text style and then type Ctrl+I to apply the italic text style, the bold format is replaced with the italic format. With direct character formats, the sequence Ctrl+B, Ctrl+I results in bold italic text.

If you use any other character formats routinely, create character styles for them, too. For example, if you frequently use the Strikethrough format, create a Strikethrough character style and assign a keyboard shortcut to it. If you like to interject a little Greek here and there, create a Greek Text character style that sets the font to Symbol and assign it a keyboard shortcut.

Searching for and replacing style formatting

Want to quickly find every paragraph formatted with the Heading 1 style? You can activate the style area and scroll through the document, watching the style area to see whether the Heading 1 style comes up. But there's an easier way: just use the Edit⇨Find command.

Here's the procedure for finding paragraphs tagged with a particular style:

1. **Invoke the Edit⇨Find command.**

   The keyboard shortcut is Ctrl+F. Either way, the Find dialog box shown in Figure 3-9 appears.

2. **Click the Format button and then choose the Style command from the pop-up menu.**

   The Find Style dialog box appears, as shown in Figure 3-10.

3. **In the Find Style dialog box, scroll through the list of styles until you locate the one you're looking for. Click it; then click OK.**

   Make sure that the Find What text box is blank; otherwise, the Find command searches for specific text that's formatted with the style you specify.

4. **Click the Find Next button to find the next occurrence of the style.**

   Click it again to find the next occurrence. It's like déjà vu all over again.

5. **Press Esc when you're done.**

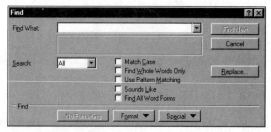

Figure 3-9:
The Find dialog box.

Figure 3-10:
The Find Style dialog box.

To replace paragraph styles, follow a similar procedure with the Edit⇨Replace command:

1. **Invoke the Edit⇨Replace command.**

   The keyboard shortcut is Ctrl+H. The Replace dialog box appears.

2. **Click in the Find What text box; then use the Format button to choose the style you want to find and replace.**

3. **Click in the Replace With text box; then use the Format button to choose the style you want to replace the Find What style with.**

4. **Click the Find Next button.**

   WinWord finds the first paragraph formatted with the style you specified and asks whether you want to replace its style.

5. **Click Replace if you want to replace the style.**

   WinWord replaces the style; then it finds the next paragraph formatted with the style and asks again. If you don't want to replace it, click Find Next. Either way, WinWord finds the next paragraph and asks again. Keep it up until all paragraphs have been found.

When replacing one style with another, you can click the Replace All button to have WinWord replace all occurrences of the style without asking your permission. I suggest you start by clicking Find Next just to make sure that WinWord is finding and replacing styles the way you intended. After you're sure, click Replace All to finish the laborious Find and Replace operation without your intervention.

Make sure that you leave both the Find What and Replace With fields blank. You're looking for all paragraphs formatted with a particular style; it doesn't matter what text is in the paragraphs. If you accidentally leave text in the Replace With text box, WinWord replaces the entire paragraph with the Replace With text. If that happens, press Ctrl+Z and go fishing.

Storing styles in a template

You can store styles directly in a document file or in a *template* file. When you apply a template to a document, you can copy all the styles in the template into the document, replacing any existing styles with the same name. You can change the entire look of a document simply by applying a different template.

Keep these hints in mind when using templates:

- To store a style in the current template rather than the current document, check the Add to Template button in the New Style dialog box when you use the Format⇨Style command to create the style.

- To copy styles from the document to the template, use the Format⇨Style command and then click the Organizer button.

- To apply a different template to the document, use the File⇨Templates command.

- For much more information about using templates, read ahead to Chapter 4.

Ten Points to Remember about Using Styles

Here are ten (or so) points to remember when you use styles, in no particular order.

Always use styles

This is kind of redundant, because with WinWord, you *have* to use styles. Whether you realize it or not, all paragraphs in WinWord are based on a style. If you don't use styles, the paragraphs are based on the utilitarian Normal style.

My point here is that for all but the simplest of documents, create and apply styles instead of applying direct formatting to your paragraphs. In the long run, using styles rather than direct formatting saves you a great deal of time and grief. You may curse the computer while you climb the steep-at-times learning curve that comes along with using styles, but when you get to the top, you'll say to yourself, "That wasn't so hard."

Avoid the Format⇨Style command at all costs

I hate the Format⇨Style command. It's much easier to create styles by example: format a paragraph, click in the style list box on the Formatting toolbar, and type a new style name. To apply a style, use a keyboard shortcut or choose the style name from the style list box.

The Format➪Style command is useful in the following circumstances:

- ✔ You want to assign a keyboard shortcut to a style, and you can't remember that Ctrl+Alt+gray plus is the shortcut.
- ✔ You want to specify a style for the following paragraph.
- ✔ You want to use a different base style.
- ✔ You want to delete a style.

You can perform most other routine style chores more easily without the Format➪Style command.

Check out the templates that come with WinWord

Microsoft has already done a great deal of the hard work creating styles for you. Check out the various templates that come with WinWord to see whether any of them are suitable. If not, pick one that's close and modify it to suit your needs.

Use the Style for Following Paragraph field to automate your formatting

The fastest way to assign styles is to have WinWord do it automatically. Set the Style for Following Paragraph field in the Modify Style or New Style dialog box. Then, when you press the Enter key to create a new paragraph, WinWord automatically assigns the style.

Use keyboard shortcuts to assign styles quickly

The second fastest way to assign styles is to use keyboard shortcuts. Assign a keyboard shortcut to each style that you use frequently. Don't bother with the ones you use infrequently, though. It's hard enough to remember the keyboard shortcuts you use frequently.

Use the built-in Heading 1, Heading 2, and Heading 3 styles for your headings

WinWord has three predefined heading styles. If you don't like the way they look, redefine them. By using Heading 1, Heading 2, and Heading 3, you can work with your headings in Outline view or use them to create a Table of Contents. (See Chapters 6 and 21 for more information.)

Base all text variants on the Normal style

Most documents have several different types of paragraphs that are minor variations on normal text. For example, the bullet-list paragraphs in this book are variations of the book's normal-text paragraphs: They have the same typeface, point size, and line spacing, but the margins are different and they have bullets. Paragraphs like this should be formatted with styles that are based on the Normal style. That way, if you decide to make a sweeping change, such as moving from 10 to 11 point type or switching from Times New Roman to Palatino, you can change the Normal style rather than changing each style individually.

Use Space Before or Space After, but not both

When you create your paragraph styles, decide in advance whether you prefer to add extra space before or after the paragraphs. As much as possible, stick to your decision. If you have two adjacent paragraphs, the first with extra space after and the second with space before, you may end up with more space than you intended between the paragraphs.

Chapter 4

More about Templates

In This Chapter

▶ Understanding templates

▶ Applying a template to a document

▶ Creating a new template

▶ Using global templates

▶ Using the Organizer to move stuff between templates

▶ Learning ten (more or less) template tips

A *template* is not a place of worship, though an occasional sacrifice to the WinWord gods may make your word processing life a bit easier. Rather, a template is a special type of Word document that holds styles, boiler-plate text, macros, keyboard shortcuts, and other customized Word settings.

You can probably get by for years without knowing or caring about templates, but a solid understanding of what templates are and how they work helps remove the shroud of mystery from many of Word's most useful features, especially styles. As a result, this chapter presents the basics of working with templates: what they are, how to create them, and how to use them.

Understanding Templates

A *template* is a special type of document file used as the basis for formatting your documents. Whenever you create a new document, a template file is used as the starting point for the new document. The following items are copied from the template into the new document:

✔ The template's styles

✔ Margins and other page layout information specified in the File⇨Page Setup command, including paper size and orientation, headers and footers, and so on

 ✔ Columns set by the Format⇨Columns command

 ✔ AutoText entries

 ✔ Text and graphics

 ✔ Macros

 ✔ Keyboard shortcuts, as well as menu and toolbar customizations

A template is really no different than a normal document, except that it is saved with a filename extension of DOT rather than DOC, as normal documents are. You can open a template and edit it just as you can any other document, and you can convert a document to a template simply by saving it as a template rather than as a document. The real difference between templates and documents is in how they are used.

Each document has one and only one template attached to it. If you don't specify a template to attach to a new document, WinWord attaches the generic template NORMAL.DOT, which contains the standard styles such as Normal, Heading 1, Heading 2, and Heading 3, plus default margins, keyboard shortcuts, toolbars, and so on. You can attach a different template to a document later, and you can copy the styles from the new template into the existing document, if you wish. Then you have access to the styles from the new template as well as the existing document.

The NORMAL.DOT template is always available in WinWord, even if you're working with a document that's based on some other template. Computer nerds call NORMAL.DOT a *global template.* (Computer nerds love the term *global* because they have visions of dominating the planet someday.)

Attaching Templates to Your Documents

Before you get into templates too deep, here's a quick review of the basics of attaching templates to your documents.

Creating a new document based on a template

To create a document based on a template other than NORMAL.DOT, follow these steps:

1. Conjure up the File⇨New command.

You are greeted by the ever-familiar New dialog box shown in Figure 4-1.

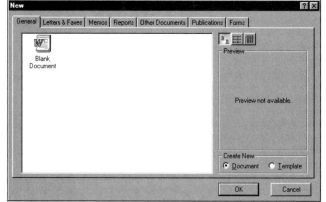

Figure 4-1:
The File
New dialog
box.

2. Select the template you want to base the new document on. If the template doesn't appear in the New dialog box, click one of the tabs that appears at the top of the dialog box.

3. Click OK.

You're done.

If you create a new document using the New button on the Standard toolbar or the Ctrl+N shortcut, WinWord automatically assigns the NORMAL.DOT template. The only way to create a new document based on a different template is to wade through the murky menu waters.

When you create a new document, any text or graphics that appears within the template is copied into the new document. This is a great way to include a letterhead in all your letters, a standard header in all your memos, a title on all your reports, and so on. When you attach a different template to an existing document (see the next section), text and graphics contained in the template are *not* copied into the document.

If you pick a wizard rather than a template from the New dialog box, the wizard leads you through a series of prompts to gather information about the document that you want to create. It then creates the document for you. When the wizard is finished, the document is fully formatted and loaded with styles, but it is based on the Normal template. In this case, the formatting and styles are created by the wizard, not drawn from a template.

Attaching a different template

If you decide that you want to change the template assigned to a document, follow these steps:

1. Fire up the File⇨Templates command.

You are greeted by the Templates and Add-ins dialog box, shown in Figure 4-2.

2. Click the Attach button.

A dialog box listing available templates appears.

3. Choose the template that you want to attach.

You may have to rummage around your disk a bit to find the template you want.

4. Click Open to return to the Templates and Add-ins dialog box.

5. If you want to copy styles from the new template, check the Automatically Update Document Styles check box.

If you leave this box unchecked, the styles from the new template are ignored. Usually, the reason you're attaching a new template is to get its styles, so you probably want to check this box.

6. Click OK.

You're done. If you updated styles, the results of attaching the new template should be immediately apparent as the paragraphs are reformatted according to the new styles.

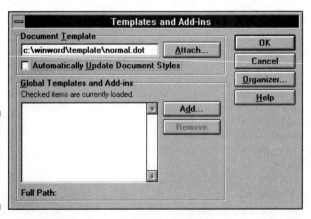

Figure 4-2:
The
Templates
and Add-ins
dialog box.

Here are some idiosyncrasies about using templates that you should know:

✔ When you attach a different template to an existing document, text and graphics from the template are not copied into the document. To include text and graphics from a template, create a new document based on the template.

✔ If you want to see the effects of applying styles from a template without actually attaching the template, use the Format⇨Style Gallery command. It displays a preview of your document formatted with styles from a template you choose. From the gallery, you can copy styles into your document from a template, but you can't actually attach the template to your document. To do that, you must note the name of the template you want to attach, exit the gallery (click Cancel), and then use the File⇨Templates command to attach the template.

✔ The Organizer button whisks you off to the Organizer, the ultimate tool for managing templates. The Organizer is described in detail later in this chapter, in the section "Using the Organizer."

Creating Your Own Templates

If you're not content with the templates provided with WinWord, you can create your own. The sections that follow explain the ins and outs of creating templates.

Creating a new template to store your styles

Let's say you've toiled for hours on a document, and now you want to make its styles available to other documents that you may someday create. The simplest solution is to create a template that contains the styles in your document. Here's how:

1. **Open the document that has all the styles you want to save in a template.**

2. **Invoke the File⇨Save As command.**

   The Save As dialog box appears.

3. **Way down at the bottom of the Save As dialog box, find the Save File as Type drop-down list box. Choose Document Template as the file type.**

4. **Choose the folder in which you wish to store the template.**

   If you want to create a new folder for the template, click the Create New Folder button and type a name for the new folder.

5. Type a filename for the template.

Don't forget that you aren't limited to eight characters anymore. So instead of SLSRPT.DOT, you can use a more meaningful name such as Sales Report.dot.

6. Click OK.

The document is saved as a template file.

7. Delete unnecessary text from the file.

Press Ctrl+A to select the entire document and then press Del to delete it. Or, if you prefer, leave a small amount of boilerplate text behind.

Remember that all the text that you leave in the document appears in your new document when you use the template.

8. Save the file again.

Click the Save button on the Standard toolbar or press Ctrl+S.

Don't forget that besides text and styles, templates also store page setups, column settings, keyboard shortcuts, macros, and toolbars.

Creating a new template from scratch

To create a new template from scratch, follow these steps:

1. Use the File⇨New command.

The New File dialog box appears.

2. Choose the Template radio button.

That way, WinWord creates a new template rather than a new document file.

3. Click OK.

4. Create whatever styles you want to include in the template.

See Chapter 2 for detailed instructions on creating styles.

5. Type some text if you want to include boilerplate text in your template.

6. Save the file.

Use the File⇨Save command. Type a name for the template and click Save.

7. Close the file.

Use the File⇨Close command.

Boring details about where to store templates

By default, Word stores its templates in the \MSOffice\Templates folder. But how does Word know how to divvy up the templates among the zillions of tabs that appear across the top of the New dialog box? The answer is actually pretty easy: Each of those tabs represents a folder within the \MSOffice\Templates folder. Thus, the memo templates are located in \MSOffice\Templates\Memos, while the Letter templates are located in \MSOffice\Templates \Letters.

(The templates that appear under the General tab appear in the \MSOffice\Templates folder, not in \MSOffice\Templates\General. See the following figure.)

When you create your own templates, you have three choices as to where you can store the templates:

1. In \MSOffice\Templates, so that they appear along with "Blank Document" (that is, Normal.dot) under the General tab. This is probably the best place to store your templates, especially if you only need a few. (If you need more than a few custom templates, you may be beyond help anyway.)

2. In one of the existing folders under \MSOffice\Templates. For example, if you create a template named Angry Letter to The Editor.dot, store it in \MSOffice\Templates\Letters folder. That way, the new template appears with your other letter templates under the Letters tab.

3. In a new folder. Click the Create New Folder button when you save the template. The folder you create appears as a tab in the New dialog box.

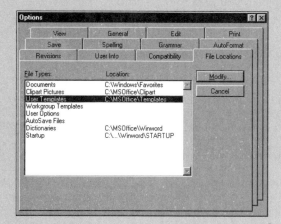

Modifying an existing template

If you want to create a template that's similar to an existing template, the easiest way is to open the template and save your modifications under a new name. Here's the procedure:

1. Invoke the File⇨Open command.

Or click the Open button or press Ctrl+O. The Open dialog box appears.

2. Change the List Files of Type field to Document Templates (*.DOT).

3. Find the template that you want to model the new template on.

You may have to switch to the \MSOffice\Templates folder or the folder that contains your templates.

4. Open it.

Click the template file; then click Open.

5. Use the File⇨Save As command to save the template under a new name.

It's best to do this step before you make any modifications. That way, you don't run the risk of accidentally changing the existing template on disk.

6. Make your changes.

Use the Format⇨Style command to modify the styles, and make any other changes you want to the template.

7. Save your changes.

Press Ctrl+S or click the Save button.

8. Close the file.

Use the File⇨Close command.

Using Global Templates

The NORMAL.DOT template is a *global template,* which means that it is always available when you're working in WinWord, even if you're working with a document that is attached to a different template. You can specify that other templates become global ones, too, so that they are available even if you're not working with a document that's attached to them.

The styles and text contained in a global template are not available unless the current document is attached to that template. However, any macros, AutoText entries, toolbars, and customized menus are available whenever the global template is active.

Follow these steps to activate a global template:

1. Summon the File⇨Templates command.

The Templates and Add-ins dialog box appears.

2. Locate the Global Templates and Add-ins list box.

It contains a list of all the currently available global templates, along with buttons to Add or Remove global templates.

3. Click the Add button.

The Add Templates dialog box appears.

4. Choose the template that you want to make global; then click OK.

When you return to the Templates and Add-ins dialog box, the template you chose appears in the Global Templates and Add-ins list box.

5. Click OK.

You're done.

Some tidbits about global templates follow:

✔ To disable a global template temporarily, conjure up the File⇨Templates command and uncheck the template's check box in the Global Templates and Add-ins list box. To remove the template from the list, choose it and click the Remove button.

✔ After you've made a template global, it remains global until you quit WinWord. The next time you start WinWord, the template is included in the Global Templates and Add-ins list box, but its check box is unchecked so that it is not active. To activate the template to make it global, use the File⇨Templates command and check the template's check box. See the sidebar, "Stop me before I tell you about the startup directory," to find out how to set up a global template that's active each time you start WinWord.

✔ It's best not to mix global templates and templates attached to documents. If you want to create a bunch of custom macros, toolbars, and menus for global use, place them in a separate template that you don't use for documents.

Stop me before I tell you about the startup directory

When you add a template to the Global Templates and Add-ins list, the template remains in the list each time you start Word. However, you must use the File➪Templates command and check the check box next to the template in the list to make the template global. If you don't want to do that each time you start Word, follow these steps:

1. Exit Word using the File➪Exit command.

2. Double-click on the My Computer icon on your desktop. Double-click on the C drive and navigate to the \MSOffice\Templates folder.

3. Double-click on My Computer again to open a second My Computer window. Double-click on the C drive, then navigate to the \MSOffice\Winword\Startup folder.

4. Drag any templates you want to be global ones from \MSOffice\Templates to \MSOffice\Winword\Startup.

5. Close both My Computer windows and then start Word.

Any template files in the \MSOffice\Winword \Startup folder are automatically loaded and made global. If you previously added the template to the Global Templates and Add-ins list, you should remove it before following the preceding procedure.

Using the Organizer

If you want to move styles en masse from one document or template to another, the easiest way to do it is to use the Organizer — WinWord's tenacious tool for taming templates. The organizer is especially useful when you create several new styles in a document and you want to copy those files to the document's template.

To copy styles from your document to a template, follow these steps:

1. **Summon the Format➪Style command.**

   The Style dialog box appears.

2. **Click the Organizer button.**

   The Organizer dialog box, shown in Figure 4-3, appears.

3. **If you want to copy styles to a template other than NORMAL.DOT, click the right Close File button, click the Open File button, choose the template file, and click Open.**

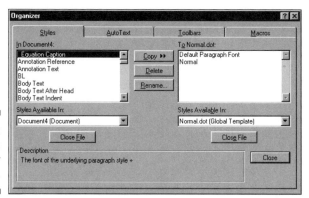

4. **Choose the styles you want to copy in the left style list (the In list box).**

   To choose several styles, hold down the Ctrl key while clicking style names. To choose a block of styles, click the first style in the block; then hold down the Shift key and click the last style.

5. **Click the Copy button.**

   The styles are copied from the document to the template.

6. **Click the Close button.**

The Organizer is a helpful beast:

✔ You can copy styles from either list in the Organizer dialog box. If you choose styles in the right box, the In and To designations switch and the arrows on the Copy button change to indicate that styles are copied from the right list to the left list.

✔ To move styles from the current document to NORMAL.DOT, skip Step 3 in the preceding procedure.

✔ Click the down arrow next to the Styles Available In list box on the left side of the Organizer dialog box to reveal a list of style sources that includes the current document, the currently attached style, and NORMAL.DOT. To move styles from the attached template to NORMAL.DOT, choose the template in the Styles Available In list.

✔ You can also use the Organizer to delete or rename styles. To delete styles, choose them in either the left or right list; then click the Delete button. If you've been good, WinWord asks for confirmation before it deletes the styles. To rename a style, choose it and click the Rename button. When WinWord asks for a new name, start typing. (Notice that you can rename only one style at a time.)

✔ The Organizer is also handy for copying toolbars, macros, and AutoText settings from one template to another. Just click the appropriate Organizer tab and have at it.

Chapter 5

More about Bullets and Numbers

In This Chapter

▶ Creating bulleted lists or numbered lists the easy way

▶ Using deviant bullets

▶ Using crazy numbering schemes

▶ Creating a multilevel numbered list

▶ Numbering headings

*B*ullets and numbered lists are great ways to add emphasis to a series of important points or to add a sense of order to items that fall into a natural sequence. Glance through this book and you see what I mean. It's loaded with bulleted and numbered lists.

In WinWord, you can add a bullet or a line number to each paragraph. The bullet or number is a part of the paragraph format, and WinWord adds the bullet character or the number so that you don't have to. WinWord even keeps the numbers in a numbered list in sequence, so if you add or delete a paragraph or rearrange paragraphs in the list, the numbers are automatically reordered.

The Easy Way to Create a Bulleted or Numbered List

Nothing is easier than clicking a toolbar button, and that's about all there is to creating a simple bulleted or numbered list. With the click of a button, you can create a bulleted list like this one:

- Cheery disposition
- Rosy cheeks
- No warts
- Plays games, all sorts

Click another button, and you transform the whole thing into a numbered list:

1. Cheery disposition

2. Rosy cheeks

3. No warts

4. Plays games, all sorts

Do *not* type bullet characters (either asterisks or special Wingding characters) or numbers yourself. Instead, use the following procedures to create bulleted or numbered lists.

Creating a bulleted list the easy way

To create a bulleted list, follow this procedure:

1. **Type one or more paragraphs that you want to add bullets to.**

2. **Select the paragraphs that you want to add bullets to by clicking and dragging the mouse over them.**

 3. **Click the Bullet button on the Formatting toolbar (shown in the margin).**

4. **You're done.**

When you create a bulleted list this way, WinWord uses a default bullet character (normally a small dot) and creates a ¼ inch hanging indent. (If the paragraphs already have hanging indents, the original indentation settings are preserved.) To learn how use oddball bullets, find the section "Using Deviant Bullets" later in this chapter.

To add additional items to the bulleted list, position the cursor at the end of one of the bulleted paragraphs and press Enter. Because the bullet is part of the paragraph format, it is carried over to the new paragraph.

You can remove bullets as easily as you add them. The Bullet button works like a toggle: press it once to add bullets, press it again to remove them. To remove bullets from an entire list, select all the paragraphs in the list and click the Bullet button.

Ever notice how the good guys never run out of bullets in the movies? Bad idea. The old notion of the six shooter is a pretty good one. More than six bullets in a row is pushing the limits of most reader's patience. (Of course, I've routinely disregarded that advice throughout this book, but what are you going to do, shoot me?)

Oh, and by the way, you probably shouldn't leave one bullet standing by itself. Bullets are used to mark items in a list, and it takes more than one item to make a list.

If you want to create a bulleted list as you go, start by formatting the first paragraph with a bullet. Then the bullet format is propagated to subsequent paragraphs as you type them. When you're done, press the Enter key and then click the Bullet button again to deactivate bullets.

Without doubt, the best way to work with bullets is to create a bullet style. This way, you can customize the bullet style all you want. With a bit of work, you can even mimic the check mark and gray-line look of the bullets in this book or create your own custom bullet design. Assign a keyboard shortcut such as Ctrl+Shift+B to your custom bullet style, and you're on your way.

Creating a numbered list the easy way

To create a numbered list, follow this procedure:

1. **Type one or more paragraphs that you want numbered.**

2. **Select them all.**

    Drag the mouse over all the paragraphs you want numbered.

 3. **Click the Numbering button on the Formatting toolbar.**

4. **That's all!**

When you use the Numbering button to create a numbered list, WinWord uses a default numbering format and establishes a ¼ inch hanging indent for each paragraph. (If the paragraphs are already formatted with hanging indents, the original indentation settings are kept.) You can use all sorts of crazy numbering schemes if you want; to find out how, skip ahead to the section "Using Crazy Numbering Schemes."

WinWord is really cool about keeping the list in order. If you add or delete a paragraph in the middle of the list, WinWord renumbers the paragraphs to preserve the order. If you add a paragraph to the end of the list, WinWord assigns the next number in sequence to the new paragraph.

The Numbering button works like a toggle: Click it once to add numbers to paragraphs, click it again to remove them. To remove numbering from a numbered paragraph, select the paragraph and click the Numbering button. To remove numbering from an entire list, select all the paragraphs in the list and click the Numbering button.

Hahahaha! Even Word goofs up once in a while!

I hate to be the bearer of bad news, but Word's Bullets and Numbering feature has a rather annoying bug. I discovered it one day when I was typing a list of my favorite Disney movies. I typed:

Snow White

Cinderella

101 Dalmatians

The Jungle Book

Then I selected the entire list and clicked the Numbering button. Here's what I got:

1. Snow White

2. Cinderella

3. Dalmatians

4. The Jungle Book

Did you notice that Word decided to remove the *101* from *101 Dalmatians*? Just a bit pretentious, don't you think?

The trouble is that Word thinks you might try to type some of the numbers yourself, and so it removes anything that looks like a number. Always be on the lookout for disappearing text whenever you use the bullet or numbering feature.

If you insert a nonnumbered paragraph in the middle of a numbered list, WinWord breaks the list in two and begins numbering from one again for the second list. However, if you simply turn off numbering for one of the paragraphs in a list, WinWord suspends the numbering for that paragraph and picks up where it left off with the next numbered paragraph.

Using Deviant Bullets

If you don't like the default bullet format that you get when you click the Bullet button, change it! Here's how:

1. Invoke the F̲ormat⇨Bullets and N̲umbering command.

The Bullets and Numbering dialog box appears, as shown in Figure 5-1. This dialog box has three tabs. If the bullet options don't appear, click the B̲ulleted tab to bring them forth. The Bulleted tab presents six possible bullet formats.

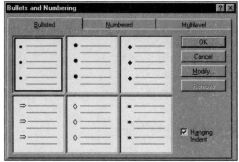

Figure 5-1:
The Bullets
and
Numbering
dialog box
(the Bulleted
tab).

2. **If one of the six bullet formats shown in the dialog box suits your fancy, click it and then click OK. You're done.**

3. **Otherwise, click the Modify button.**

   The Modify Bulleted List dialog box appears, as shown in Figure 5-2.

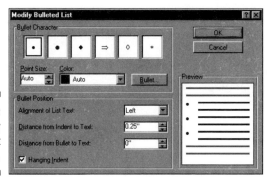

Figure 5-2:
The Modify
Bulleted List
dialog box.

4. **Modify the bullet format as you see fit.**

   Play with the bullet character, point size, color, and indentation. As you play, the preview box shows you how your bulleted list appears.

5. **If you don't like any of the bullet characters shown in the Modify Bulleted List dialog box, click the Bullet button.**

   The Symbol dialog box, shown in Figure 5-3, appears.

6. **Pick the bullet character you want; then click OK.**

   You can change the font by choosing the Symbols From list box; you find the best bullet characters in the Wingdings font. Click the character you want to use and then click OK.

Figure 5-3:
The Symbol
dialog box.

7. OK your way back to the document.

Click OK to return to the document and to see the results of your bullet formatting efforts.

This is a lot of work, isn't it? Better do it once and then save it in a style.

Keep these points in mind when changing your bullets:

✔ If the characters in the Symbol dialog box seem too small to read, fear not. When you click one of them, WinWord blows it up about four times normal size so that you can see it.

✔ The Wingdings font, which comes with Windows 3.1, is filled with great bullet characters: pointing fingers, smiley faces, grumpy faces, thumbs up, thumbs down, peace signs for folks who were at Woodstock, time bombs, and a skull and crossbones. (Yo ho, yo ho, a pirate's life for me!)

Using Crazy Numbering Schemes

Most of us like to count 1, 2, 3, and so on. But some people count A, B, C, or maybe I, II, III, like a Roman. Not to fear. With WinWord, you can count just about any way you like.

Follow these prudent steps to create your own crazy numbering schemes:

1. Invoke the Format⇨Bullets and Numbering command.

The Bullets and Numbering dialog box appears. Figure 5-4 shows the Bullets and Numbering dialog box with the Numbered tab up front. (If the Numbered tab isn't showing, click it.)

2. If one of the six numbering formats shown in the dialog box is acceptable, click it; then click OK. You're home free.

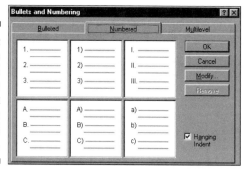

Figure 5-4:
The Bullets
and
Numbering
dialog box
with the
Numbered
tab showing.

3. Otherwise, click the Modify button.

The Modify Numbered List dialog box appears, as shown in Figure 5-5.

4. Modify the numbering scheme to suit your fancy.

You can type text to be included before and after the number, change the number format, and play with the indentation.

5. Click OK.

Happy numbering!

Figure 5-5:
The Modify
Numbered
List dialog
box.

I wouldn't want to do this more than once. Put it in a style so you can call up your hard-earned number format with the touch of a key.

Keep these points in mind when using numbered lists:

✔ Besides normal number formats like 1, 2, 3 . . . or A, B, C . . . or I, II, III . . .; you can specify One, Two, Three . . .; 1st, 2nd, 3rd; or even First, Second, Third as the number format. Believe it or not, these oddball formats work even with unreasonably long lists. Try it and see for yourself: WinWord knows how to spell one thousand one hundred eighty-seventh. It also knows that the Roman numeral equivalent is MCLXXXVII. Isn't that amazing?

✔ If you want to specify a different font for the numbers, click the <u>F</u>ont button when the Modify Numbered List dialog box appears. The font is applied not only to the number, but also to the Text <u>B</u>efore and Text <u>A</u>fter.

Creating a Multilevel List

You can create compulsive multilevel lists that would satisfy even the most rigid anthropology professor using WinWord's numbering feature. I wouldn't wish this task on anyone, but if you must create these types of lists, this feature is a godsend.

Here's the multistep procedure for creating a multilevel list (I created my own multilevel list in the text for a visual example):

1. **Type the text that you want to make into a multilevel list.**

   a) Type the top-level paragraphs as you normally do.

   b) Don't worry about numbers yet.

2. **Adjust indentation using the Increase and Decrease buttons to reflect numbering levels.**

    a) Use the Increase Indent button to create second- or third-level paragraphs.

    b) Use the Decrease Indent button to promote a paragraph to a higher numbering level.

3. **Use the Format⇨Bullets and <u>N</u>umbering command to apply the multilevel list format.**

   a) The Bullets and Numbering dialog box appears, as shown in Figure 5-6.

Figure 5-6: The Bullets and Numbering dialog box with the Multilevel tab shown.

b) If the Multilevel tab options don't appear, click the Multilevel tab.

c) Click the multilevel numbering format that you like.

d) Click OK.

4. To create a custom multilevel numbering scheme, click the Modify button.

a) The Modify Multilevel List dialog box appears, as shown in Figure 5-7.

b) This dialog box enables you to customize each level of a multilevel list.

c) The Level box indicates which level is shown. To change levels, move the scroll bar.

d) You can format each level as a bullet or a number. Choose the bullet or number format from the Bullet or Number drop-down list box.

e) When you've had enough, click OK.

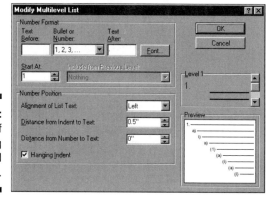

Figure 5-7:
The agony of customizing a multilevel list.

Some notes on multilevel lists:

✔ You can create styles for bulleted or numbered lists, but not for multilevel lists. Too bad.

✔ The multilevel list feature is good for small lists with two or three levels. But if what you really want to do is create an outline, use the Outline feature instead. See Chapter 6 for details on how to create an outline.

✔ Speaking of outlines, maybe what you really want to do is number your headings. That you *can* do with styles. See the next section, "Numbering Your Headings," for details.

Numbering Your Headings

A separate but related feature of WinWord enables you to add numbers to your document's headings. To use this feature, you must apply the appropriate heading styles — Heading 1, Heading 2, Heading 3, and so on — to your heading paragraphs. Then, when you apply heading numbering, all the heading paragraphs in the document are numbered according to the numbering scheme you pick. This feature is great for legal documents like bylaws and contracts.

Heading styles are inherently multilevel, so the heading numbering feature is similar to the multilevel numbering feature. Don't confuse these two features, however. Heading numbering applies numbers to all the headings in your document, whereas a multilevel list applies numbers only to the paragraphs that you indicate.

Follow these steps to add heading numbers to your document:

1. **Use WinWord's standard heading styles to format your document's headings.**

   You can vary the formatting applied by the styles, but you must use the style names Heading 1, Heading 2, Heading 3, and so on to format your headings.

2. **Summon the Format⇨Heading Numbering command.**

   The Heading Numbering dialog box appears, as shown in Figure 5-8.

3. **Pick the heading style you want and then click OK. You're done!**

   All the heading paragraphs in your document are numbered according to the scheme you pick.

Figure 5-8:
The
Heading
Numbering
dialog box.

4. If you don't like any of the predefined numbering styles, click <u>M</u>odify.

The Modify Heading Numbering dialog box appears, which bears a remarkable resemblance to the Modify Multilevel List dialog box. To set the number format for a particular heading level, move the scroll bar in the <u>L</u>evel box. When you're done, click OK.

Keep these points in mind when using heading numbering:

✔ You can add heading numbers to your heading styles if you want. Call up the F<u>o</u>rmat⇨<u>S</u>tyle command and choose any of the heading styles. Then click the <u>M</u>odify button, click the F<u>o</u>rmat button, choose the <u>N</u>umbering command, and pick the number format you want.

✔ Heading numbering is an all-or-nothing proposition; you can't selectively apply it to some heading paragraphs and not others. However, you can tell WinWord to omit numbers for specific heading levels. To do that, call up the F<u>o</u>rmat⇨<u>H</u>eading Numbering command, click the <u>M</u>odify button, slide the <u>L</u>evel scroll bar to choose the heading level for which you want numbers omitted, and pick None for the Bullet or <u>N</u>umber field.

✔ To remove heading numbers, call up the F<u>o</u>rmat⇨<u>H</u>eading Numbering command and click the <u>R</u>emove button in the dialog box.

Chapter 6
More about Outlining

Some writers have the outlining gene — others don't. Some writers manage to concoct at least a rudimentary outline only through an extraordinary act of self-will. Other writers spend days polishing the world's most perfect outline before they write a word. Their outlines are so good that they can write with their eyes closed after finishing the outline. Hmph. I fall somewhere in between. I spin a fairly decent outline up-front, but I'm not compulsive about it. I rarely write with my eyes closed and usually revise the outline substantially as I go, sometimes beyond the point of recognition.

Word for Windows has a built-in outlining tool that's handy whether you like to create detailed outlines in advance, or you just want to check occasionally on the overall structure of your document to see how it is evolving. I use it all the time, even though I'm not an outline fanatic. If you use WinWord to create reports, proposals, or other types of documents that have some sense of structure to them, you owe it to yourself to learn the basics of working with outlines.

Switching to Outline View

Word for Windows usually runs in *Normal view,* which displays your document in a manner that's most convenient for on-screen editing. *Outline view* shows the contents of your document in the form of an outline. You can switch to Outline view in three ways:

- ✔ Using the View➪Outline command
- ✔ Clicking the Outline View button (shown in the margin) next to the horizontal scroll bar, near the bottom left corner of the document
- ✔ Typing the keyboard shortcut Ctrl+Alt+O

Figure 6-1 shows an example of a document in Outline view.

Outlining toolbar

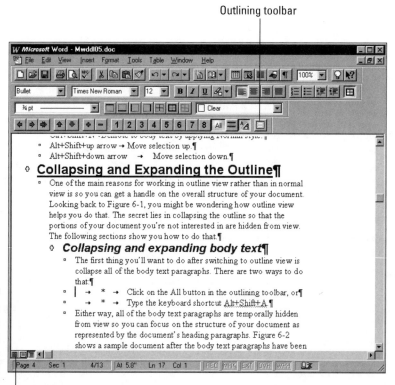

Figure 6-1:
A document
in Outline
view.

Normal view

◼ To return to Normal view, use the View⇨Normal command, click the Normal button (shown in the margin), or press the keyboard shortcut Ctrl+Alt+N.

Understanding Outline View

The key to understanding WinWord's Outline view is realizing that an outline is just another way of looking at a document. The outline is not a separate entity from the document. Instead, when you switch to Outline view, WinWord takes the headings from your document and presents them in the form of an outline. Any changes you make to your document while in Outline view are reflected automatically in the document when you return to Normal view, and any changes you make in Normal view automatically appear when you switch to Outline view. The reason is because Normal view and Outline view are merely two ways of displaying the contents of your document.

There are some important concepts to note about Outline view:

🖊 The outline is made up of the headings and body text of the document. Any paragraph formatted with one of the built-in heading styles (Heading 1, Heading 2, Heading 3, and so on) is considered to be a heading; any other paragraph is considered body text.

🖊 When you switch to Outline view, an extra toolbar appears on-screen, replacing the ruler (which isn't needed in Outline view). This toolbar, appropriately called the Outlining toolbar, contains buttons for performing routine outlining tasks.

🖊 Initially, a document in Outline view may not appear dramatically different than it does in Normal view. That's the case in Figure 6-1. Just wait, though: In the following sections, you see how Outline view enables you to view your document quite differently from the way you view it in Normal view.

🖊 While in Outline view, you can type new text or edit existing text just as you do in Normal view. You can also apply character formatting such as bold or italic and you can apply styles to paragraphs. However, you can't apply direct paragraph formats like indentation, tab stops, alignment, and so on. To apply these types of formats, you must return to Normal view.

🖊 Outline view has its own set of keyboard shortcuts to help you move things along. They are summarized in Table 6-1.

Table 6-1	Keyboard Shortcuts for Outline View
Keyboard Shortcut	*What It Does*
Ctrl+Alt+O	Switches to Outline view
Ctrl+Alt+N	Switches back to Normal view
Alt+Shift+A	Collapses or expands all text
Alt+Shift+gray minus	Collapses the selection
Alt+Shift+gray plus	Expands the selection
Alt+Shift+1	Collapses/expands to Heading 1
Alt+Shift+*(number)*	Collapses/expands to specified heading level
/ (on numeric keypad)	Hides/shows formatting
Shift+Tab	Promotes the selection
Alt+Shift+left arrow	Promotes the selection
Tab	Demotes the selection
Alt+Shift+right arrow	Demotes the selection
Ctrl+Shift+N	Demotes selection to body text by applying Normal style
Alt+Shift+up arrow	Moves the selection up, similar to cutting and pasting it
Alt+Shift+down arrow	Moves the selection down, similar to cutting and pasting it

Collapsing and Expanding the Outline

One of the main reasons for working in Outline view rather than in Normal view is so that you can get a handle on the overall structure of your document. Looking back to Figure 6-1, you may be wondering how Outline view helps you do that. The secret lies in collapsing the outline so that the portions of your document you're not interested in are hidden. The following sections show you how to do this.

Collapsing and expanding body text

Probably the first thing you want to do after switching to Outline view is collapse all of the body text paragraphs. There are two ways to do so:

✔ Clicking the All button on the Outlining toolbar (shown in the margin)

✔ Pressing the keyboard shortcut Alt+Shift+A

Either way, all the body text paragraphs are hidden temporarily so that you can focus on the structure of your document as represented by the document's heading paragraphs. Figure 6-2 shows a sample document after someone has collapsed the body text paragraphs.

Here are some important features to note about Outline view:

✔ Notice that some of the headings have fuzzy lines under them. These fuzzy lines represent collapsed body text.

✔ Notice also that each heading has a large plus sign or minus sign next to it. Headings with plus signs have other headings or body text subordinate to them. Headings with minus signs do not. Body text paragraphs always have a hollow square bullet next to them.

✔ To restore body text paragraphs, click the All button or press the Alt+Shift+A keyboard shortcut again.

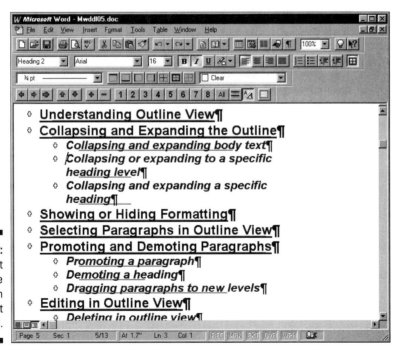

Figure 6-2:
A document in Outline view with body text collapsed.

Collapsing or expanding to a specific heading level

The eight numbered buttons on the Outlining toolbar enable you to collapse or expand an outline to a specific heading level. For example, if you want to see just the top level headings (paragraphs formatted with the Heading 1 style), click the Show Heading 1 button (shown in the margin). Figure 6-3 shows what the document looks like with only Heading 1s showing.

Collapsing and expanding a specific heading

You also can selectively collapse or expand specific headings in Outline view so that you can focus on specific portions of your document. For example, you can collapse the entire document to Heading 1 and then expand only the heading that you want to work on.

To collapse and subsequently expand a heading, follow these simple steps:

1. Select the heading that you want to collapse.

Click anywhere in the heading to select it.

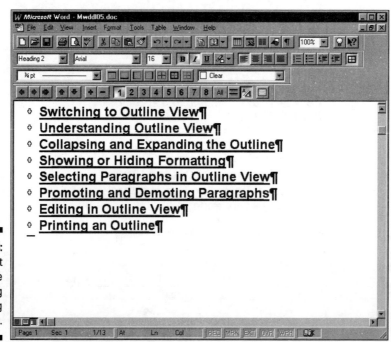

Figure 6-3:
A document in Outline view showing only Heading 1s.

2. Click the Collapse button (shown in the margin).

All the subordinate heading and body text paragraphs text for the heading are hidden temporarily.

3. To expand the heading again, click the Expand button (shown in the margin).

The hidden paragraphs reappear.

Another way to collapse a heading is to double-click the big plus sign next to it. Double-click it again to expand the heading. You can also use the keyboard shortcuts:

Alt+Shift+gray minus	Collapse
Alt+Shift+gray plus	Expand

Showing or Hiding Formatting

Collapsing body text from an outline gives you a bird's eye view of a document's structure, but you can focus more closely on the structure if you remove the formatting associated with each heading style.

To remove formatting from an outline, click the Show Formatting button or press the gray slash key on the numeric keypad. Figure 6-4 shows what an outline looks like with formatting removed.

Keep these tips in mind when using the Show Formatting button:

✔ To restore formatting, click the Show Formatting button or press the gray slash key again.

✔ You don't need the formatting to distinguish among heading levels because the headings are indented for you. So I usually work in Outline view with formatting off.

✔ When you hide formatting, you're doing just that: hiding it. You're not actually removing it. When you click the Show Formatting button again or return to Normal view, all the formatting that you so carefully applied to your document is restored.

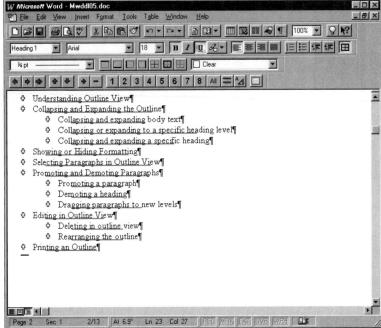

Figure 6-4:
A document
in Outline
view with all
formatting
removed.

Selecting Paragraphs in Outline View

When you work in Outline view, it's easy to become confused about how to select various portions of the document. This section is a quick summary of the techniques.

Most of the techniques for selecting text that work in Normal view also work in Outline view. For example, you can select a block of text by dragging the mouse or holding down the Shift key while using the keyboard arrows.

To select an entire heading or body text paragraph, point the mouse to the left of the paragraph in the invisible zone (actually, the left margin) called the *selection bar* and click. (The mouse arrow points Northeast when it's in the selection bar.)

To select a heading paragraph and all its subordinate paragraphs, click the big plus sign next to the paragraph or double-click to the left of the paragraph in the selection bar. This action selects subordinate heading paragraphs as well as body text paragraphs.

It isn't necessary to select an entire paragraph to perform most outline operations. For example, you can select a paragraph for promotion or demotion just by clicking anywhere in the paragraph.

Promoting and Demoting Paragraphs

To *promote* a paragraph means to move it up one level in the outline. If you promote a Heading 2, it becomes a Heading 1. If you promote a body text paragraph, it becomes a heading paragraph at the same level as the heading it is subordinate to. Thus, if you promote a body text paragraph that follows a Heading 2, the body text paragraph becomes a Heading 2.

To *demote* a paragraph is to move the paragraph down one level in the outline. If you demote a Heading 1, it becomes a Heading 2. Demote it again and it becomes a Heading 3. You cannot demote a body text paragraph, but you can demote any heading to a body text paragraph.

When you promote or demote headings, the body text paragraphs that fall under the heading always go along for the ride. There's no need to worry about losing a heading's body text. Whether or not subordinate headings get swept up in the move depends on how you handle the promotion or demotion.

Promoting a paragraph

To promote a paragraph, place the cursor anywhere in the paragraph and then perform any of the following techniques:

- ✔ Click the Promote button (shown in the margin) on the Outlining toolbar.
- ✔ Press Shift+Tab.
- ✔ Use the keyboard shortcut Alt+Shift+left arrow.

The paragraph moves up one level in the outline pecking order.

You cannot promote a Heading 1; it is already at the highest level in the outline hierarchy.

If you want to promote a heading *and* all its subordinate headings, click the big plus sign next to the paragraph or double-click in the invisible selection bar to the left of the paragraph. Then promote it. If you promote a body text paragraph, it assumes the heading level of the heading paragraph it used to belong to.

You also can promote paragraphs by dragging them with the mouse. See the section "Dragging paragraphs to new levels" later in this chapter.

Demoting a heading

To demote a heading, place the cursor anywhere in the heading and then do one of the following:

- ✔ Click the Demote button (shown in the margin) on the Outlining toolbar.
- ✔ Press Tab.
- ✔ Use the keyboard shortcut Alt+Shift+right arrow.

The heading moves down a level in the outline pecking order.

To demote a heading *and* any headings unfortunate enough to be subordinate to it, click the paragraph's big plus sign or double-click in the hidden selection bar just left of the paragraph. Then demote it.

Don't be insensitive when you demote a paragraph. It can be a traumatic experience.

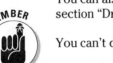

You can also demote paragraphs by dragging them with the mouse. See the section "Dragging paragraphs to new levels" later in this chapter.

You can't demote a body text paragraph. It's already at the bottom of the rung.

You can quickly demote a heading paragraph to body text by clicking the Demote to Body Text button (shown in the margin) on the Outlining toolbar or by pressing the keyboard shortcut Ctrl+Shift+N. (Recognize this shortcut? Demoting a paragraph to body text is accomplished by assigning the Normal style to it.)

Dragging paragraphs to new levels

When you move the mouse pointer over the big plus or minus sign next to a heading or body text paragraph, the pointer changes from a single arrow to a four-cornered arrow. This arrow is your signal that you can click the mouse to select the entire paragraph (and any subordinate paragraphs) and then use the mouse to promote or demote a paragraph along with all its subordinates.

To promote or demote with the mouse, follow these steps:

1. **Point to the big plus or minus sign for the paragraph you that want to demote or promote.**

   The mouse pointer changes to a four-cornered arrow.

2. **Click and hold the mouse button down.**

3. Drag the mouse to the right or left.

The mouse pointer changes to a double-pointed arrow, and a vertical line appears that shows the indentation level of the selection. Release the button when the selection is indented the way you want. The text is automatically assigned the correct heading style.

If you mess up, press Ctrl+Z to undo the promotion or demotion. Then try again.

You can't demote a heading to body text using the preceding technique. You must use the Demote to Body Text button or Ctrl+Shift+N.

Editing in Outline View

Outline view is a great place to perform large-scale editing on your document, such as rearranging or deleting whole sections of text. If you edit a document while the body text is hidden, any edits you perform on headings are automatically extended to the body text that belongs to them. Thus, if you delete a heading, all its body text is deleted, too. If you move a heading to a new location in the document, the body text moves as well.

Deleting in Outline view

To delete large portions of your document quickly, switch to Outline view. Select the text that you want to delete; then press the Del key and — Pow! — the text is gone.

Some helpful hints when using Outline view to delete text:

- ✔ Click the mouse in the magic invisible selection bar just left of a heading paragraph to select the entire paragraph. Then press Del and kiss the paragraph good-bye. Any body text that belonged to the heading is subsumed under the previous heading.

- ✔ Click the big plus sign next to a heading paragraph to select it *and* all its subordinate headings and body text. Press the Del key to send everything — headings and body text alike — into oblivion.

- ✔ Click and drag the mouse over a block of heading paragraphs to select them and then press Del to delete everything that you selected.

- ✔ Obviously, using the Del key in Outline view is risky business. Don't do it unless you're certain that the body text and subordinate paragraphs are preserved. When in doubt, switch to Normal view and delete text the old-fashioned way.

Rearranging the outline

To rearrange your document on a large scale, switch to Outline view and move entire headings up or down in the outline. Remember, body text always travels with its headings. Whether subordinate headings travel as well depends on whether you select them before moving headings around.

To move just one paragraph, click anywhere in the paragraph. To move a paragraph along with its subordinates, click the big plus sign next to it. Then use one of the following techniques.

To move the selected paragraphs up, use one of these methods:

- ✔ Click the Up button (shown in the margin) on the Outlining toolbar.
- ✔ Press Alt+Shift+up arrow.
- ✔ Drag the text with the mouse.

To move the selected text down, use one of the following techniques:

- ✔ Click the Down button (shown in the margin) on the Outlining toolbar.
- ✔ Press Alt+Shift+down arrow.
- ✔ Drag the text with the mouse.

If you don't like the result of your move, you can always undo it by pressing Ctrl+Z.

Printing an Outline

You can quickly print an outline of your document by following this procedure:

1. **Switch to Outline view.**

2. **Click the All button (shown in the margin) to hide body text.**

3. **Collapse or Expand any other headings that you want to include or exclude in the printout.**

4. **Click the Show Formatting button if you don't want the outline to include heading formats.**

5. **Click the Print button on the Standard toolbar.**

    The outline prints.

A printed outline is no substitute for a Table of Contents. See Chapter 21 for details on printing a table of contents — complete with page numbers.

Chapter 7
More about Mail Merge

Mail merge. Just the sound of those two words is enough to drive even veteran Word for Windows users into a state of utter and complete panic. Just when you think that you've figured out enough about mail merge to put out a simple form letter, along comes Word for Windows 95 with a bunch of new mail-merge features. Arghhhh! What next?

This chapter covers some of the more interesting things you can do with WinWord's mail-merge feature, such as print mailing labels, choose only certain names to print letters for, use data from sources other than Word for Windows, and create an address directory.

This chapter is *not* a gentle introduction to mail merge. It does have a section called "Understanding Mail Merge" that quickly reviews the basics, but if you're completely new to mail merge, stop where you are. Back up very slowly, make no sudden moves, and get yourself a copy of *Word For Windows 95 For Dummies* by Dan Gookin. It has an entire chapter devoted to the basics of using mail merge.

Understanding Mail Merge

When most people say *mail merge,* they mean merging a file that contains a list of names and addresses with another file that contains a model letter to produce a bunch of personalized form letters. Suppose that you decided to do some volunteer work for the local public library, and the library decided to put you in charge of getting deadbeats to return long overdue books. A personalized letter would be the ideal way to communicate your message to these good-for-nothings. And Word's mail-merge feature is ideal for preparing such a personalized letter.

Mail merge is a three-step affair, greatly assisted by the Mail Merge Helper dialog box, which appears when you summon the Tools⇨Mail Merge command. Figure 7-1 shows the Mail Merge Helper.

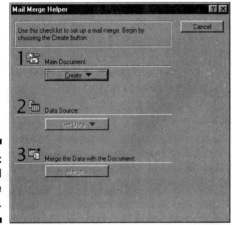

Figure 7-1:
The Mail
Merge
Helper.

These steps summarize the three mail-merge steps the Mail Merge Helper guides you through:

1. Write the form letter.

First you have to figure out what to say to all those recalcitrant patrons. You can create a new letter or call up the letter you sent last time when you volunteered for the PTA fundraising campaign. Either way, you have to create a *main document.* You toil over the letter for hours, trying to be firm yet inoffensive. As you write the letter, you leave blank spaces in the spots that will be filled in with personalized information, such as the inside address and salutation ("Dear John"). Figure 7-2 shows an example of a typical form letter.

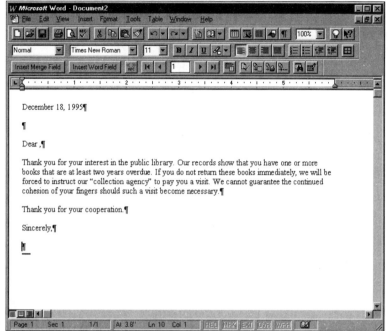

December 18, 1995¶

¶

Dear ,¶

Thank you for your interest in the public library. Our records show that you have one or more
books that are at least two years overdue. If you do not return these books immediately, we will be
forced to instruct our "collection agency" to pay you a visit. We cannot guarantee the continued
cohesion of your fingers should such a visit become necessary.¶

Thank you for your cooperation.¶

Sincerely,¶

Figure 7-2:
A typical
form letter.

2. Get the names and addresses.

Hope to God that someone has already typed the names and addresses of
all the deadbeats into a computer. In the best of all worlds, that person
typed the names into a Word for Windows 95 document so that you're all
set. In the OK-but-still-a-long-shot world, someone has indeed already
entered the names, but he did it by using PC CheaperBase or some other
database program you never heard of. You have to figure out a way to
convert the data into a format you can use with WinWord.

After the main document is composed, you return to the Mail Merge
Helper and click the Get Data button, which enables you to set up a *data
source:* a WinWord document that contains all the names and addresses
neatly formatted in a table. The good news is that WinWord sets up this
table for you; all you have to do is tell it which *fields* to include (such as
first and last names, address lines, city, state, postal code, and so on).
Then WinWord pops up the Data Form dialog box, shown in Figure 7-3.
You spend the next two weeks working in this dialog box, typing names
and addresses.

2a. Insert field names in the main document.

Did I say that there were just three steps? I guess I didn't mention that
some of the steps have substeps. Sorry.

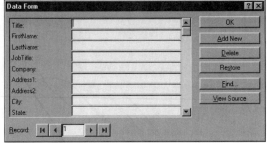

Figure 7-3:
Using the
Data Form
dialog box
to enter
names and
addresses.

After you enter all the names and addresses (saving the file frequently, of course), WinWord complains that you didn't enter any field names in your main document and whisks you back to your form letter. There you add the field names to the blank spaces you left in the form letter by positioning the cursor in one of the blank spots, clicking the Insert Merge Field button from the Mail Merge toolbar, and choosing the appropriate field name from the list of field names that appears. When you're finished, the document looks something like Figure 7-4.

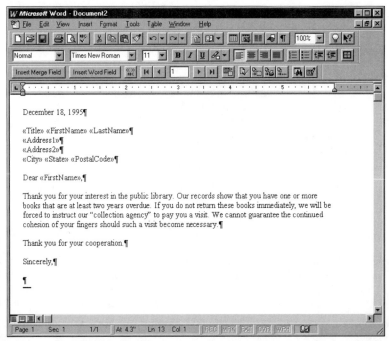

Figure 7-4:
The form
letter with
field names
inserted.

3. Merge the addresses with the form letter.

This is the easy part. After you've set up the main document and the data source, click the Merge button in the Mail Merge Helper. WinWord creates a personalized letter for each name in the address list. You can send the personalized letters directly to the printer or you can put them all in a new document, which you can then examine before you print.

Creating Form Letters with Pizzazz

Usually, you think of mail merge only in terms of adding an inside address and personalized salutation to a form letter. You can also personalize the body of the letter, however, if you have information you want to include in the letter and you plan ahead carefully. You can include fields from the data source, for example, in the body of the letter. You can tell WinWord to pause as it prepares each merge letter so that you can type custom text. And you can include an IF field to customize each letter based on the results of a condition test.

Using merge fields in the body of a letter

Suppose that in addition to the names and addresses of all the deadbeat library patrons, you also have the titles of their overdue books. To make the letter seem more personalized, why not mention the books in the body of the letter?

Figure 7-5 shows how this type of letter looks. As you can see, I included the merge field Books in the body of the paragraph. When you merge the letters, the contents of each record's Books field is inserted into the middle of the sentence.

For example:

```
Our records show that you checked out A Tale of Two Cities
more than two years ago, and we have not heard from you
since.

Our records show that you checked out The Killer Angels and
Roots more than two years ago, and we have not heard from you
since.

Our records show that you checked out Networking For Dummies,
PowerPoint For Windows 95 For Dummies, and MORE Word For
Windows 95 For Dummies more than two years ago, and we have
not heard from you since.
```

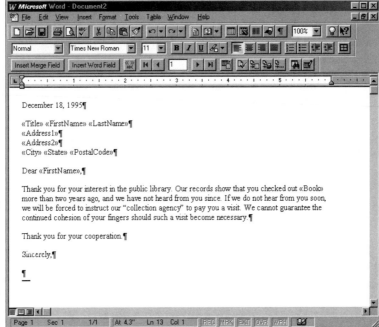

Figure 7-5:
The form letter with a merge field inserted in the body of the letter.

The secret to inserting fields in the middle of sentences is carefully planning all the grammatical possibilities to avoid an embarrassing faux pas. Suppose that you write a sentence like this one:

```
Our records show that you checked out the book «Books» more
than two years ago and haven't returned it yet.
```

Then you'd end up with sentences like these:

```
Our records show that you checked out the book A Tale of Two
Cities more than two years ago and haven't returned it yet.

Our records show that you checked out the book The Killer
Angels and Roots more than two years ago and haven't returned
it yet.

Our records show that you checked out the book Networking For
Dummies, PowerPoint For Windows 95 For Dummies, and MORE Word
For Windows 95 For Dummies more than two years ago and
haven't returned it yet.
```

This works for the first sentence, but the second two aren't quite right.

People have been desensitized to personalized mail by Publishers Clearing House. Don't overdo the personalization; most people see right through it.

Personalizing each letter

Suppose that you want to add a little personal note to each letter. You can merge the letters to a document and then edit the resulting document and add a personal note to each merged letter. That's the easy way, and probably the best way if you want to do it only once. But if you want to add a personal note to each letter of a mail merge you run every Friday, consider doing it the cool computer-geek way: by adding a FILLIN field to your main document.

A FILLIN field causes WinWord to prompt you for text to be inserted into each document as the mail merge proceeds. A dialog box like the one in Figure 7-6 appears for each letter as it is merged. When you type a personalized message here, it is inserted into the letter.

Figure 7-6:
How
WinWord
prompts you
to enter
personalized
text for each
letter.

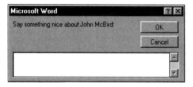

Follow these steps to prompt for personalized text for each letter:

1. **Set up a main document and data source as you normally do.**

   See the first section in this chapter, "Understanding Mail Merge," for a review of how to do that. If you're still completely perplexed, see *Word For Windows 95 For Dummies.*

2. **Edit the main document.**

   Use the Window command to switch to the window that holds the main document or use the Mail Merge Helper's Edit button to edit the main document.

3. **Call up the Tools⇨Options command, click the View tab (if the View options are not already displayed), and check the Field Codes box if it is not already checked. Then click OK.**

You must be able to see field codes as they are inserted into your document. All the beautiful merge field placeholders, such as «FirstName», are replaced by less elegant merge fields, such as {MERGEFIELD FirstName}. Have no fear — the merge fields are intact. Checking the Field Codes box in the View Options dialog box simply tells WinWord to display these fields in greater detail.

4. **Position the cursor at the spot where you want personalized text to be inserted for each letter.**

It's usually best to insert the personalized text in its own paragraph so that you don't have to worry about leaving too many or too few spaces before or after it.

5. **Click the Insert Word Field button in the Mail Merge toolbar and then choose Fill-in as the type of field to insert.**

The Insert Word Field: Fill-in dialog box appears, as shown in Figure 7-7.

Figure 7-7:
This dialog box appears when you insert a FILLIN field.

6. **Type a friendly prompt and then click OK.**

Type whatever text you want WinWord to display when it prompts you for text during the merge. In Figure 7-7, I entered "Say something nice about:" as the Prompt text.

7. **Insert the FirstName and LastName merge fields in the FILLIN field so that you know to whom each letter is addressed.**

This part of the procedure is the most difficult. You may have noticed that the prompt text in Figure 7-6 included the name of the person to whom the letter is addressed. These names are usually available as the merge fields FirstName and LastName. To insert the name, find the FILLIN field you inserted in Step 6. It should look something like this:

```
{ FILLIN "Say something nice about:" }
```

Move the cursor to the point in the field's prompt text where you want the name inserted (in this case, just before the colon). Then click the Insert Merge Field button to insert the FirstName and LastName fields. Also, insert a space before each field. When you're finished, the FILLIN field should look like this:

```
{ FILLIN "Say something nice about { MERGFIELD FirstName }
         { MERGEFIELD LastName }:" }
```

8. **Use the File⇨Save command to save the main document. Then call up the Mail Merge Helper dialog box (Tools⇨Mail Merge) and click the Merge button to merge the letters.**

9. **When you're prompted, type a personal message for each letter.**

   Pay attention to the name that appears in the dialog box so that you know which message to type.

If you check the Ask Once check box in the Insert Word Field: Fill-in dialog box, WinWord prompts you for the fill-in field just once. It then inserts the same text in each letter created during the mail merge. This procedure is useful if you want to insert a different message every time you run a mail merge, but the message is the same for each letter in the merge run.

Using a condition test

A *condition test* enables you to insert different text into a merge letter based on the contents of some field in the data source. If you have a field named *Party,* for example, you may include one message for records in which the Party field is Republican and a completely different message for records in which the field is Democrat. (I would offer appropriate messages for both cases, but I would probably offend half my loyal readers, so I'll pass.)

To incorporate a condition test into a mail-merge document, you use a WinWord IF-THEN-ELSE field. This procedure sounds like computer programming to me, so you had better grab your pocket protector and close your door. You don't want your friends to see you doing this or you'll lose their respect forever.

Follow these steps to add a conditional test to your mail merge:

1. **Set up a main document and data source as you normally would.**

   Look back to the section "Understanding Mail Merge" at the beginning of this chapter for a quick review. Or consult *Word For Windows 95 For Dummies.*

Make sure that the data source contains a field that you can use as the basis for a condition test. If you want to include one message for people who owe you money and another for people who are all paid up, for example, make sure that the data source has a field that provides the balance due.

2. **Edit the main document.**

   Use the Window command to pop up the main document or use the Mail Merge Helper's Edit button.

3. **Summon the Tools⇨Options command. If the View options are not already displayed, click the View tab. Then check the Field Codes box if it is not already checked and click OK.**

   You need to see the merge codes that you insert into your document, so you may as well activate the Field Codes option now.

4. **Move the cursor to where you want to insert the conditional text.**

5. **Use the Insert Word Field button from the Mail Merge toolbar to insert an IF-THEN-ELSE field.**

   Click the Insert Word Field button and then choose If...Then...Else. A dialog box similar to the one in Figure 7-8 appears.

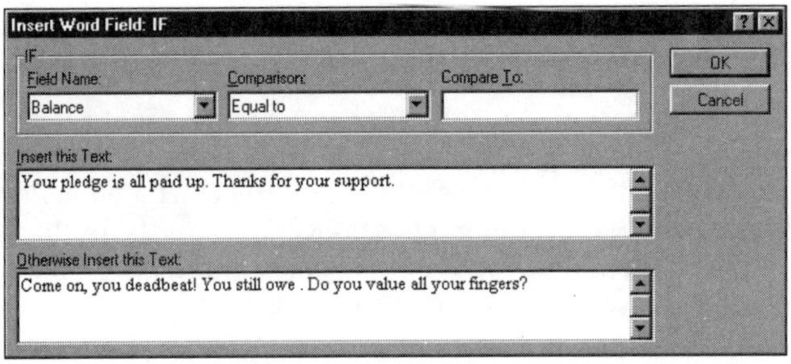

Figure 7-8:
This dialog box appears when you insert an IF-THEN-ELSE field.

   If the conditional text is based on the balance due, for example, choose the Balance field (or whatever field contains the balance due).

6. **Set up the condition test in the Field Name, Comparison, and Compare To fields.**

   Start by choosing in the Field Name field the field you want to test. Then set the conditional equation in the Comparison field and the value to be compared in the Compare To field.

7. **In the Compare To text box, type the value to which you want to compare the field.**

8. **In the Insert this Text field, type the text you want inserted if the condition is true.**

   In Figure 7-8, I typed, "Your pledge is all paid up. Thanks for your support."

9. **In the Otherwise Insert this Text box, type the alternative text you want included if the condition is *not* true.**

, I typed "Come on you deadbeat! You still owe . Do you value
ers?" (In this example, the second sentence is incomplete
an to insert the Balance field in the next step. Bear with me.)

n document and insert field names into the IF-THEN-ELSE

e field inserted in Figure 7-8 should look like this in the main

```
FIELD Balance ] = 0 "Your pledge is all paid up.
for your support." "Come on you deadbeat! You
we . Do you value all your fingers?"
```

ursor after the word *owe* and then click the Insert Merge
he Mail Merge toolbar to insert the Balance field. When
d, the IF merge field should look like this:

```
IELD Balance ] = 0 "Your pledge is all paid up.
or your support." "Come on you deadbeat! You
e { MERGEFIELD Balance }. Do you value all your
fingers?"
```

11. **Save the main document by using the File⇨Save command; then call up
the Mail Merge Helper dialog box and click the Merge button to merge
the letters.**

12. **Put away your pocket protector and don't tell anyone that you did this.**

Printing Mailing Labels and Envelopes

Ever spent 30 minutes printing 50 personalized letters by using mail merge and
then spent another 30 minutes hand-addressing envelopes? Never again!
WinWord can easily transform a mail-merge address list into mailing labels or
envelopes.

These steps show the procedure for creating mailing labels:

1. **Call up the Tools⇨Mail Merge command.**

   The familiar Mail Merge Helper dialog box appears.

2. **Click the Create button under Main Document and choose Mailing Labels.**

3. **When WinWord asks whether you want to use the active window or
   create a new main document, choose New Main Document.**

4. **Back at the Mail Merge Helper, click Get Data under Data Source and
   choose Open Data Source. Choose the file that contains your mailing
   addresses and click OK.**

If you haven't yet created your mailing list, choose the Create Data Source option instead. Then choose the fields to be included in the mailing list and enter your names and addresses.

5. **When WinWord complains that it has to set up the main document, obey its wishes. Click the Set Up Main Document button.**

6. **When WinWord displays the Label Options dialog box, choose the label type you use and click OK.**

   Figure 7-9 shows the Label Options dialog box. Click Dot Matrix if you use a dot-matrix printer or Laser if you use a laser printer. Then scroll through the Product Number list to choose the specific Avery label type you plan to use.

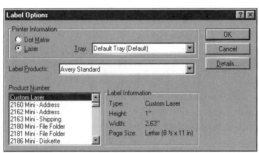

Figure 7-9:
The Label
Options
dialog box.

If the labels you use aren't in the list, choose Custom Dot Matrix or Custom Laser as the label type and then click the Details button. This step pops up a dialog box in which you type detailed measurements for the labels. Measure your labels carefully and then type the measurements and click OK.

7. **When WinWord displays the Create Labels dialog box, use the Insert Merge Field button to insert merge fields where you want them to appear on the labels. Then click OK.**

   As you insert each merge field, it is copied into the Sample Label box (see Figure 7-10). If you include more than one field on a line, be sure to press the spacebar to leave a space between the fields. To begin a new line, press Enter. Click OK when you're finished.

8. **Back at the Mail Merge Helper, click the Merge button to create the labels.**

   WinWord displays the Merge dialog box, from which you can tell WinWord to merge to a new document or directly to the printer. Choose the option you want, click the Merge button and watch while WinWord creates your labels.

The procedure for creating envelopes is the same, except that you choose Envelopes from the Create button under Main Document. Also, rather than specify Label Options, you specify Envelope Options. The procedures are otherwise identical.

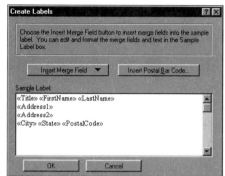

Figure 7-10:
The Create
Labels
dialog box.

If you want to include a postal bar code on your labels or envelopes, click the Insert Postal Bar Code on the Create Labels or Create Envelopes dialog box. This code is not a secret password that gets you into pubs where mail carriers hang out — it's a bar code that speeds mail delivery. If you do bulk mailing and have the proper permits, using this bar code can earn postage discounts.

You can use the same data source to print both personalized letters and labels or envelopes. If you do, however, be very careful to stuff each letter into its corresponding envelope. Nothing spoils a personalized mailing more than to send personalized letters to the wrong addresses.

When you print labels, you can save yourself a great deal of grief if you use Avery label products. Nope, I don't get an under-the-table kickback for this blatant endorsement. It just so happens that Word for Windows comes with most Avery label sizes and formats predefined.

Fun Things to Do with the Data Source

Mail merge would be useful enough if all you could do with the data source was use it to store your names and addresses. But WinWord's data sources have more tricks up their sleeves than meet the eye. With a little chutzpah and a bit of wrestling with the dialog boxes, you can do several cute and moderately useful tricks with the data source. The following sections explain these amazing feats.

Sorting data

Suppose that you enter all the names in whatever sequence they were sitting in the pile, but you want to print the letters in alphabetical order. No problem! Just sort the data source. Here's how you do it:

1. **Set up the mail merge as you normally would.**

   Call up the Tools⇨Mail Merge command, use the Create button in the Main Document section to set up the main document, and click the Get Data button to create the data source or open an existing data source.

2. **Don't click the Merge button yet!**

3. **Click the Query Options button instead to summon the Query Options dialog box. If the sort options aren't visible, click the Sort Records tab.**

   Figure 7-11 shows the sort options in the Query Options dialog box.

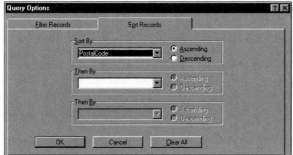

Figure 7-11:
Sorting the
data source.

4. **In the Sort By list box, choose the merge field that you want the data source to be sorted by.**

   Click the down arrow next to the sort field box to reveal a list of all the merge fields in the data source and then choose the one you want to sort the data by (LastName, for example).

5. **If you want a second or third sort field, set them in the Then By and Then By fields.**

   The Then By field is used as a tiebreaker when two or more records have the same main Sort By field. If the data source has more than one record with the same LastName, they are sorted into sequence by their first names, like this:

   ```
   King   Larry
   King   Martin Luther
   King   Stephen
   ```

   If you have a third field you can use as a tiebreaker, set it in the Then By field.

6. **Click OK.**

   You return to the Mail Merge Helper dialog box.

7. Click the Merge button to continue with the mail merge.

If you want to sort records in reverse order, click the appropriate Descending button. Records are then sorted on that field in reverse order, beginning with the *Z*s and working back up to the *A*s.

If you want to sort your data source on a particular field, such as LastName, make sure that you set that field up as a separate merge field. It may be tempting to replace the separate Title, FirstName, and LastName fields with a single Name field. But if you do, you can't sort your records by the last name.

Using a merge query

Merge query sounds like some ominous computer database feature that you have to have a Ph.D. to figure out, but all it really means is that you send letters to only a certain select group of names from your data source. You may want to send letters only to left-handed San Francisco 49er fans born in February, for example. Sending letters to this group is possible if you have fields in your data source for handedness, favorite football team, and birthday.

WinWord uses the term *filter* to mean the process of choosing the records you want to include in a mail merge. Unlike the filters in your car, mail-merge filters don't fill up with gunk, so you don't have to change them every 5,000 miles. You do have to be careful about how you set them up, though, to be sure that they choose just the records you want included in your mail merge.

To mail letters to only those lucky few, follow these steps:

1. Set up the mail merge just like you usually do.

Summon the Tools⇨Mail Merge command and then click the Create button in the Main Document section and specify the main document. Then use the Get Data button to set up the data source.

2. Don't click the Merge button yet!

3. Click the Query Options button instead to summon the Query Options dialog box. If the Filter Records options aren't visible, click the Filter Records tab.

Figure 7-12 shows the Filter Records options in the Query Options dialog box.

4. Set the criteria for including records in the mail merge by specifying a Field, Comparison, and Compare To value for each criteria.

To create a letter only for people who live in the 93711 ZIP code, for example, set the first Field to PostalCode, the first Comparison to Equal To, and the Compare To field to 93711. This filter means that only records whose PostalCode field is equal to 93711 are included in the mail merge.

Figure 7-12:
Filtering the
data source.

5. **Click OK.**

   You return to the Mail Merge Helper dialog box.

6. **Click the Merge button to continue with the mail merge.**

I've never been very good at relationships

You can set up different kinds of tests in the Comparison fields, as summarized in Table 7-1. Computerniks call these tests *relational tests* because they test the relationships between two things (in this case, a merge field and a specific value). You can use these relational tests to create different kinds of selection filters.

You can set up complicated queries that check the contents of several fields. You may want to mail letters only to people who live in a particular city and state, for example. You set up the query like this:

```
City Equal to Bakersfield
    And State Equal to CA
```

In this query, only records whose City field is equal to *Bakersfield* and whose State field is equal to *CA* are included in the merge.

You can also set up queries that test the same field twice. To mail to addresses with ZIP codes 93711 or 93722, for example, set up the query like this:

```
PostalCode Equal to 93711
    Or PostalCode Equal to 93722
```

Notice that I change the And/Or field from And to Or. That way, a record is selected if its PostalCode field is 93711 or 93722. If you test the same field for two or more specific values, do not leave the And/Or field set to And. If I had left the And/Or field set to And in the preceding example, a record would be selected only if its Postal Code was equal to 93711 and if it was also equal to 93722. Obviously, this can't be: Each record in the data source can have only one value for the PostalCode field. It's natural to want to leave the And/Or field set to And because you want to "mail letters to everyone in the 93711 *and* 93722 ZIP codes." But when you fill in the Query dialog box, you have to use Or, not And.

On the other hand, suppose that you want to mail to anyone whose ZIP code is 93711, 93722, or any value in between. In that case, you use two condition tests linked by And, as shown in this example:

```
PostalCode Greater Than or
    Equal to 93711

And PostalCode Less Than or
    Equal to 93722
```

Table 7-1	Relational Tests
Comparison Setting	*What It Means*
Equal To	Selects only those records in which the value of the specified Field exactly matches the Compare To value
Not Equal To	Selects only those records in which the value of the specified Field does not exactly match the Compare To value
Less Than	Selects only those records in which the value of the specified Field is less than the Compare To value
Greater Than	Selects only those records in which the value of the specified Field is greater than the Compare To value
Greater Than or Equal To	Selects only those records in which the value of the specified Field is greater than or equal to the Compare To value
Is Blank	Selects only those records in which the value of the specified Field is blank
Is Not Blank	Selects only those records in which the value of the specified Field is not blank

Editing the data source directly

When you edit the data source by clicking the Edit button in the Data Source portion of the Mail Merge Helper dialog box, you are presented with the Data Form dialog box, which provides a convenient way to add names and addresses to your mailing list. If you want, you can fiddle directly with the data in the data source by clicking the View Source button in the Data Form dialog box. When you do, the data source document is displayed in a document window so that you can edit it just like any other document (see Figure 7-13).

Data is stored in the data source as a Word table. Each field is represented by a table column, and each record is represented by a row. The first row of the table contains the field names. You can edit data directly in the table if you want, but I find it easier to edit the table data by using the Data Form dialog box.

Word formats the table so that most of the columns are not wide enough to display their contents on one line. However, the line breaks in the fields don't affect the way the merged letters are printed. If you want, you can adjust the width of each field by dragging the boxes between columns in the ruler.

When you view the data source, WinWord activates the Database toolbar, just beneath the Formatting toolbar. The function of each button on the Database toolbar is summarized in Table 7-2.

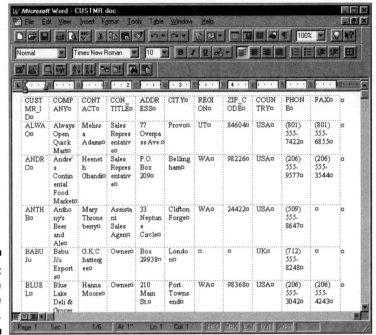

Figure 7-13:
Editing the
data source
directly.

Table 7-2	Buttons on the Database Toolbar
Button	*What It Does*
	Calls up the Data Form dialog box so that you can quickly enter new records
	Calls up the Manage Fields dialog box so that you can add new fields to the table or delete fields from the table
	Adds a new record to the table
	Deletes the chosen record
	Sorts the table into ascending sequence
	Sorts the table into descending sequence
	Imports data from a database program
	Updates the contents of any Word fields included in the data source
	Finds data in a specific field
	Switches to the mail-merge main document

You can add or delete fields from the table by clicking the Manage Fields button. When you do, the Manage Fields dialog box appears, as shown in Figure 7-14. To add a field to the table, type the field name in the Field Name box and click the Add button. To remove a field, choose the field in the Field Names in Header Row list and click the Remove button.

Figure 7-14:
The Manage
Fields dialog
box.

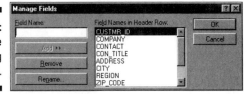

Importing data from another source

Word for Windows enables you to use name and address records that you created with another program for your mail merges. If you use Paradox for Windows to keep a customer list, for example, you can open the Paradox database file as the data source. You can do the same with files created with dBASE, Microsoft Excel, Microsoft Access, Microsoft FoxPro, Lotus 1-2-3, WordPerfect, and earlier versions of Microsoft Word.

All you have to do to use a file created by one of the preceding programs as a mail-merge data source is follow these steps:

1. **Create a name and address database by using your program of choice.**

   Use whatever commands are necessary to create the data and keep it up-to-date.

2. **Call up Word for Windows and begin a mail merge.**

   Use the Tools➪Mail Merge command to begin the mail merge. Click the Create button to create a new main document or open an existing one.

3. **Use the Get Data button to open an existing data source.**

4. **When the Open Data Source dialog box appears, use the List Files of Type field to choose the type of file you want to use.**

   If you create the database file with Paradox, for example, choose Paradox Files as the file type.

5. **Choose the file you want and click OK.**

   Word for Windows opens the database file and converts it to a mail-merge data source.

6. **Continue as usual.**

   Finish the mail merge by completing the main document (if necessary) and clicking the Merge button to begin the merge.

Unprecedented nonsense about precedence

If you set up a query that uses three or more field tests and mixes And and Or, you had better grab your pocket protector first so that you're prepared to deal with the advanced computer science graduate degree subject of precedence.

Precedence means, in layman's terms, "what to do first." You may suppose that WinWord would test the conditions you list in the Query Options dialog box in the order in which you list them. Not necessarily. WinWord groups any condition tests linked by And and checks them out before combining the results with tests linked by Or.

Confused? So am I. Let's walk through an example to see how it works. Suppose that you open the menu at a restaurant and see that the fried chicken dinner comes with a "leg or wing and thigh." Which of the following statements represents the two possible chicken-dinner configurations the restaurant could sell you:

✔ You can order a meal with a leg and a thigh, or you can order a meal with a wing and a thigh.

✔ You can order a meal with a leg, or you can order a meal with a wing and thigh.

Hmm. Tough one. According to the way WinWord processes queries, the answer is the second one. WinWord lumps together as a group the two options linked by And. If you were a computer science grad student, you would put parentheses around "wing and thigh," like this: "leg or (wing and thigh)."

If you want the first example to be the right answer, you have to state the menu choice as "leg and thigh or wing and thigh."

For a more realistic Word for Windows example, suppose that you want to mail to everyone who lives in Dallas or Fort Worth. To do that, you have to set up the query like this:

```
City Equal to Dallas
And State Equal to TX
Or  City Equal to Fort Worth
And State Equal to TX
```

When you open a Microsoft Access file as a data source, Word for Windows asks whether you want to include the entire file or access specific records based on an Access query. If the data table is large and you don't need all the records, consider setting up an Access query to select just the records you want to include in the mail merge. This procedure is more efficient than importing the entire file into Word for Windows and then using a mail-merge query.

If the file you open is a Microsoft Excel worksheet, Word for Windows asks whether you want to include the entire worksheet file or whether you want to include only those cells that fall within a certain range.

You can also open text files in which the data for each field is separated by commas, tabs, or other characters. This is your bridge to foreign database programs that aren't included in the List Files of <u>T</u>ype field. Almost all database programs let you *export* data to a text file. You can use the export feature to create a file that Word for Windows can open as a text file data source.

Ten Things That Often Go Wrong with Mail Merge

When you use the mail-merge feature, here are ten or so things that sometimes go wrong, along with suggested cures.

Blank lines

Mailing addresses are funny. Some have two address lines, some have one. For records that omit the second address line, you don't want to leave a blank line where the second address line should be. If that happens, make sure that the *Don't print blank lines when data fields are empty* box in the Merge dialog box is checked.

Fields get all jumbled up

If the name prints where the address should print and the ZIP code prints where the city name should print, you may have jumbled up your data source. Switch to the data source window and quickly check the table that holds the data records. Is the correct data in the proper columns? Is the correct data source opened? If that technique doesn't pinpoint the problem, switch over to the main document and make sure that you inserted the merge fields correctly.

Nothing merges

If the mail merge comes up empty, it could be that you set up a merge query that can't be satisfied. Maybe you tried, for example, to mail to everyone whose city is either Sacramento or Davis by setting up a query like this:

```
        City Equal To Sacramento
And     City Equal To Davis
```

The And should have been Or.

Missing spaces or too many spaces

When you insert a merge field in the body of the letter, you have to plan carefully how the merged fields fit into the letter text. If the field is in the middle of a sentence, leave a space before and after the field. Then make sure that you do *not* add a space to the end of the field when you type it in the data source.

If you do, you have two spaces where you need only one. On the other hand, if you omit the space from both the main document and the data source fields, you miss a space where one is needed.

Unexpected page breaks

What if the letter should fit on one page, but the last line or two of some letters prints on a second page? The problem could be that one or more of the merge fields resulted in extra lines you didn't count on. Suppose that you set up a main document which just barely fits on one page, and a merge field is inserted into the body of the letter. If the contents of this field are unusually long, the paragraph that contains it may wind up running one line long. And sometimes one extra line is enough to send the last line of the letter to the next page.

Not enough memory

Run out of memory during a mail merge? Welcome to Windows. The first thing to do is shut down everything else. Don't attempt a large mail merge while Excel, PowerPoint, Doom, and Solitaire are all running. Shut down everything (except perhaps Solitaire) and try again.

If that still doesn't solve the memory crunch, try merging in smaller chunks. If the merge runs out of memory at 500 letters, for example, try merging 100 at a time.

Letters stuffed into wrong envelopes

Be especially careful when you merge letters with personalized inside addresses and then merge envelopes. When you stuff the envelopes, it's all too easy to shove Joe Deadbeat's final dunning notice into the wrong envelope.

Chapter 8

More about Footnotes

. . . .

In This Chapter

▶ Adding footnotes

▶ Changing the appearance of footnotes

▶ Changing the reference marks

▶ Changing the footnote separators

▶ Finding a footnote reference

. . . .

*F*ootnotes. Back when I was in college, typing them was a major pain in the derriere[1]. You had to count out the lines just right to make sure that you left enough room at the bottom of the page. I never did figure out how to deal with footnote references that fell right at the bottom of the page, too close to the margin to place the note on the same page.

Footnotes are one of the neatest features of word processors, at least while you're in college. After that, they're a pretty useless appendage, unless you happen to work at the college, in which case the footnote feature becomes a source of resentment — just one among many examples of how easy kids have it today. Hmph.

Adding a Footnote

There's really not much to using footnotes, unless you want to get fancy with them. Here's the down-and-dirty procedure for adding plain-vanilla footnotes:

1. **Put the cursor where you want the little footnote reference number to appear in your text.**

2. **Call up the Insert⇨Footnote command.**

---

[1] Hind part; rear appendage; stern.

The Footnote and Endnote dialog box appear, as shown in Figure 8-1. You can choose between footnotes and endnotes (footnotes appear at the bottom of the page on which the footnote reference appears; endnotes are printed together at the end of the document) and fiddle with numbering options, but usually you just give this dialog box a bothered glance before clicking OK.

Figure 8-1:
The
Footnote
and Endnote
dialog box.

3. **Click OK.**

This step opens a separate footnote window at the bottom of the screen, as shown in Figure 8-2. Type your footnote in the space provided.

4. **Click Close when you're finished.**

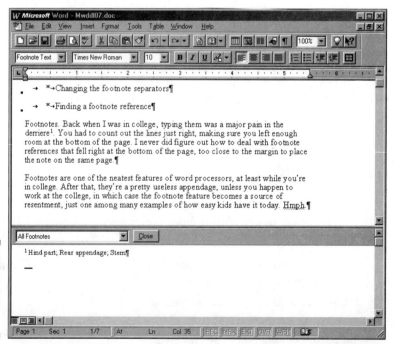

Figure 8-2:
Typing a
footnote in
the footnote
window.

Word automatically numbers footnotes for you. Heck, that's the point. When you use the Insert⇨Footnote command, Word inserts the little footnote reference number in the text and pairs it with a number in the footnote itself. If you go back later and insert a new footnote in front of an existing one, Word automatically juggles the footnote numbers to keep everything in sync.

Here are some more tips to remember when using footnotes:

- ✔ For an extra-quick way to create a footnote, use the keyboard shortcut Ctrl+Alt+F. This keyboard shortcut means "go directly to the footnote window. Do not display the Footnote and Endnote dialog box; do not collect $200."

- ✔ To look at your footnotes, use the View⇨Footnotes command.

- ✔ If you start off with Endnotes but then decide that you want to convert your endnotes to footnotes (or vice versa), fear not! Just call up the Insert⇨Footnote command, click the Options button, and then click the Convert button. When you click OK three times, your notes are converted.

- ✔ If you made a goof in the footnote, double-click the footnote reference in the text. That action pops open the footnote window so that you can fix the note.

- ✔ To delete a footnote, select its footnote reference in the text and press the Del key.

Changing the Footnote Format

The formatting of footnotes is governed by the Footnote Text style. You can change the appearance of all the footnotes in your document, therefore, by simply modifying the Footnote Text style.

Similarly, footnote reference numbers are formatted by using the Footnote Reference style. This style is a character style, so it doesn't affect formatting for the entire paragraph.

For details on how to change a style, see Chapter 3.

The initial setting for Footnote Text is Normal + 10 point. Therefore, footnotes are formatted by using the same font as in your Normal paragraphs, except that they are 10 point regardless of the Normal text size. If you want your footnotes to appear in a different font from the rest of the document, change the font for the Footnote Text style.

The initial setting for Footnote Reference is Default Character Format + Superscript. As a result, footnote references are printed using the same font as the rest of the text in the paragraph, except that the superscript attribute applies.

If you would rather see footnote references in a different font, all you have to do is change the Footnote Reference style.

Both Footnote Text and Footnote References are applied automatically when you create footnotes, so you shouldn't have any cause to apply these formats directly.

Changing the Reference Marks

Most footnotes are numbered 1, 2, 3, and so on, but WinWord enables you to change this standard numbering format to use letters, roman numerals, or the special reference symbols *, †, ‡, and §.

Follow these steps to change reference marks:

1. Summon the Insert⇨Footnote command.

The Footnote and Endnote dialog box appears.

2. Click the Options button.

The Note Options dialog box appears, as shown in Figure 8-3.

3. Choose the Number Format you want.

This list shows your choices:

> 1, 2, 3 . . .
>
> a, b, c . . .
>
> A, B, C . . .
>
> i, ii, iii . . .
>
> I, II, III . . .
>
> *, †, ‡, § . . .

4. Click OK all the way home.

You have to click twice — once to return to the Footnote and Endnote dialog box and then a second time to return to your document.

All the footnotes in a section must use the same numbering scheme. You can't mix and match.

If you choose the special symbols *, †, ‡, and § for your reference marks, WinWord doubles them if necessary to create unique reference marks. The first four footnotes, therefore, use the symbols singly. The mark for the fifth through eighth notes are **, ††, ‡‡, and §§. After that, the symbols are tripled.

Figure 8-3:
The Note
Options
dialog box.

To keep this doubling and tripling of symbols in check, choose the Restart Each Page button in the Note Options dialog box. That way, the mark for the first note on each page is always an asterisk (*).

You can bypass WinWord's automatic footnote-numbering scheme at any time by checking the Custom Mark button in the Footnote and Endnote dialog box and then entering any text that you want to use for the mark in the Custom Mark text box. If you want to enter a symbol that's not readily available from the keyboard, click the Symbol button and choose the symbol you want from the resulting Symbol dialog box.

Changing the Footnote Separators

Word for Windows automatically adds a short horizontal line called the *footnote separator* to separate footnotes from the text on a page. If the footnote is too long to fit at the bottom of the page, Word automatically continues the footnote to the next page and adds a *footnote continuation separator*, a longer horizontal line. You can customize the appearance of these separators by following this procedure:

1. **Create at least one footnote.**

   There's no point in bothering with customized separators for a document that doesn't yet have any footnotes. Word doesn't let you anyway.

2. **Summon the View⇨Footnotes command.**

   The footnote window appears.

3. **In the list box at the top of the footnote window, choose the separator that you want to edit.**

   You can choose the footnote separator, the footnote continuation separator, or the footnote continuation notice. (The continuation notice is printed beneath a footnote that is being continued to the next page; the continuation separator is printed atop the continued note on the next page.)

4. Edit it.

Delete the horizontal line if you want. Add text, such as "Footnotes," above or below it. Or change the amount of space before or after the separator. Whatever.

5. Click Close.

You're finished.

If you mess with a separator and then wish that you hadn't, use the View⇨Footnotes command, choose the separator you messed up, and click the Reset button.

Finding a Footnote Reference

To quickly find the reference mark for a particular footnote, follow these steps:

1. Call up the Edit⇨Go To command.

The keyboard shortcut is Ctrl+G. The Go To command displays a dialog box that isn't worthy of a separate figure here.

2. In the Go To What list box, choose Footnote.

3. In the Enter Footnote Number text box, type the number of the footnote that you want to go to.

If the notes are numbered with reference symbols (*, †, ‡, and §), type the corresponding number (1, 2, 3, and so on).

4. Click OK.

There it is.

Chapter 9

More about Tables

I couldn't figure out what to call this chapter: Setting the table? Turning the tables? Sliding under the table? Dancing on the table? Tabling the motion? The periodic table? Table for two? So I gave up and decided to call it just *More about Tables.*

All the basic kid stuff about using tables is in *Word For Windows 95 For Dummies,* by Dan Gookin (IDG Books Worldwide). Read this chapter when you're ready to move up from the kids' table to the grown-ups' table so that you can learn how to do grown-up table stuff, such as add borders, create headings, and pretend that the table is a spreadsheet or database. (After all, pretending that you're something you really aren't is what being at the grown-up table is all about, isn't it?)

If you're going to sit at my table, you have to remember the same two rules of table manners I've been trying to teach my kids for years: No talking with your mouth open and no eating with your mouth full.

Help, Mr. Wizard!

Word comes with a nifty built-in Table Wizard which can do much of the dirty work involved in setting up and formatting a table. Just follow these steps:

1. Move the insertion pointer to where you want the table to be inserted.

2. Summon the Table⇨Insert Table command.

The Insert Table dialog box appears, as shown in Figure 9-1.

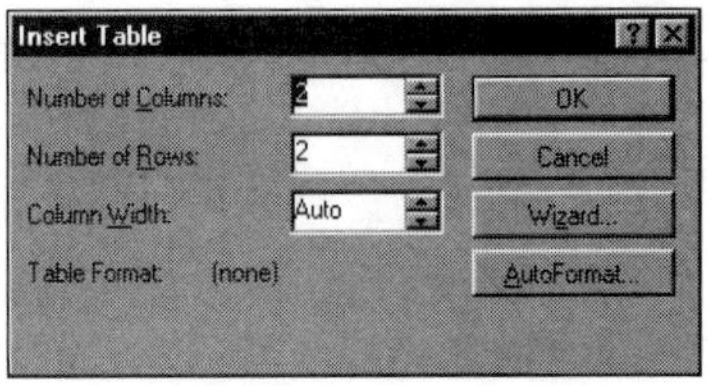

Figure 9-1:
The Insert
Table dialog
box.

3. Click the Wizard button.

The Table Wizard, as shown in Figure 9-2, replaces the Insert Table
dialog box.

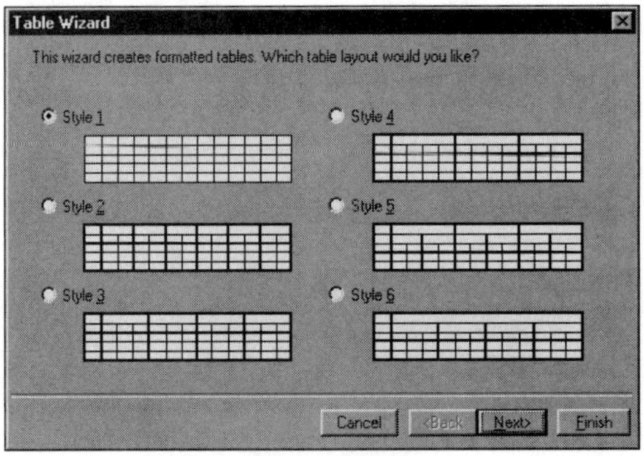

Figure 9-2:
The Table
Wizard
makes a
grand
entrance.

4. Answer the Wizard's questions, one by one.

The Table Wizard walks you through a series of dialog boxes, each asking
for different information about the table you're creating. You get to pick a
style for column headings, row headings, data alignment, salad forks, and
cloth or paper napkins. After you complete each query, click Next to
proceed to the next dialog box.

5. When you reach the end of the Table Wizard, click Finish.

Word creates the table for you. Before it finishes, however, Word pops up
the Table AutoFormat dialog box so that you can apply even more formatting to the table. Table AutoFormat is covered, er, well, next!

Autoformatting a Table

You can create great-looking tables in two ways:

 ✔ Use the Table⇨Table AutoFormat command and skip the rest of this chapter.

 ✔ Pretend that you didn't read this section and toil away at the table for hours until you get it just the way you want.

Get the picture?

Here are the steps to instant awe-inspiring tables:

1. Create a table.

Use the Insert Table button on the Standard toolbar or the Table⇨Insert Table command. Create the correct number of rows and columns and type your data. If appropriate, devote the first row and column to headings.

2. Click the mouse anywhere in the table.

3. Summon the Table⇨Table AutoFormat command.

The Table AutoFormat dialog box appears, as shown in Figure 9-3.

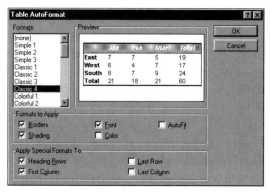

Figure 9-3: Simplify your table life with the Table AutoFormat command.

4. Choose the table format that you like from the Formats list box.

As you scroll through the list of available formats, a preview of how a sample table will appear with the format applied is shown in the preview box.

5. If you want to change the formatting elements applied to the table, check or uncheck the appropriate check boxes.

If you don't have headings in the first column, for example, uncheck the First Column check box. Or if you don't have a printer that can do justice to shading, uncheck the Shading check box.

6. Click OK.

You return to the document, where you can admire your work.

7. Don't tell your friends how you did it.

Make them think that you toiled for hours with WordPerfect 5.1's table feature.

You can change the AutoFormat applied to a table at any time. Just click anywhere in the table and summon the Table⇨Table AutoFormat command again.

The Table⇨Table AutoFormat command works by setting the formatting individually for each cell in the table. If you're still not satisfied, you can easily adjust the formatting by using the commands on the Format menu.

Amazingly, the formatting applied by the Table⇨Table AutoFormat command can withstand severe table editing in the form of inserting and deleting entire columns and rows. Remarkable! Microsoft should patent some of this stuff.

Adding Borders and Shading to a Table

If you must linger at the table, manually adding your own borders and shading, that's your business. Here's the procedure:

1. Click the Border button (shown in the margin) on the Formatting toolbar.

The Borders toolbar appears.

2. Select the cell or cells to which you want to add a border or shading.

3. To add a border to the cell or cells, click the appropriate border button.

You can add a border above or below, on the left or right of, on the interior borders of, or around an entire range of cells.

4. To shade a cell or cells, pull down the shading list box and choose the shading you want.

5. You're finished.

Click the Border button again to make the Border toolbar go away.

You can also apply borders and shading by using the Format⇨Borders and Shading command, although I'm not sure why you would. Then again, I'm not sure why you would want to add borders and shading cell by cell when the Table AutoFormat command does such a great job. So you may as well go ahead and use the Format⇨Borders and Shading command. Or just draw the table by using a fountain pen and straight edge.

You can remove borders as well as create them by using the Borders toolbar. Just select a cell that has a border you want to remove and click the appropriate border button.

Merging Cells to Create Headings

Some tables have headings that span more than one column. To create this type of heading, you use the Table➪Merge Cells command. Check out Figure 9-4 to see what I mean. In this example, the cell that contains the heading "Shipments By Region (millions)" has been merged so that it spans three columns.

Figure 9-4:
A table with
a heading
that spans
three
columns.

	Shipments By Region (millions)		
	Western	Eastern	Central
Paper bags	103	87	98
Plastic bags	120	93	92
Dirt bags	43	38	129
Scum bags	204	44	31

To create a multicolumn heading, follow these simple steps:

1. **Create the table as usual.**

   Type the data into the cells as usual. For the heading that spans several columns, type the text into the cell over the first column that you want the heading to span.

2. **Highlight the cells in the row in which you want to create a multicolumn heading.**

3. **Use the Table➪Merge Cells command.**

   The cells are merged into one super cell that spans several columns.

4. **If you want the heading centered over the cells, click the Center button on the Formatting toolbar.**

   Or press Ctrl+C.

Change your mind? Select the big cell and use the Table➪Split Cells command. When WinWord asks you in how many columns to split the cell, specify the number of columns that the heading cell spans.

If you have a really long table, so long that it doesn't all fit on one page, select the heading row and use the Table➪Headings command. Then WinWord duplicates the heading row at the top of the table on each page.

Merged cells don't get along well with the Table⇨Table AutoFormat command. Format the table with Table⇨Table AutoFormat first; then merge the cells to create a multicolumn heading.

Sorting Data in a Table

If you entered rows into a table in the wrong order, you can sort them by using the Table⇨Sort command. These steps show you how to do it:

1. Select the rows you want to sort.

It's best if you select entire rows and leave out any heading rows you don't want sorted.

2. Summon the Table⇨Sort command.

The Sort dialog box, shown in Figure 9-5, appears.

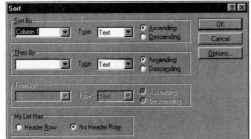

Figure 9-5:
The Sort
dialog box.

3. Set both the column you want to sort the table by and the type of sort you want.

The Sort By list box allows you to choose any of the columns you selected. Under Type, you can choose Text, Number, or Date. And you can choose Ascending or Descending sequence.

4. Click OK.

The data is sorted according to your specs.

Made a mistake? Table sorting is a little error-prone. It's all too easy to include heading rows accidentally in the sort range or to pick the wrong column. If you should be so unlucky, fret not. Just press Ctrl+Z to undo the whole thing.

You can sort as many as three columns. You can sort a table, for example, that shows sales data by Sales Rep within Region. You can specify a different sort type and sequence for each column, too.

Pay no attention to the My List Has selections at the bottom of the dialog box. If your table has one or more header rows, don't select them when you sort the table.

Pretending That a Table Is a Spreadsheet

If you can't afford a real spreadsheet program, you can pretend that WinWord's table feature is sort of like a spreadsheet. After all, it does let you enter data into rows and columns, just like a spreadsheet does. If only you could create simple formulas that total data in several cells — oh, I almost forgot — you can!

Follow these steps to total the contents of a row or column of cells:

1. **Select the cell in which you want to place the sum.**

2. **Choose the Table➪Formula command.**

   The Formula dialog box appears, as shown in Figure 9-6.

Figure 9-6:
The
Formula
dialog box.

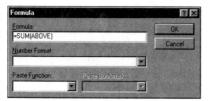

3. **Briefly review the formula and number format proposed by WinWord.**

   WinWord takes its best guess at the cells you want to total. If you insert a formula to the right of an entire row of numbers, WinWord figures that you want to sum up the numbers to the left. If you place it beneath a column of numbers, WinWord thinks that you want to sum the cells above. WinWord also looks at the numbers in the cells and guesses at the number format. If you don't like the formula or number format, you can change them.

4. **Click OK.**

   The formula is inserted into the cell, and the value is calculated.

5. **Double-check the results.**

   Make sure that the numbers look good. You can never trust a computer to add things up right.

In addition to summing numbers, WinWord has a host of other fancy functions it can do. The most useful are Average, Count, Max, and Min. Use the Paste Function list box in the Formula dialog box to choose functions other than Sum.

You can also create simple math expressions in the Formula field, such as C3+C5*100. When you create expressions like this, you can refer to specific cells just as you would in a spreadsheet program: A1, C4, and so on.

Don't throw away your copy of Excel or Lotus just yet. Formulas are useful for summing or averaging cells in small tables, but that's about as far as their usefulness goes. A WinWord table is no substitute for an Excel spreadsheet.

Pretending That a Table Is a Database

WinWord also likes to pretend that it's a database program. After all, databases are nothing more than tables of information, so why not call a WinWord table a *data table?* This enables Microsoft to increase the price of WinWord by about $50.

To use a table as a database, use the first row in the table to specify a field name for each column. Then use the View➪Toolbars command to activate the Database toolbar. This toolbar has a bunch of useful buttons that let you treat a table like a database. The most useful is the Data Form button, which enables you to insert and delete table rows as though they were database records.

Isn't this what you do when you use the Mail Merge feature? You bet. So I'm not going to repeat myself here. If you want to know more about using a table as a database, shuffle on over to Chapter 7.

Part II
WinWord's Gee-Whiz Desktop Publishing Features

The 5th Wave   By Rich Tennant

"It says,' Seth- Please see us about your idea to
wrap newsletter text around company logo. Production.'"

In this part . . .

Used to be that if you wanted to do desktop publishing, you bought a desktop publishing program. Nowadays, though, most word processors have enough fancy text-formatting features to qualify as rudimentary desktop publishing programs. WinWord is no exception. With a little effort, you can produce spiffy-looking newsletters, brochures, manuals, and even books without ever touching a high-end (and high-stress) desktop publishing program.

The chapters in this part show you how. It might be like trying to find gold in a silver mine or trying to drink whiskey from a bottle of wine, but it works. So get back.

Chapter 10

Bluffing Your Way through Typography School

*B*ack where I came from, there were people who did nothing all day but study type. They were called *typographers*. They worked in musty type foundries that smelled of molten lead and spent most of their free time cleaning their hands and coming up with cute names for new type designs like *Pandemonium* or *Bologna Book* or *Vogon Old Style*.

Now, through the magic of Windows, you too can be a typographer. Why print all your documents using Arial and Times New Roman like everybody else, when typefaces that are more attractive and more useful are readily available. A surprising number of Windows application programs come with extra typefaces, so odds are that you already have a few alternatives to pick from. Some programs, such as Corel DRAW!, come with *hundreds* of typefaces. Just today I was in an office supply store and saw a collection of 400 typefaces on a CD-ROM for $29.95.

Of course, the dark side of this story is that once you have all those typefaces, you don't know what to do with them. The proper use of typefaces can make your documents look like they were done by a professional with impeccable taste. Improper use can have the same effect as hanging a yellow "Amateur Desktop Publisher On Board" sign on your computer.

Typography (the study of type) can be a fascinating subject. Whole books have been written about it, books that are worthy of a quiet evening read while resting in a lush, leather recliner with a glass of sherry and a pipe nearby. If you don't have a leather recliner and you're fresh out of sherry and quiet evenings, this chapter has to suffice. It gives you a few quick pointers that don't make you an expert in typography, but should help you avoid the most obvious typographical blunders.

Two basic kinds of type fonts are used in desktop publishing: *PostScript* and *TrueType*. PostScript is the more popular among desktop publishing gurus, but TrueType is far and away the more popular among normal people, because support for TrueType is built into Windows. Using PostScript requires not only a more expensive PostScript printer, but also special software that you don't want to contend with. This chapter focuses on TrueType fonts, conveniently ignoring PostScript so that I don't have to buy an expensive printer.

Two Uses for Type

Before jumping into the various types of type, I want to distinguish between the two uses of type.

Body text: Body text is the main text of your document. The most important criteria for selecting a typeface for body text is legibility. In most documents, body text consists of paragraph upon paragraph of rather ordinary-looking words. You should choose a body text typeface that doesn't distract the readers as they read.

Display type: Display type is used for headings, captions, titles, and anything else that isn't body text. Text set in display type is usually brief — often just a few words — so legibility isn't the only factor to consider. The display type usually contrasts in some way with the body text type, adding variety to a page that would otherwise be filled with boring and lifeless body text.

When selecting type for body and display text, keep these points in mind:

✔ The typefaces you use for body text and display type need to be carefully coordinated. One of the easiest ways to mess up an otherwise good-looking page is *typeface clash*. (And the Typeface Clash Police are everywhere, you know.) See the section, "Avoiding Typeface Clash," later in this chapter for advice on picking typefaces for body text and display type that work well together.

✔ Some documents have more than one kind of display type. For example, a newsletter has display type in the nameplate, masthead, headings, pull quotes, jumplines, and so on. Try to limit the number of different typefaces you use for these elements. If you don't, your document ends up looking like a ransom note.

About face

To a normal person, the terms *font* and *typeface* mean the same thing. But don't use them interchangeably around typography nuts. They're liable to throw a case of hot lead type in your face. Here's a rundown on the proper way to use these terms:

Typeface: A typeface is a design for a set of letters, along with numerals and punctuation marks to go along with it. The typeface includes both upper and lowercase letters. For example, Times Roman is the name of one of the most popular typefaces.

Typeface family: A group of closely related typefaces. For example, Times Roman, Times Bold, Times Italic, and Times Bold Italic. The bold, italic, and bold italic forms of a family are considered separate typefaces, but members of the same family.

Font: A complete set of type for a particular typeface and size. For example, 10-point Avant Garde and 12-point Avant Garde are two distinct fonts.

In the days of lead type, the distinction between font and face was important because a typesetter had only certain fonts representing a particular family. For example, the typesetter had only 9-, 10-, 12-, and 14-point Times fonts for each face in the Times family. If you wanted 13-point Times Roman, you were out of luck.

The distinction between font and face is not so important anymore because Windows can create fonts of any point size you want. Thus, if you have the Times Roman typeface, you can display it in any size you want.

Windows actually muddles the terminology by using the term *font* to mean *typeface family*. When you format characters in Word for Windows, you specify the font (such as Times New Roman), the size (such as 11 point), and the style (bold, italic, or bold italic). Actually, all three of these characteristics combined is what a typographer calls a *font*.

✔ When you set up the styles for a document, set the Normal style to the body text font and base other styles that are variations of body text on Normal. Then create a style named Display that uses the typeface you want for display type and base styles that define display text (such as Heading 1, Heading 2, and so on) on the Display style. This enables you to change your typefaces later simply by changing the Normal and Display styles. (For more information about styles, see Chapter 3.)

Type Types

Typography is kind of like wine tasting: It has its own fancy terminology. Typographers say things like, "*Vogon Old Style* has a delicately balanced variation in stroke weight, with just a hint of angularity in the serifs to drive the message forward without being pretentious. This, combined with its full but gentle bouquet and a tangy but fruity finish, makes it the ideal choice for your yard-sale signs."

Then they'll look at you, expecting you to nod your head knowingly and say, "Ah."

You certainly don't need to have such refined taste when it comes to picking type, but you should at least understand the differences between the basic kinds of type — serif, sans serif, script, and decorative/novelty.

Serif type

Serif type is type that has little feet at the bottom of the letters. These little feet enable the type to walk smoothly across the page in Michael Jackson moon-walking style. Figure 10-1 shows the difference between a serif and sans serif *y* up close so that you can see what I am talking about.

Figure 10-1:
What a serif
really is.

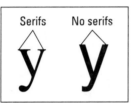

Figure 10-2 shows some examples of typefaces with serifs.

In each of the typefaces in Figure 10-2, the serifs at the bottoms of the letters create the faint illusion of a baseline that aids the eye as it moves across the page.

Figure 10-2:
Some
typefaces
that include
serifs.

Times New Roman is ubiquitous and universal, too.

Book Antiqua is not antiquated.

Bookman Old Style is a classic.

Century Schoolbook is an excellent study.

Garamond is gentle.

Who cares about all those type parts?

Ever wonder what all the doohickeys and deelybobs found in a typical type design are called? Probably not. But just in case, the accompanying figure and the following definitions give you the lowdown.

Serifs: The little feet at the tops and bottoms of letters.

Descender: The part of the letter that hangs down below the line (such as the lines in *j, p,* and *y*).

Ascender: The part of the letter that rises above the body of the letter (such as the lines in *b, d,* and *h*).

X-height: The height of a lowercase letter *x*, which usually governs the height of other lowercase letters and the appearance of the ascenders.

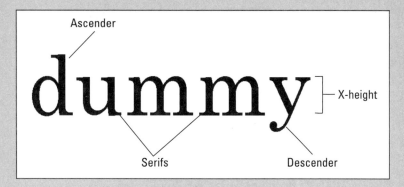

Serif type is usually the best kind of type to use in paragraphs of text. The serifs make it easier for the eye to follow a line of text across the page and then jump down to the next line.

Serifs also occur at the tops of some letters, like at the top of a capital *T* or *F* and a lowercase *p* or *y*. Serifs at the tops of letters are called *head serifs*. That means they get to boss the lowly *foot serifs* around.

Sans serif type

Sans serif typefaces don't have serifs. Figure 10-3 shows some examples.

Arial is a bit overused.

Arial Narrow fits in tight places.

Century Gothic goes around in circles.

Haettenschweiler (bless you!)

Figure 10-3:
Sans serif
typefaces.

All serif typefaces look the same to me!

Serif typefaces used to look alike to me, until I got interested in them and started looking at them more closely. Actually, there's a world of difference between various serif typefaces. The shapes of the serifs vary from face to face, as does the x-height, the design of ascenders and descenders, the thickness of the strokes, the contrast between thick and thin portions of the stroke, the shape of the enclosed spaces in letters like *a* and *e*, and other subtle details of the design.

Collectors love to classify things, and type collectors are no different. Here are a few of the categories commonly used to group related typefaces.

Old Style: Old Style typefaces are influenced by the very first typefaces, originating in the late 15th century. One of the great type designers of this era was Aldus Manutius, after whom the software company Aldus (the folks who make PageMaker) is named.

Many typefaces identify themselves as Old Style faces; for example, Bookman Old Style, Century Old Style, and Goudy Old Style. Others, such as Garamond, Palatino, Times Roman, and ITC Souvenir, do not.

Note that some of these typefaces were developed in the 20th century. The designation *Old*

Style doesn't mean that the typeface is old; it just means that it uses design elements common to other Old Style typefaces.

Transitional: This style was originated in the mid-18th century by John Baskerville. Baskerville pioneered improved printing techniques, which enabled typefaces to use finer strokes safely. Examples of Transitional typefaces are Americana, Baskerville, and Caledonia.

Modern: The Modern style isn't really modern, but dates to the 18th century and the type designer Giambattista Bodoni. Modern typefaces have a strong vertical orientation that some say gives the entire category a picket-fence look. It includes serifs that are very thin and nearly flat. The most commonly used modern typeface today is Bodoni.

Clarendon: Clarendon typefaces were first used in the mid-19th century. Like Modern typefaces, they have a strong vertical orientation. However, they also have generous serifs, usually cut square off the edge, and are not so flat. This makes them exceptionally readable, and among the most widely used typefaces categories. Examples include Bookman, Century Schoolbook, and Cheltenham.

Here are some things to keep in mind concerning sans serif type:

- ✔ Without serifs to scoot the eye across the line, sans serif types are difficult to read in large stretches. Sans serif types are best used for headlines, captions, notes, and other short bursts of text. Use them in full paragraphs only if you want to appear trendy.

- ✔ The best-known sans serif typeface is Arial, which is built into many laser printers. Arial is a versatile typeface, but it's overused. Some designers would rather cut off their ear than use Arial. Suitable alternatives include Folio and Univers.

- ✔ Notice in Figure 10-3 how Century Gothic has a very geometrical look to it. It's almost as if the whole typeface is constructed of perfect circles and straight lines. Appearances can be deceiving, though. Study this typeface carefully and you'll notice subtle variations in the seemingly perfect circles and lines. (Try turning the book around and looking at the type upside-down.)

Scripts

Scripts are typefaces that are designed to mimic handwriting. Some scripts look like ornate, hand-drawn calligraphy; they are usually used in formal invitations. Other scripts look like they were spontaneously drawn. Figure 10-4 shows examples of both.

Brush Script

BriemScript

Lucida Caligraphy

Vivaldi

Zap-Chance

Figure 10-4:
Various
script
typefaces.

Don't use script typefaces until you've considered these points:

✔ Scripts are usually difficult to read, especially in smaller sizes. Don't use them for large expanses of text.

✔ Don't use script types to imitate a hand-written signature. It's too much of a desktop cliché. If you want to add a computer printed signature to your documents, use a scanner to scan your signature and then include it as a graphic. If you don't have a scanner, take your signature to a copy center that has computers. They'll scan it for you, probably for about $10.

Novelty types

Novelty types are types that are so weird they defy categorization. Figure 10-5 shows some examples.

See? There are hundreds of typefaces like this to choose from.

Be careful about how you use these typefaces. Most of them are intended only for decorative use. Some of them can evoke a certain atmosphere, such as the Gold Rush days. Others just look goofy.

You can often find typefaces that represent your favorite TV show: *Star Trek, The Brady Bunch, The Flintstones, The Jetsons,* and so on. These are fun for a comical effect.

Figure 10-5:
Some really
cool
typefaces.

ENVISION HAS A VERY ODD LOOK

Tekton is a bit overused

GOLD MINE IS A REAL RUSH

Hobo sort of Hangs Around

KeyPunch is Very Punchy

KEYSTROKES: BOXY BUT GOOD

There's More to Typography Than Picking a Typeface

Picking a typeface is only the first step in creating type that looks good. Other aspects to consider are the point size, line length, line spacing, and alignment.

Point size

When you create a new document by clicking the New button, WinWord bases the new document on the Normal template (NORMAL.DOT). The default text format for documents based on the NORMAL.DOT is 10-point Times New Roman. Considering that the left and right margins in the Normal template are 1¼ inches, creating text lines a full 6 inches long, this font is way too small. Type a few paragraphs of text in 10-point Times New Roman on a 6-inch line and you'll see what I mean.

One obvious way to improve the legibility of documents based on NORMAL.DOT is to increase the point size to 11- or 12-point type. As you increase the point size, the amount of text that fits on each line naturally goes down and the text becomes more readable. This increase eases the burden on the eye, probably saving you money in the long run by reducing your need for eyeglasses. (See Chapter 4 for details on how to modify the NORMAL.DOT template.)

Note, however, that not all typefaces appear to be the same size at a given point size. For example, consider the examples in Figure 10-6, both set in 11-point type.

Figure 10-6:
Some
typefaces
look bigger
than others.

Times New Roman (11 point)

The Old Grey Donkey, Eeyore, stood by himself in a thistly corner of the forest with his front feet well apart and his head on one side, and thought about things.

Century Schoolbook (also 11 point)

The Old Grey Donkey, Eeyore, stood by himself in a thistly corner of the forest with his front feet well apart and his head on one side, and thought about things.

Notice how much larger the second example looks, even though both samples are the same point size? This is partly because the design of Century Schoolbook has a slightly larger x-height than Times New Roman, but also because Century Schoolbook has longer serifs than Times New Roman, which leaves more space between the letters.

- ✔ Increasing the point size isn't the only way to make NORMAL.DOT more legible. Another alternative is to shorten the line length by increasing the margins. See the next section, "Line length," for more about the relationship between point size and line length.

- ✔ There is no magic point size to use in all circumstances. Some typefaces are very readable in 9-point type, and others are not. Most of the time, your body text should be set in 10-, 11-, or 12-point type.

Line length

The NORMAL.DOT template sets the left and right margins to 1¼ inches each, which results in a 6-inch line length. That's almost always too wide, especially if you stick with the NORMAL.DOT default 10-point Times New Roman font. You need to reel 'er in a bit.

Unfortunately, there is no hard and fast rule for setting the proper line length. It varies depending on the typeface, point size, and the spacing between lines. All these factors work together. In other words, if you use a larger typeface and a larger point size and increase the amount of space between the lines, you can use a longer line length.

For example, here are two samples of text set in 10-point Times New Roman, with different line lengths:

> The Old Grey Donkey, Eeyore, stood by himself in a thistly corner of the forest, his front feet well apart, his head on one side, and thought about things.

> The Old Grey Donkey, Eeyore, stood by himself in
> a thistly corner of the forest, his front feet well apart,
> his head on one side, and thought about things.

The only real test for getting the line length right is to print some samples and read them.

- ✔ There are a few rules of thumb that graphics designers follow when setting the line length. One is that the length of the line should average about 50-60 characters; another is that each line should hold about eight to ten words. Yet another rule of thumb is the one-and-a-half-alphabets rule: Type the lowercase alphabet one and a half times, like this:

  abcdefghijklmnopqrstuvwxyzabcdefghijklm

That should be about the length of one line. Note, however, that these rules of thumb are meant to be applied to two- or three-column layouts. For single-column layouts, these rules usually result in lines that are too short.

✔ To adjust the line length, set the page layout margins using the File⇨Page Setup command, instead of grabbing the margin doohickeys on the ruler and sliding them. Dragging the ruler's margin doohickeys sets the left and right indents on a paragraph-by-paragraph basis, instead of adjusting the margins for the entire page. If you want to adjust only one paragraph, using the ruler is the way to go.

Line spacing

Line spacing refers to the amount of space added between lines of text. Consider these samples, each set in 10-point Times New Roman but with varying amounts of line spacing:

Line spacing: exactly 10 points

The Old Grey Donkey, Eeyore, stood by himself in a thistly corner of the forest with his front feet well apart and his head on one side, and thought about things. Sometimes he thought sadly to himself, "Why?" and sometimes he thought, "Wherefore?" and sometimes he thought, "Inasmuch as which?"

Line spacing: exactly 12 points

The Old Grey Donkey, Eeyore, stood by himself in a thistly corner of the forest with his front feet well apart and his head on one side, and thought about things. Sometimes he thought sadly to himself, "Why?" and sometimes he thought, "Wherefore?" and sometimes he thought, "Inasmuch as which?"

Line spacing: exactly 14 points

The Old Grey Donkey, Eeyore, stood by himself in a thistly corner of the forest with his front feet well apart and his head on one side, and thought about things. Sometimes he thought sadly to himself, "Why?" and sometimes he thought, "Wherefore?" and sometimes he thought, "Inasmuch as which?"

Increasing the line spacing enables you to run the line longer and use a smaller point size, or use a larger point size on a smaller line. In both cases, the extra line spacing adds definition to each line. To change the line spacing in Word for Windows, use the Format⇨Paragraph command and adjust the Line Spacing and At settings.

> ✔ Extra line spacing beyond the type size is called *leading,* because back in the old days of lead type, the extra space was added by inserting thin strips of lead between the lines of type.
>
> ✔ If you set the line spacing to *Single,* WinWord adds a bit of extra leading. How much depends on the size of the type and the typeface you've selected. It usually works out pretty well, but if you want precise control, set the line spacing to *Exactly* instead. (You then also have to set the number of points for the line spacing.)

Alignment

The type of paragraph alignment you use affects the legibility of type, too. WinWord enables you to use four types of alignment: Left, Centered, Right, and Justified. Body text is either left-aligned or justified. Headings are usually either left-aligned or centered. You can set the text alignment by clicking one of the alignment buttons in the formatting toolbar or by calling up the Format⇨Paragraph command and adjusting the Alignment setting.

Justified text gives your document a more formal appearance, but it has another important benefit as well: justified text usually crams more text onto each line, resulting in fewer lines of text. That's why almost all newspapers set text in justified columns. If you're tight on space, consider using justified text.

Be careful about justified text in narrow columns, though. WinWord sometimes throws in an excessive amount of space between words to get the line to justify, as shown here:

> Sometimes he thought
> sadly to himself, "Why?"
> and sometimes he thought,
> "Wherefore?"   and
> sometimes he thought,
> "Inasmuch as which?"

Notice the humongous gap in the fourth line. You could throw a Linotype machine through it.

You can fix problems like this usually by throwing in an optional hyphen. To do that, press Ctrl+– where you want the word to be hyphenated. If the word is anywhere near the end of the line, WinWord hyphenates it. For example:

> Sometimes he thought
> sadly to himself, "Why?"
> and sometimes he thought,
> "Wherefore?" and some-
> times he thought,
> "Inasmuch as which?"

In this example, I hyphenated the word *sometimes*. That solved the problem from the fourth line, but introduced a new problem in the fifth line. To correct the new problem, hyphenate again:

> Sometimes he thought
> sadly to himself, "Why?"
> and sometimes he thought,
> "Wherefore?" and some-
> times he thought, "Inas-
> much as which?"

This is a lot of work, isn't it? That's why I avoid justified type whenever possible.

You can set up WinWord to hyphenate your documents automatically. Skip ahead to the next chapter to find out how.

Avoiding Typeface Clash

Faced with a bewildering array of typographical choices, what's the poor WinWord user to do? Following is some well-intentioned advice on picking fonts to use for body text and display type.

The good news is that you don't have to run out and invest $40 in a font collection to apply the advice contained here. Word 7 comes with a fairly decent collection of fonts right on the CD, so you can break right out of the "Times and Arial Duldrums."

Picking the body text type

The main criterion for selecting a body type is legibility. Unfortunately, legibility is not an either/or proposition. Some typefaces are easy to read in some circumstances and hard to read in others. Several factors work together to make text easy or hard to read. The typeface, the point size, the length of the line, and the amount of space between the lines all work together to create or destroy legibility.

That being said, here are a few rules of thumb for picking a good, legible typeface for body type:

> ✔ *Use a serif typeface for body text.* The point of serifs is to make text more legible. You can use sans serif typefaces for body text if you know what you're doing, but the safest way to create legible body text is to stick to a serif typeface.

✔ *Whatever typeface you use, adjust the point size, line length, and line spacing to improve legibility.* No type looks good when set in 9 point on a 6-inch line with no additional line spacing.

✔ *Don't bother with Times New Roman.* Times was originally designed for newspapers (the *London Times,* actually). The design goals were something like this: design a typeface that enables us to cram as much text as possible onto one line and print the newspaper on cruddy presses and cheap paper. Unless you're trying to save paper or you want a newspaper look, you can almost certainly find a better typeface. As an added bonus, you'll stand out from the crowd. *Everybody* has Times New Roman, but not everybody has Vogon Old Style.

Picking the display type

Display type is usually used in short bursts: short headings, captions, titles, and so on. So legibility isn't necessarily the most important consideration when choosing a display type. Other factors, such as how much it contrasts with the body text and what kind of atmosphere is created, are important as well.

The safest way to pick a display type is to opt for a sans serif typeface. That's why Windows includes Arial, a Helvetica look-alike. Arial works with Times New Roman and just about any other serif typeface. Like Times New Roman, though, it's a bit overused. For a more distinctive look, use a different sans serif typeface, such as Univers, Optima, or Avant Garde.

If you want, you can also safely use a variation of the body text typeface for display type. For example, if the body text is 11-point Century Schoolbook, you may set headings as 14-point Century Schoolbook Bold and captions as 10-point Century Schoolbook Italic.

Don't mix different serif typefaces unless you know what you're doing. Some serif typefaces work well together, but others do not, and the subtleties are beyond the reach of most of us. Some designers marvel at your ingenuity in combining Goudy Old Style with Cheltenham, while others turn pale and begin to feel nauseous just thinking about it. Don't risk it.

Typefaces That Come with Windows 95 and Word 95

The following sections show samples of the typefaces that are available to all Word 95 users. Times New Roman and Arial are supplied with Windows 95; the others are supplied with Word 95 or Office 95. All samples are shown in 12-point type.

Algerian

Algerian
Algerian Italic

ABCDEFGHIJKLMNOPQRSTUVWXYZ
abcdefghijklmnopqrstuvwxyz
1234567890

ABCDEFGHIJKLMNOPQRSTUVWXYZ
abcdefghijklmnopqrstuvwxyz
1234567890

Arial

Arial
Arial Bold
Arial Italic
Arial Bold Italic

ABCDEFGHIJKLMNOPQRSTUVWXYZ
abcdefghijklmnopqrstuvwxyz
1234567890

ABCDEFGHIJKLMNOPQRSTUVWXYZ
abcdefghijklmnopqrstuvwxyz
1234567890

Arial Narrow

Arial Narrow
Arial Narrow Bold
Arial Narrow Italic
Arial Narrow Bold Italic

ABCDEFGHIJKLMNOPQRSTUVWXYZ
abcdefghijklmnopqrstuvwxyz
1234567890

ABCDEFGHIJKLMNOPQRSTUVWXYZ
abcdefghijklmnopqrstuvwxyz
1234567890

Arial Rounded MT Bold

Arial Rounded MT Bold
Arial Rounded MT Bold Bold
Arial Rounded MT Bold Italic
Arial Rounded MT Bold Bold Italic

ABCDEFGHIJKLMNOPQRSTUVWXYZ
abcdefghijklmnopqrstuvwxyz
1234567890

ABCDEFGHIJKLMNOPQRSTUVWXYZ
abcdefghijklmnopqrstuvwxyz
1234567890

Book Antiqua

Book Antiqua
Book Antiqua Bold
Book Antiqua Italic
Book Antiqua Bold Italic

ABCDEFGHIJKLMNOPQRSTUVWXYZ
abcdefghijklmnopqrstuvwxyz
1234567890

ABCDEFGHIJKLMNOPQRSTUVWXYZ
abcdefghijklmnopqrstuvwxyz
1234567890

Bookman Old Style

Bookman Old Style
Bookman Old Style Bold
Bookman Old Style Italic
Bookman Old Style Bold Italic

ABCDEFGHIJKLMNOPQRSTUVWXYZ
abcdefghijklmnopqrstuvwxyz
1234567890

ABCDEFGHIJKLMNOPQRSTUVWXYZ
abcdefghijklmnopqrstuvwxyz
1234567890

Braggadacio

Braggadacio
Braggadacio Italic

ABCDEFGHIJKLMNOPQRSTUVWXYZ
abcdefghijklmnopqrstuvwxyz
1234567890

ABCDEFGHIJKLMNOPQRSTUVWXYZ
abcdefghijklmnopqrstuvwxyz
1234567890

Britanic Bold

Britanic Bold
Britanic Bold Bold
Britanic Bold Italic
Britanic Bold Bold Italic

ABCDEFGHIJKLMNOPQRSTUVWXYZ
abcdefghijklmnopqrstuvwxyz
1234567890

ABCDEFGHIJKLMNOPQRSTUVWXYZ
abcdefghijklmnopqrstuvwxyz
1234567890

Brush Script MT

Brush Script MT
Brush Script MT Bold

ABCDEFGHIJKLMNOPQRSTUVWXYZ
abcdefghijklmnopqrstuvwxyz
1234567890

Century Gothic

Century Gothic
Century Gothic Bold
Century Gothic Italic
Century Gothic Bold Italic

ABCDEFGHIJKLMNOPQRSTUVWXYZ
abcdefghijklmnopqrstuvwxyz
1234567890

ABCDEFGHIJKLMNOPQRSTUVWXYZ
abcdefghijklmnopqrstuvwxyz
1234567890

Century Schoolbook

Century Schoolbook
Century Schoolbook Bold
Century Schoolbook Italic
Century Schoolbook Bold Italic

ABCDEFGHIJKLMNOPQRSTUVWXYZ
abcdefghijklmnopqrstuvwxyz
1234567890

ABCDEFGHIJKLMNOPQRSTUVWXYZ
abcdefghijklmnopqrstuvwxyz
1234567890

Colona MT

Colona MT
Colona MT Bold
Colona MT Italic
Colona MT Bold Italic

ABCDEFGHIJKLMNOPQRSTUVWXYZ
abcdefghijklmnopqrstuvwxyz
1234567890

ABCDEFGHIJKLMNOPQRSTUVWXYZ
abcdefghijklmnopqrstuvwxyz
1234567890

Desdemona

Desdemona
Desdemona Bold
Desdemona Italic
Desdemona Bold Italic

ABCDEFGHIJKLMNOPQRSTUVWXYZ
abcdefghijklmnopqrstuvwxyz
1234567890

ABCDEFGHIJKLMNOPQRSTUVWXYZ
abcdefghijklmnopqrstuvwxyz
1234567890

Footlight MT Light

Footlight MT Light
Footlight MT Light Bold
Footlight MT Light Italic
Footlight MT Light Bold Italic

ABCDEFGHIJKLMNOPQRSTUVWXYZ
abcdefghijklmnopqrstuvwxyz
1234567890

ABCDEFGHIJKLMNOPQRSTUVWXYZ
abcdefghijklmnopqrstuvwxyz
1234567890

Garamond MT

Garamond MT
Garamond MT Bold
Garamond MT Italic
Garamond MT Bold Italic

ABCDEFGHIJKLMNOPQRSTUVWXYZ
abcdefghijklmnopqrstuvwxyz
1234567890

ABCDEFGHIJKLMNOPQRSTUVWXYZ
abcdefghijklmnopqrstuvwxyz
1234567890

Haettenschweiler

Haettenschweiler
Haettenschweiler Italic

ABCDEFGHIJKLMNOPQRSTUVWXYZ
abcdefghijklmnopqrstuvwxyz
1234567890

ABCDEFGHIJKLMNOPQRSTUVWXYZ
abcdefghijklmnopqrstuvwxyz
1234567890

Impact

Impact
Impact Italic

ABCDEFGHIJKLMNOPQRSTUVWXYZ
abcdefghijklmnopqrstuvwxyz
1234567890

ABCDEFGHIJKLMNOPQRSTUVWXYZ
abcdefghijklmnopqrstuvwxyz
1234567890

Kino MT

Kino MT
Kino MT Bold
Kino MT *Italic*
Kino MT Bold Italic

ABCDEFGHIJKLMNOPQRSTUVWXYZ
abcdefghijklmnopqrstuvwxyz
1234567890

ABCDEFGHIJKLMNOPQRSTUVWXYZ
abcdefghijklmnopqrstuvwxyz
1234567890

MS Linedraw

MS Linedraw
MS Linedraw Bold
MS Linedraw Italic
MS Linedraw Bold Italic

ABCDEFGHIJKLMNOPQRSTUVWXYZ
abcdefghijklmnopqrstuvwxyz
1234567890

ABCDEFGHIJKLMNOPQRSTUVWXYZ
abcdefghijklmnopqrstuvwxyz
1234567890

Matura MT Script Capitals

Matura MT Script Capitals
Matura MT Script Capitals Bold
Matura MT Script Capitals Italic
Matura MT Script Capitals Bold Italic

ABCDEFGHIJKLMNOPQRSTUVWXYZ
abcdefghijklmnopqrstuvwxyz
1234567890

ABCDEFGHIJKLMNOPQRSTUVWXYZ
abcdefghijklmnopqrstuvwxyz
1234567890

Playbill

Playbill
Playbill Bold
Playbill Italic
Playbill Bold Italic

ABCDEFGHIJKLMNOPQRSTUVWXYZ
abcdefghijklmnopqrstuvwxyz
1234567890

ABCDEFGHIJKLMNOPQRSTUVWXYZ
abcdefghijklmnopqrstuvwxyz
1234567890

Times New Roman

Times New Roman
Times New Roman Bold
Times New Roman Italic
Times New Roman Bold Italic

ABCDEFGHIJKLMNOPQRSTUVWXYZ
abcdefghijklmnopqrstuvwxyz
1234567890

ABCDEFGHIJKLMNOPQRSTUVWXYZ
abcdefghijklmnopqrstuvwxyz
1234567890

Wide Latin

Wide Latin
Wide Latin Bold
Wide Latin Italic
Wide Latin Bold Italic

ABCDEFGHIJKLMNOPQRSTUVWXYZ
abcdefghijklmnopqrstuvwxyz
1234567890

ABCDEFGHIJKLMNOPQRSTUVWXYZ
abcdefghijklmnopqrstuvwxyz
1234567890

Chapter 11

More Than You Ever Wanted to Know about Columns and Hyphenation

● ●

In This Chapter

▶ Creating columns

▶ Adjusting column width

▶ Forcing a column break

▶ Hyphenating your text

● ●

*I*f you use WinWord to create newsletters, brochures, and other stuff that you really should be using a desktop publishing program like PageMaker or Ventura Publisher for, you'll be happy to know that WinWord enables you to create beautiful two- or three-column layouts. (Actually, you can create as many as 11 columns on a page, but unless you're using *really* wide paper, that's not such a good idea.)

WinWord refers to two- and three-column layouts as *newspaper-style columns*, but that's just a bit misleading. To implement a true newspaper style column feature, WinWord would have to edit your prose automatically as you type it so that it focused on bad news and added a distinct left-wing slant to your text.

This chapter jumps head-first into setting up newspaper-style columns in WinWord and tackles a related feature: hyphenation. Hyphenation isn't such a big deal in single-column layouts, but after you add two or three columns to a page, hyphenation can be the key to making the columns look good. Plus, hyphenation didn't really fit anywhere else and this chapter was kind of short without it.

Creating Columns

Columns are a sectional thing: When you create multiple columns, the column layout is applied to the entire section. If the entire document consists of but one section, the column layout applies to the entire document. If you want part of the document to have one column and another part to have two or three columns, you have to create two or more sections to accommodate the different column layouts.

Creating columns the easy way

Here is the easiest way to create multiple columns in your document:

1. Click the Columns button (shown in the margin) on the Standard toolbar.

The drop-down menu shown in Figure 11-1 appears.

Figure 11-1: The Columns button.

2. Click and drag the mouse to pick the number of columns you want.

3. Let go.

Voila! The document is formatted with the number of columns you chose.

Some notes on using multiple columns:

✔ When you create a two-column layout, you probably expect to see both columns side by side on-screen. That happens only if you switch to Page Layout view using the View⇨Page Layout command. In Normal view (View⇨Normal), the text is formatted according to the width of the column, but the columns are not displayed side by side on-screen.

✔ For a quick glimpse of how the columns appear when printed, use the File⇨Print Preview command. When you've seen enough, click the Close button to return to your document.

✔ Did you choke when you saw what your document looked like in columns? You can revert to single-column mode by pressing Ctrl+Z (the magic Undo command) or by using the Columns button to set the layout to one column.

✔ The Columns button enables you to set the number of columns, but it doesn't enable you to control the size of each column or the amount of space between columns. To do these latter actions, you need to use the Format⇨Columns command, described next.

Creating columns the hard way

For more control over the appearance of columns, use the Format⇨Columns command. Grab a cup of coffee and follow these steps:

1. **Move the cursor to the point in the document where you want the columns to begin.**

   If you want to apply columns to the entire document, it doesn't matter where you put the cursor.

2. **Hail the Format⇨Columns command.**

   You are greeted with the Columns dialog box, shown in Figure 11-2.

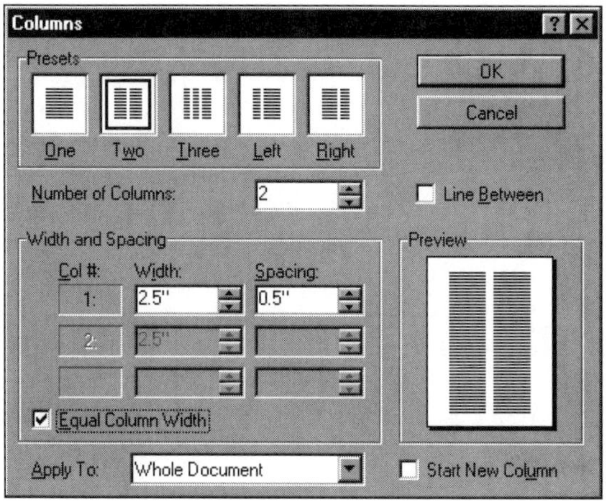

Figure 11-2:
The
Columns
dialog box.

3. **Click one of the five preset column layouts.**

   If you want more than three columns, drop everything. Take a long lunch; clear your head of such nonsense. If you still want four or more columns when you return, use the Number of Columns control to set the number of columns you want.

4. **Change the Width or Spacing fields if you must.**

   If you want to change the width of the columns, change the Width field. To change the amount of space between columns, change the Spacing field.

5. **Click the Line Between button if you want a line between the columns.**

   This is the line between the stuff you read, not the stuff you read between the lines.

6. **Here's the tricky part: If you want the new column layout to begin at the cursor position, choose This Point Forward from the Apply To list box.**

   If you choose This Point Forward, Word adds a section break at the cursor position and applies the column layout to the new section. Thus, text that follows the cursor is formatted in columns, but text that comes before it is not.

7. **Periodically peer at the preview box to see whether you like the column layout.**

8. **Click OK.**

   Excellent!

Here are some things to remember as you twiddle with the Columns dialog box:

- ✔ If you check the Equal Column Width check box, WinWord balances the columns evenly. If you uncheck this check box, you can create columns of uneven width.

- ✔ Using the Apply To: This Point Forward option is the way to create a headline or title that spans the width of two or three columns. Start by creating the headline, using a large font and centering it. Then use the Format⇨Columns command to create a two- or three-column layout. Set the Select Apply To field to This Point Forward to throw the columns into a new section so that the headline remains in a single column.

Adjusting Column Width

If you don't like the width of columns you've created, you can change them at any time. You have two ways to change column width:

- ✔ Call up the Format⇨Columns command and play with the Width and Spacing fields.

- ✔ Click and drag the *column marker,* the box-like separator between columns in the ruler (shown in the margin). If you check the Equal Column Width check box in the Columns dialog box, all the column markers move in concert so that equal column widths are preserved. Otherwise, you can adjust the column markers individually.

Some things to remember when you adjust column width:

- ✔ Even if you use unequal column widths, try to keep the gap between the columns the same widths. Otherwise, you create an unbalanced look.

- ✔ When adjusting column width by dragging the column marker, hold down the Alt key before clicking the mouse. Doing so causes WinWord to display measurements that show the width of each column and the size of the space between columns.

- ✔ Remember that any formatting applied to paragraphs in columns is still in effect. If you gave a paragraph a left indent of ½ inch, the paragraph is indented ½ inch from the left column margin. This reduces the column width.

Forcing a Column Break

Left to its own devices, WinWord decides when to jump text from the bottom of one column up to the top of the next column. There are times, however, when you want to intervene and insert a column break of your own.

Follow these steps to force a column break:

1. **Place the cursor where you want the new column to begin.**

2. **Press Ctrl+Shift+Enter.**

   Or use the Insert⇨Break command, check the Column Break feature, and click OK.

In Normal view, a column break is indicated in the text by a solid line running all the way across the screen. In Page Layout view, the column break is obvious when you see the text jump to the next column.

Don't try to create two or three columns of equal length by inserting column breaks where you think the bottom of each column should fall. Instead, insert a continuous section break at the end of the last column. A continuous section break balances all the columns in the section so that they're of equal length and then starts a new section without forcing a page break. To insert a continuous section break, call up the Insert⇨Break command, choose Continuous, and click OK.

Hyphenating Your Text

WinWord has the capability of automatically hyphenating words. You can set it up so that words are hyphenated as you type them, or you can wait until after you've typed your text and then automatically hyphenate the document. Hyphenating as you type can slow WinWord down, especially if you don't have a blazingly fast computer. Thus, I suggest you type your document first and then hyphenate it.

Here's how:

1. **Type your text.**

   Don't worry about hyphens during this step.

2. **Activate the Tools⇨Hyphenation command.**

   The Hyphenation dialog box, shown in Figure 11-3, appears.

Figure 11-3:
The
Hyphenation
dialog box.

Hyphenation	? ✕
☑ Automatically Hyphenate Document	OK
☐ Hyphenate Words in CAPS	Cancel
Hyphenation Zone: 0.25"	Manual...
Limit Consecutive Hyphens To: No Limit	

3. **Check the Automatically Hyphenate Document check box.**

4. **Check the Hyphenate Words in CAPS check box if you want words made entirely of capital letters to be hyphenated.**

   Uncheck this option if your writing includes specialized jargon that appears in all capitals and should not be hyphenated. For example, if you use terms like TECHNOBABBLE VOCABULATOR, which must not under any circumstances be hyphenated, you'll love this option.

5. **Adjust the Hyphenation Zone if you're picky.**

   This zone is the area within which WinWord tries to end each line. If necessary, WinWord hyphenates words that cross into this zone.

6. **Set the Limit Consecutive Hyphens To list box to 3 or 4.**

   There's nothing wrong with two hyphens in a row, and three is OK once in awhile. But WinWord's default setting for this field places no limit to the number of consecutive lines that WinWord can hyphenate. You don't want to see a column of 20 hyphenated lines, do you?

7. Click OK.

WinWord hyphenates the document.

8. Check the results.

You may not be happy with WinWord's hyphenations. You should always check the results and make any necessary corrections.

Here are some hyphenation pointers to keep in mind:

✔ WinWord uses its dictionary to determine where to hyphenate words. It probably spells better than you do. (I know it spells better than *I* do!)

✔ If you want to cause WinWord to hyphenate a word at a particular spot, place the cursor where you want the word hyphenated and press Ctrl+–. Pressing this creates an *optional hyphen,* which is displayed only when the word falls at the end of a line.

✔ Do *not* hyphenate words simply by typing a hyphen. It may work for the time being, but if you later edit the text so that the hyphenated word no longer falls at the end of a line, the hyphen still appears, now in the middle of the line where it does not belong. Use Ctrl+– instead.

✔ Sometimes you want to use a hyphen in a compound word, but you don't want the word to be split up at the end of the line because it might look funny. For example, *G-Men.* In that case, you should use Ctrl+Shift+– to create the hyphen rather than the hyphen key alone. WinWord displays the hyphen, but does not break the word at the hyphen.

✔ If you click the <u>M</u>anual button in the Hyphenation dialog box, WinWord leads you through the entire document, asking you about each word it wants to hyphenate. This is tiresome beyond belief. Better to just hyphenate the document and then review it and remove any hyphens you don't like.

Chapter 12

I've Been Framed!
(How to Put Text and Pictures
Where You Want Them)

In This Chapter

▶ Putting text in a frame

▶ Putting a picture in a frame

▶ Creating an empty frame

▶ Aligning a frame

I know I should start this chapter with a silly joke about Roger Rabbit, but I'm not in the mood for it. One of my dogs just dug up one of the few remaining green plants in my backyard, so I'd rather fume and pout and just get on with the exciting computer stuff.

This chapter is all about frames. What, you ask, is a frame? It's a bit of text or a picture that's detached from the main flow of text in your document so that you can place it anywhere on the page. The main text of your document can skip right over the frame, or you can cause the text to flow smoothly around the frame for a spiffy desktop publisher appearance. Frames are used to plop pretty pictures down in the middle of a column or two of text, or to pull out a bit of text — perhaps a great quote, a heading, or a complete paragraph — and give it special highlighting.

This chapter covers the rudiments of using frames. For a compendium of ideas for using frames in concert with WinWord's other desktop publishing features, head straight for Chapter 13 after you finish this chapter. Do not pass Go, do not collect $200.

Inserting a Text Frame

Suppose you're writing along, minding your own business, when it occurs to you that the sentence you just wrote — about how many men have more hair than wit — would benefit from special highlighting. Instead of just making the sentence bold or setting it in 98-point Screaming Yellow Zonker, you think it would be great to put it in a box alongside the main text and make the main text flow around it, just like in Figure 12-1.

The following steps provide the framework for inserting text into a frame:

1. Type the text you want to frame as a separate paragraph.

Type the text in the document at a point that's near where you want the final framed text to appear. The positioning doesn't have to be exact, though, because you can move it once you've placed it in a frame. In Figure 12-1, I typed the quote I want to frame as a separate paragraph just before the heading "Inserting a Text Frame."

2. Select the paragraph and call up the Insert⇨Frame command.

Select the entire paragraph by triple-clicking it. Then use the Insert⇨Frame command to place the text in a frame.

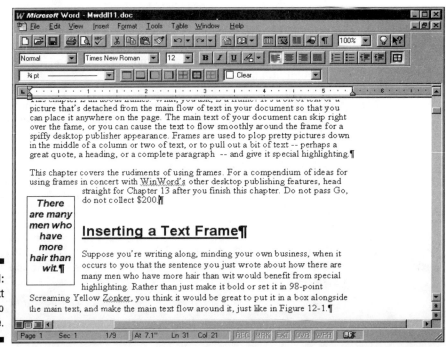

Figure 12-1:
Some text dropped into a frame.

3. **If WinWord asks whether you want to switch to Page Layout view, respond Yes.**

   You can work with framed text in Normal view, but you can't adjust its positioning on the page. Because moving the text around on the page is the main reason for framing it, it only makes sense to switch to Page Layout view now. After you've finished playing with the frame, you can switch back to Normal view if you want.

4. **WinWord inserts a frame and places the text in it.**

5. **Drag the frame kicking and screaming to its new size and location.**

   When the frame is initially created, WinWord automatically selects it. This is what the frame looks like when selected:

   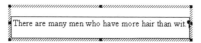

   You can change the size and shape of the frame by dragging any of the love handles at the corners or on the sides of the gray frame box. To move the frame, drag the frame from any point on the gray frame box other than the love handles.

6. **Reformat the text within the frame to suit your fancy.**

   In Figure 12-1, I changed the font and centered the paragraph. (The border was automatically added by WinWord when I created the frame.)

7. **Switch back to Normal view for a real shocker.**

    Use the View⇨Normal command or click the Normal View button (shown in the margin). When you return to Normal view, you see that the framed paragraph is formatted properly, but it is not displayed in its final location on the page. Instead, it's displayed in the location at which you originally typed the text in Step 1. You can see the frame's position on the page only when you switch to Layout view.

Here are some issues to keep in mind when you create a text frame:

- ✔ Be careful that you don't shrink the frame so small that the text gets cut off.

- ✔ Don't forget that WinWord automatically adds a border to framed text. You can change or remove the border or add shading by using the Format⇨Borders and Shading command.

- ✔ A frame can contain more than one paragraph of text. If you try to create a frame from *less* than a paragraph of text, WinWord inserts a paragraph mark at the end of the text you framed.

- ✔ WinWord keeps track of the location and size of a frame by stuffing the necessary information into the paragraph mark for the last paragraph in the frame.

Putting a Picture in a Frame

Suppose that you're rambling along, typing some boring prose about a dull subject, such as using frames in WinWord, when it occurs to you that a picture of a Heffalump would be most appreciated right about now. You conjure up the Insert⇨Picture command and discover that WinWord does indeed come with a clipart picture of a Heffalump. But when you insert it, the Heffalump stands there all by itself, on its own line. It's as if all the text in the document is stuffed with fluff, afraid to meet the Heffalump face to face, probably aware that wherever you find a Heffalump, a Woosle is usually not far off.

Well, just slap a frame on that picture and the text cuddles up right next to it as if Heffalumps are what text likes best of all. Look at Figure 12-2, and you see what I mean. Putting a picture in a frame and letting the text flow around it is a sure-fire way to get your friends to ooh and ahh and marvel at your wonderful desktop-publishing skills. Don't tell them how it's done; make them buy their own copy of this book.

To frame a picture, follow these steps:

1. **Use the Insert⇨Picture command to insert a picture.**

   If the top of the picture looks like it has been cut off, use the Format⇨ Paragraph command to set the Line Spacing to anything other than Exactly.

2. **Click the picture to select it.**

3. **Use the Insert⇨Frame command to slap a frame on the picture.**

4. **Drag the frame by the love handles to resize it or drag it by the frame box to move it.**

   Watch the text flow around the frame. Experiment with different locations and sizes until you get just the effect you want.

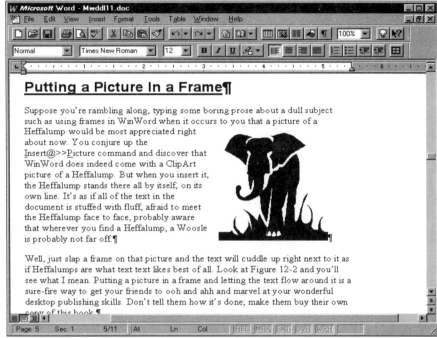

Figure 12-2:
Making
the text
surround
the picture.

5. Congratulate yourself on your ingenuity.

You've earned it.

Some random thoughts to ponder as you frame pictures:

✔ To edit a picture, double-click it. WinWord launches into its drawing mode, where you can fuss with the picture a bit. For Figure 12-2, I didn't like the way the Heffalump was facing, so I flipped him around to make him run the other direction. See Chapter 14 for tips on playing with WinWord's drawing tools.

✔ To delete a framed picture, just click the frame and press the Del key.

✔ Unlike text frames, WinWord does not automatically wrap a border around picture frames. If you want the frame to have a border, use the Format⇨Borders and Shading command.

✔ You can stretch a picture all out of proportion by dragging the love handles on one of the sides of the frame box rather than one of the corners.

Creating an Empty Frame

If you want to create an empty frame, which you can later fill with text or a picture, follow these steps:

1. Use the View➪Page Layout command to switch to Page Layout View.

You must be in Page Layout View to insert a frame. If you skip this step, WinWord nags you about it when you try to insert the frame.

2. Don't select anything.

If you select text or graphics, WinWord tries to put the selection into the frame when you perform the next step. To create an empty frame, make sure no graphics or text is selected.

3. Call up the Insert➪Frame command.

Watch the cursor change to a gunsight.

4. Drag the gunsight cursor to create your frame.

Place the gunsight cursor where you want the top-left corner of the frame to be placed. Then click and drag the mouse to create a frame of the correct size.

5. Move the frame if you didn't get it placed right.

Drag the frame by the edges.

6. Put something in the frame.

Select the frame and start typing text or use the Insert➪Picture command to put a picture in the frame.

Some tantalizing tidbits concerning empty frames:

✔ Frames aren't much good unless you put something in them. Whether you create the frame and then insert text or a picture into it — or type the text or insert the picture and then create the frame — doesn't matter much.

✔ When you first create an empty frame, WinWord draws a border around it. However, if you later insert a picture into the frame, WinWord removes the border.

Aligning a Frame

You can use your mouse to drag a frame to any location on-screen, but if you want to ensure that the frame is placed at a specific location, use the Format⇨Frame command instead. This command awakens the Frame dialog box, pictured in Figure 12-3. Its controls enable you to regiment the position of a frame on the page.

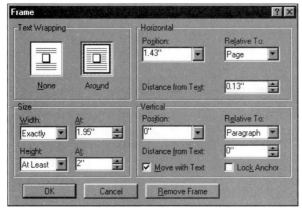

Figure 12-3:
The Frame
dialog box.

Here's the lowdown on the various Frame dialog box controls.

Text Wrapping: Read this carefully: It's text *wrapping*, not text *warping*. To warp your text, you must dig deeply into your own deviant sense of humor. To wrap your text around a frame, click Around. To interrupt your text when the frame appears and resume it after the frame, click None.

Size: Controls the Width and Height of the frame. You can leave both fields set to Auto to make WinWord figure out how big the frame should be. Or you can change either field to *Exactly* and then type a number in the corresponding At field to set the width or height precisely.

Horizontal: Controls the horizontal left-to-right position of the frame. In the Position field, you can type a measurement or you can choose Left, Right, Center, Inside, or Outside and allow WinWord do the measuring for you. (Inside and Outside are used when even- and odd-numbered pages have different margins. Inside means left on a right-hand page and right on a left-hand page; outside means left on a left-hand page and right on a right-hand page.)

In the Relative To field, you can choose Page, Margin, or Column. This option tells WinWord where to measure from when applying the Position setting. For example, to place the frame flush left against the margin, set Position to Left and Relative To to Margin. To line it up against the right edge of the column, set Position to Right and Relative To to Column.

Distance from Text is where you tell WinWord how much empty space to leave between the right and left edges of the frame and any text that wraps around the frame. Increase this option if the text seems too crowded.

Vertical: Sets the vertical, up-and-down position of the frame. You can type a number in the Position field or set it to Top, Bottom, or Center and let WinWord figure it out.

Set the Relative To field to Page, Margin, or Paragraph to control placement of the frame. For example, to set the frame down on the bottom margin, set Position to Bottom and Relative To to Margin. To place a frame one inch below a particular paragraph, set Position to 1" and Relative To to Paragraph.

Check the Move With Text check box if you want the frame to travel along with the paragraph it's anchored to. If extensive editing causes the anchor paragraph to move to the next page, the frame is moved to the next page too. If you want to force the frame to stay on the same page even if the anchor paragraph jumps pages, uncheck the Move With Text check box. See the sidebar, "Stop me, Smee, before I drop the anchor!" if you're not sure what I mean by *the anchor paragraph*.

Tonight, as you drift off to sleep wondering about the marvels of the Frame dialog box, consider these amazing facts:

- ✔ The Frame dialog box is a bit much, especially if you're a very small animal like Piglet. Avoid it if you can. Use the mouse to drag your frames into position.

- ✔ If you must use the Frame dialog box, consider using it in a style. Once you get it set up right, you can recreate your bizarre frame settings just by applying the style.

- ✔ This procedure would be much easier if you'd just break down and buy PageMaker.

Stop me, Smee, before I drop the anchor!

Every frame is *anchored* to a particular paragraph. When you move a frame around on the page, WinWord automatically picks up the frame's anchor and drops it on the nearest paragraph. This is the paragraph that is referred to when you set the Frame dialog box's Vertical Relative To field to Paragraph. When you switch to Normal view, the frame is displayed immediately before the paragraph it is anchored to.

If you don't want WinWord to change the paragraph that a frame is anchored to when you move the frame, check the Lock Anchor field in the Frame dialog box. Then the frame anchor remains in the same paragraph even if you move the frame around the page.

You can actually see the anchors in Page Layout View if you click the Show/Hide Paragraph Marks button on the Standard toolbar. When you select a frame, the paragraph it is anchored to has a little anchor next to it. You can change the anchor paragraph by dragging the anchor from paragraph to paragraph, and you can pop up the frame dialog box by double-clicking the anchor. Shiver me timbers!

Getting Rid of a Frame

The easiest way to get rid of a frame is to select it and press the Del key. However, that deletes not only the frame but its contents, as well. WinWord enables you to delete the frame without deleting the text or pictures contained in the frame. The contents of the frame are returned to their proper position on the page, and all is well.

To remove a frame without destroying its contents, follow this procedure:

1. **Select the frame.**

   Click it, kick it, or do whatever you must do to get its attention.

2. **Conjure up the Format⇨Frame command.**

   WinWord spews forth the Frame dialog box.

3. **Click the Remove Frame button.**

   The frame is blown away by a Microsoft sharpshooter, who manages to leave the frame's hostage contents unharmed.

Some fascinating points to ponder as you blow away your frames:

- ✔ Remember that the whole point of a frame is to relocate some text or graphics on the page. If you remove the frame, the text or graphics it contains is zapped back to its original location within the text.

- ✔ To blow away a frame and its contents completely, select the frame and press the Del or Backspace key.

- ✔ You can use the Format⇨Borders and Shading command to hide the border in a frame, but that's not the same as removing the frame itself. To remove the frame itself, you must use the Format⇨Frame command and click the Remove Frame button.

- ✔ That dimwit dog just chewed up another plant.

Chapter 13

Sidebars, Pull Quotes, Eyebrows, and Other Flashy Tricks

This chapter is a compendium of ideas on how to incorporate common graphic design elements into a WinWord document to make it look like you used a more expensive desktop publishing program like PageMaker or Ventura Publisher.

Although I do dive into a few new WinWord features here, most of what's in this chapter is more along the lines of "here's how to use styles, frames, borders, and other stuff you already know to create some really cool effect that only graphic artists used to be able to do." You may come across a feature or two that you're not sure how to use. That's okay; no reason to feel bad. Just hop back to the relevant chapter for a quick refresher and all will be well.

On with the show.

Sidebars

A *sidebar* is a short portion of text — usually a paragraph or two — that is incidental to the main flow of text in your document and is given special graphical treatment. This book is filled with sidebars: they're those gray boxes of text usually set off with a Technical icon.

Sidebars are frequently used in newsletters. If your newsletter has a two- or three-column layout, a sidebar can help you break up the monotony created by column after column of pure text. Figure 13-1 shows what I mean. Here, the sidebar at the bottom of the page spans two columns, breaking up the otherwise long and boring columns.

To create a sidebar like the one in Figure 13-1, follow these steps:

1. **Type the text for the sidebar.**

   Place the text near where you want the sidebar to appear, but don't worry too much about the positioning yet. You can adjust it in a later step.

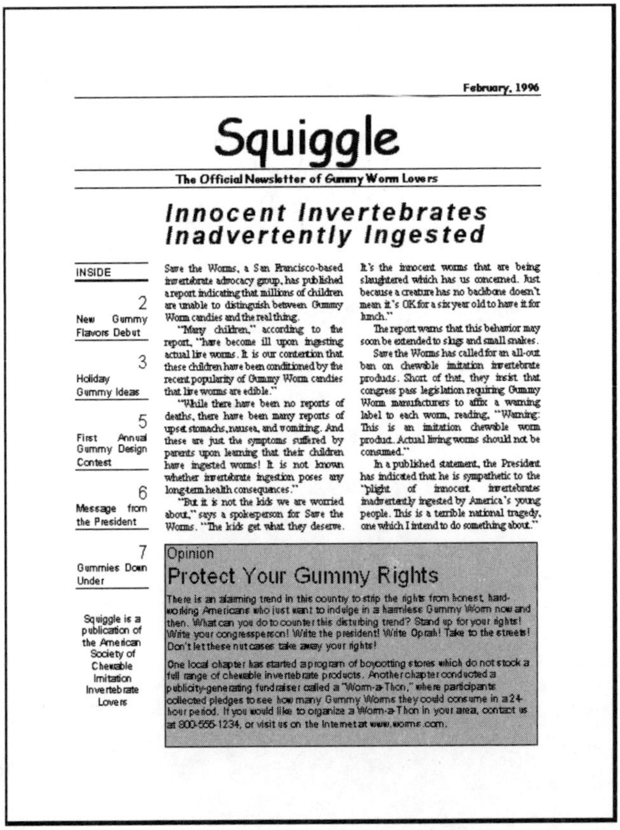

February, 1996

Squiggle

The Official Newsletter of Gummy Worm Lovers

Innocent Invertebrates Inadvertently Ingested

INSIDE

2 New Gummy Flavors Debut

3 Holiday Gummy Ideas

5 First Annual Gummy Design Contest

6 Message from the President

7 Gummies Down Under

Squiggle is a publication of the American Society of Chewable Imitation Invertebrate Lovers

Save the Worms, a San Francisco-based invertebrate advocacy group, has published a report indicating that millions of children are unable to distinguish between Gummy Worm candies and the real thing.

"Many children," according to the report, "have become ill upon ingesting actual live worms. It is our contention that these children have been conditioned by the recent popularity of Gummy Worm candies that live worms are edible."

"While there have been no reports of deaths, there have been many reports of upset stomachs, nausea, and vomiting. And these are just the symptoms suffered by parents upon learning that their children have ingested worms! It is not known whether invertebrate ingestion poses any long-term health consequences."

"But it is not the kids we are worried about," says a spokesperson for Save the Worms. "The kids get what they deserve. It's the innocent worms that are being slaughtered which has us concerned. Just because a creature has no backbone doesn't mean it's OK for a six year old to have it for lunch."

The report warns that this behavior may soon be extended to slugs and small snakes.

Save the Worms has called for an all-out ban on chewable imitation invertebrate products. Short of that, they insist that congress pass legislation requiring Gummy Worm manufacturers to affix a warning label to each worm, reading, "Warning: This is an imitation chewable worm product. Actual living worms should not be consumed."

In a published statement, the President has indicated that he is sympathetic to the "plight of innocent invertebrates inadvertently ingested by America's young people. This is a terrible national tragedy, one which I intend to do something about."

Opinion

Protect Your Gummy Rights

There is an alarming trend in this country to strip the rights from honest, hard-working Americans who just want to indulge in a harmless Gummy Worm now and then. What can you do to counter this disturbing trend? Stand up for your rights! Write your congressperson! Write the president! Write Oprah! Take to the streets! Don't let these nut cases take away your rights!

One local chapter has started a program of boycotting stores which do not stock a full range of chewable invertebrate products. Another chapter conducted a publicity-generating fundraiser called a "Worm-a-Thon," where participants collected pledges to see how many Gummy Worms they could consume in a 24-hour period. If you would like to organize a Worm-a-Thon in your area, contact us at 800-555-1234, or visit us on the Internet at www.worms.com.

Figure 13-1: A sidebar can spice up an otherwise dull page.

2. **Apply whatever formatting you want to the sidebar text.**

   The easiest way to do this is to create styles for the sidebar heading and body. Then you simply apply the styles to format the sidebar properly.

3. **Select the sidebar paragraphs.**

4. **Call up the Insert⇨Frame command.**

   The selected text is placed in a boxed frame.

5. **Move and resize the frame to its final destination.**

   Experiment a bit with the positioning and size until the sidebar lands at an interesting location.

6. **Use the Format⇨Borders and Shading command to add shading to the sidebar paragraphs.**

   10% or 20% black should do the trick. While you're at it, you might want to add some space between the border and the text — three points should do.

7. **You're done.**

   Wasn't that easy?

Here are some random thoughts about creating sidebars:

- Pick a contrasting font for the sidebar. In Figure 13-1, I used a sans-serif font (Arial) for both the sidebar heading and text.

- Unfortunately, WinWord won't let you set up a two-column text frame. If you absolutely must have two-column sidebars, it's time to switch to PageMaker.

- To keep the sidebar from moving around the page after you've found a good spot for it, uncheck the Move with Text check box in the Format⇨Frame dialog box.

- Don't overdo the sidebars. Sidebars lose their impact if they take up more space than the main text.

Pull Quotes

A *pull quote* is a short quotation pulled out of the article and given special treatment. Its purpose is to pique the reader's interest so that he or she is drawn to read the article.

Pull quotes are usually set in a larger type and are often sandwiched between columns in a two- or three-column layout, as shown in Figure 13-2. To achieve this effect, the pull quote is created in its own frame.

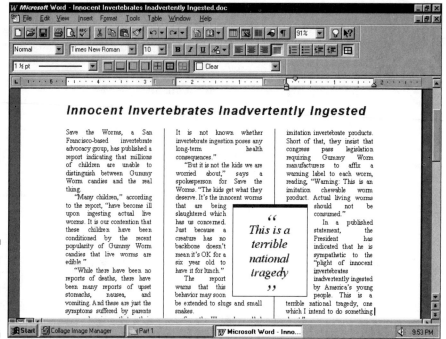

Follow these steps to create a pull quote like the one in Figure 13-2:

1. **Type the text that you want to appear in the pull quote.**

   Type the quote near the point where you want it to appear, but don't worry about the exact positioning. Once you put the quote in a frame, you can easily move it about the page.

2. **Format the pull quote however you want.**

   In Figure 13-2, I used a larger italic version of the body text typeface, centered the paragraph, and placed the quotation marks on separate lines. Then I increased the size of the quotation marks. (I didn't like the way the quotes looked when I increased their size; they seemed to float too high above the rest of the text. So I used the Format⇨Font command to adjust the position of the quotes, lowering them several points to get them to look just right.)

3. **Double-click the pull quote paragraph to select it.**

4. **Use the Insert⇨Frame command to place the pull quote paragraph in a frame.**

5. **Adjust the frame's size and position however you want.**

   Place the pull quote frame in a location that is not too close to the spot where the quote appears in the article. And make sure you place it in the middle of paragraphs, not between them. If you place the pull quote between paragraphs, the reader might think the pull quote is a heading.

6. **Use the Format⇨Borders and Shading command to add a border to the pull quote.**

   In Figure 13-2, I used a thin border for the left, right, and bottom edge of the frame and provided a thicker border at the top. Other border designs can be just as effective.

Keep these thoughts in mind when you create pull quotes:

- Remember that the purpose of the pull quote is to draw the reader into your text. Pick the most interesting or provocative quotes from the article.

- Pull quotes are typically enclosed in a box border, but sometimes a simple rule above and below does the job of highlighting the quote without imprisoning it.

- Experiment with different column positions for your pull quotes. In Figure 13-2, the pull quote is sandwiched between the columns. You can also set a pull quote within a column, or you can create pull quotes that are two full columns wide. Placing your pull quotes in frames makes this kind of experimentation easy.

Eyebrows

Eyebrows are the short department descriptions that appear over article titles in magazines and newsletters. Eyebrows are a good place to have some typographical fun (if that's possible). Since they're so short (a word or two will do), you don't have to worry much about readability.

Some eyebrows can be created using WinWord's basic formatting options. For example, you might format your eyebrows with 10-point bold Century Gothic with the letter spacing expanded 6 points, centered over the article title:

E D I T O R I A L

Or use the same typeface, but condense the letter spacing to 1 point:

EDITORIAL

Or add a special symbol from the Dixieland font to characterize the eyebrow and left-align it:

■ **EDITORIAL**

You can use borders and shading to create interesting effects:

EDITORIAL

In the preceding example, I used two paragraphs for the eyebrow. For the first paragraph, I typed the word EDITORIAL, formatted it with the right font, switched to white characters on a black background, and then played with the paragraph indents until the black shading extended just a bit past each side of the word. For the next paragraph, I added a border line above, with zero space between the line and the text. Oh, and I made sure the space after for the first paragraph and the space before for the second paragraph were both zero.

Some thoughts to think about as you ponder the meaning of eyebrows and other great issues of life:

- ✔ Format your eyebrows consistently. They can help give your publication a more unified look.

- ✔ Put the eyebrow formatting information in a style. That's the best way to format them consistently.

- ✔ If you really want to get creative with eyebrows, doodle with them using the WordArt applet. More info about Word Art can be found in *Word For Windows 95 For Dummies.*

- ✔ For a really dramatic look, try letting your eyebrows run together like Nikita Khrushchev or shaving them off completely like Whoopie Goldberg.

Captions

A *caption* is a bit of text that identifies a figure, table, chart, or other visual you've included in a document. Captions usually include a reference number, for example, Figure 58 or Table 293. Figure 13-3 shows a document with a captioned illustration.

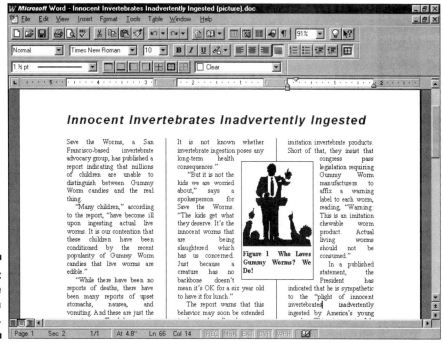

Figure 13-3:
A picture
with a
caption.

If you want, you can create captions simply by typing them in. But WinWord includes a Caption feature that automatically numbers your captions when you insert them, keeps the numbers in order, and lets you create a table of figures, tables, charts, or whatever when you're all done. You paid for this program, so you may as well learn how to use as much of it as possible.

To add a caption to a picture, table, chart, or other graphic goodie, follow these steps:

1. **If you haven't done so already, use the Insert⇨Frame command to put the picture, table, or chart into a frame.**

   You don't have to, but captions work better when they're attached to frames. Don't ask me why; go ask your mom.

2. **Select the frame that you want the caption attached to.**

3. **Call up the Insert⇨Caption command.**

   You see the dialog box shown in Figure 13-4.

4. **Type the rest of the caption.**

   WinWord gives you just the reference number. Type whatever text you want to describe the figure, table, chart, or whatever.

Figure 13-4:
The Caption
dialog box.

5. Change the Label field if it is incorrect.

WinWord keeps track of caption numbers for figures, tables, and equations separately. When you insert a caption, make sure the Label field is set to the type of caption you want to create.

6. Change the Position field if you want to change the positioning.

The two options are Above or Below the selected item.

7. Click OK.

The caption is inserted!

Here are a few rapid-fire thoughts designed to inspire your use of captions:

✔ If you want to create captions for something other than figures, tables, and equations, click the New Label button and then type a label for whatever you want to create captions for; say, for example, Limerick. Click OK, and from then on, Limerick appears as one of the Label types.

✔ When you create a caption, WinWord automatically applies the style named Caption to the caption paragraph. You can control the format of all captions in a document by modifying the Caption style.

✔ You can create a table of figures, tables, equations, or limericks by using the Insert⇨Index and Tables command. Pick the Table of Figures tab and then choose the type of caption you want to create a table for from the Caption Label field. Click OK and treat yourself to a Snickers bar.

✔ At various and sundry times, caption numbers will get out of sequence. Fear not! WinWord will put the caption numbers back into sequence when you print the document. If you're tired of looking at out-of-sequence numbers, use the Edit⇨Select All command to select the entire document and then press F9 to recompute the caption numbers.

✔ If you want WinWord to always create a caption whenever you insert a particular type of object into your document, click the AutoCaption button in the Caption dialog box. This yields a dialog box that lists all the various types of objects you can insert into a word document. Check the ones you want to automatically create captions for and then click OK.

Icons

Ever wonder how to insert icons similar to the ones found throughout the margins in this and other . . .*For Dummies* books using WinWord? Actually, it's pretty easy. You just pick a picture to use for an icon, drop it into a frame, and line it up where you want it. Figure 13-5 shows an example.

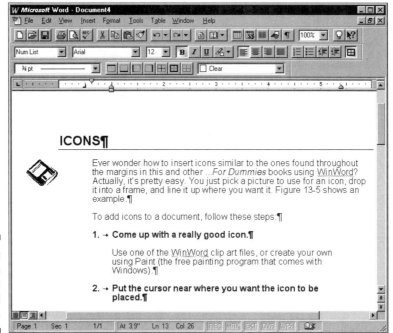

Figure 13-5:
Inserting an
icon in a
WinWord
document.

To add icons to a document, follow these steps:

1. **Come up with a really good icon.**

   Use one of the WinWord clip art files or create your own using Paint (the free painting program that comes with Windows).

2. **Put the cursor near where you want the icon to be placed.**

3. **Use the Insert⇨Picture command to insert the picture file.**

4. **Use the Insert⇨Frame command to place the picture in a frame.**

5. **Resize the frame and drag it to the margin.**

   Make sure the frame remains anchored to the paragraph in which you you created it.

As you lie awake nights thinking about icons, keep these points in mind:

✔ The purpose of icons is to call attention to text that might be of particular interest. Study the way icons are used in this book and other . . .*For Dummies* books for the ultimate example of the proper use of icons (but don't share anything you learn with other publishers).

✔ Icons work especially well in procedure manuals. For example, you might design a File Cabinet icon to use whenever you tell the reader to file something away. Or you might create a Computer icon to use whenever the reader is told to do something on a computer.

✔ The Wingdings font that comes with Windows includes quite a collection of little pictures that might be suitable for icons. To insert a Wingdings character, use the Insert⇨Symbol command, pick the character you want, click Insert, and then click OK. Adjust the point size of the symbol until it is as large as you want, and then choose the symbol and use the Insert⇨Frame command to place it in a frame. When you get the frame positioned properly, create an Icon style so you can format more icons without going through all these steps.

Side Headings

A *side heading* is a heading that appears in a separate column next to the text it relates to, as in Figure 13-6. You would think that side headings would be easy to do: Just give all your body text paragraphs a generous left indent, and format the heading paragraph with a hanging indent. But this works only when the heading consists of only one line. To create multi-line side headings, such as the ones in Figure 13-6, you have to use frames. Although it's a bear to get it set up, once you get everything just right, you can put it in a style and forget about it.

To create a side head, do the following:

1. **Use the File⇨Page Setup command to lay out your page with a generous left margin.**

   In Figure 13-6, I set the left margin to 3¼ inches.

2. **Type the heading text where you want the heading to appear in your document.**

3. **Assign the appropriate Heading style to the paragraph.**

   For top-level headings, assign Heading 1 to the paragraph. Use Heading 2 or Heading 3 for lower-level headings.

Figure 13-6:
Side
headings.

4. **Format the characters however you want.**

   In Figure 13-6, the text is 14-point Arial Bold.

5. **Select the entire paragraph and use the Insert⇨Frame command to place the heading in a frame.**

   Triple-click the paragraph to select it and then call up the Insert⇨Frame command. If you're not already in Page Layout view, WinWord will offer to switch for you. Go ahead and switch to Page Layout view.

6. **Call up the Format⇨Frame command or double-click the frame to call up the Frame dialog box.**

   The Frame dialog box appears, as shown in Figure 13-7. Adjust the following settings:

   Horizontal Position and Relative To: These fields set the left edge of the heading frame. In Figure 13-7, I set the left edge of the frame at 1¼ inches from the edge of the page.

   Size Width and At: These fields set the width of the frame. The default for Width is Auto; change it to Exactly and then type the width of your heading column in the At field. In Figure 13-7, the frame width is set to 1¾ inches. Added to the horizontal position of 1¼ inches, that puts the right-hand edge of the frame at 3 inches, leaving ¼ inch empty space between the frame and the left margin (which was set to 3¼ inches in step 1).

Size Height: Leave the height of the frame set to Auto. That way, the frame will adjust its height depending on how much text is in the heading.

Move with Text: Leave this check box checked so that the heading will travel with the text.

7. **Use the Format➪Borders and Shading command to remove the border.**

When you frame text, WinWord automatically adds a border around the text. You usually want to remove this border, though you might want to leave a line above the heading.

8. **Got it just right? Reapply the appropriate Heading style to record the formatting information in the style.**

Then, whenever you apply the appropriate Heading style to a paragraph, the paragraph will automatically be framed and positioned to the left of the text.

Figure 13-7:
Frame
settings for
side
headings.

Here are some juicy tidbits to keep in mind:

✔ The hardest part about side headings is planning the layout. The best way to plan the layout is with a blank piece of paper and a ruler. Mark the location of the heading frames and the text column. Set the page margins to accommodate the text column. Set the heading frame's horizontal position and width accordingly.

✔ If you're not sure that a heading frame is anchored to the text that follows it, select the frame and look for the little anchor. If you can't see the anchor, click the Show/Hide Paragraph button.

✔ If all this talk about frames has sent your blood pressure through the roof, turn to Chapter 12, where you'll find a nice, calming explanation of how frames work.

✔ Throwing a framing hammer at your computer monitor won't help.

Chapter 14

Drawing with the Left Side of Your Mouse

· ·

In This Chapter

▶ Drawing straight and curved lines

▶ Drawing rectangles, squares, and circles

▶ Drawing polygons and freeform shapes

▶ Drawing text boxes and callouts

▶ Selecting drawing objects

▶ Setting the fill color and line style

▶ Flipping and rotating objects

▶ Changing layers

▶ Aligning objects

▶ Group therapy

· ·

Chim-chiminey, chim-chiminey, chim chim cheeroo,
I draws what I likes and I likes what I drew . . . .

Art time! Everybody get your crayons and glue and don an old paint shirt. We're going to cut out some simple shapes and paste them on our WinWord documents so that people either think we are wonderful artists or scoff at us for not using clip art.

This chapter covers WinWord's drawing features. WinWord isn't a full-featured drawing program like CorelDraw! is, but it does give you enough rudimentary drawing tools to let you spice up your documents with a little something here and a little something there.

Some General Drawing Tips

WinWord's drawing tools aren't as powerful as the tools provided with a full-featured drawing program such as CorelDraw! or Illustrator, but they are powerful enough to create some fancy pictures. Before I get into the specifics of how to use each tool, this section describes a handful of general tips for drawing pictures.

Activate the Drawing toolbar

 WinWord has an entire toolbar devoted to drawing. To make the toolbar visible, use the View⇨Toolbars command and then click the Drawing check box. Or just click the Drawing button on the Standard toolbar. Figure 14-1 shows what WinWord looks like after the Drawing toolbar has been revealed. The drawing functions provided by each of the buttons on both toolbars are explained in this chapter.

I drew the face shown in Figure 14-1 by using WinWord's drawing tools.

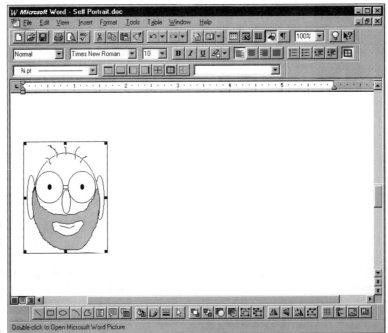

Figure 14-1:
WinWord
with the
Drawing
toolbar
enabled.

WinWord's drawing tools work only in Page Layout view. WinWord automatically switches to Page Layout view when you activate the Drawing toolbar.

After you have drawn something on your document, you probably should stick to Page Layout view for the duration. When you switch back to Normal view, drawing objects are hidden from view. This is not only disconcerting but also error prone.

Zoom in

When you work with WinWord's drawing tools, increase the zoom factor so that you can draw more accurately. I usually work at 200 percent when I'm drawing. To change the zoom factor, click the down arrow next to the zoom control tool (near the right side of the Standard toolbar) and choose a zoom factor from the list, or click the zoom factor, type a new zoom percentage, and press Enter.

Before you change the zoom factor to edit an object, select the object you want to edit. That way, WinWord zooms in on that area of the page. If you don't select an object before you zoom in, you may need to scroll around to find the right location.

Save frequently

Drawing is tedious work. You don't want to spend two hours working on a particularly important drawing, only to lose it all just because some joker on the other side of the world drops a bomb on your backyard. You can prevent catastrophic loss from incidents such as these by pressing Ctrl+S frequently while you work (and working in a hardened bunker located a minimum of 60 feet underground).

Don't forget Ctrl+Z

Don't forget that you're never more than one keystroke from erasing a boo-boo. If you do something silly — such as forget to group a complex picture before you try to move it — you can always press Ctrl+Z to undo your last action. Ctrl+Z is my favorite and most frequently used WinWord key.

Drawing Simple Lines and Shapes

WinWord provides an entire row of drawing tools, located on the Drawing toolbar. Table 14-1 shows you what each of these drawing tools does.

To draw an object, you just click the button that represents the object you want to draw and then use the mouse to draw the object. It's not always as simple as that; you can find in the following sections detailed instructions for drawing with the more important tools.

Table 14-1		WinWord's Basic Drawing Tools
Drawing Tool		*What It Does*
⬊	Line	Draws a straight line. You can later change the attributes of the line to create thick lines, dashed lines, or lines with arrowheads.
▢	Rectangle	Draws rectangles. To make a perfect square, hold down the Shift key while you draw.
◯	Ellipse	Draws circles and ovals. To create a perfect circle, hold down the Shift key while you draw.
⬀	Arc	Draws an arc (not the kind Noah used, but a curved line). To create a perfect quarter-circle arc, hold down the Shift key while you draw.
⬧	Freeform	Draws freeform shapes.
▤	Text	Draws a text box.
▤	Callout	Draws a callout, which resembles a text box but has a line sticking out from it.

If the Drawing toolbar has disappeared, you can make it appear again by using the View➪Toolbars command and checking the Drawing box, or by clicking the Drawing button on the Standard toolbar.

Made a mistake? You can delete the object you just drew by pressing the Del key and then try drawing the object again. Or you can change its size or stretch it by clicking it and dragging its love handles.

Table 14-2 summarizes some handy shortcuts you can use while you're drawing.

Table 14-2	Drawing Shortcuts
Shortcut	*What It Does*
Shift	Hold down the Shift key to force lines to be horizontal or vertical, to force arcs and ellipses to be true circles, or to force rectangles to be squares.
Ctrl	Hold down the Ctrl key to draw objects from the center, rather than from end to end.
Ctrl+Shift	Draws from center and enforces squareness.
Double-click	Double-click one of the buttons on the toolbar to draw several objects of the same type.

Drawing straight and curved lines

To draw a straight line, follow this procedure:

1. Click the Line tool.

2. Point to where you want the line to begin.

3. Press the mouse button and drag to where you want the line to end.

4. Release the mouse button.

The procedure for drawing an arc is the same as drawing a line except that you click the Arc button rather than the Line tool.

You can use the Format⇨Drawing Object command to change the line color, thickness, dashes, and arrowheads for a line or arc. Or you can use buttons on the Drawing toolbar to change these attributes. See the section "Setting the Fill Color, Line Style, and Shadow" later in this chapter.

You can force a line to be perfectly horizontal or vertical by holding down the Shift key while you draw.

The ends of an arc are always 90 degrees apart. In other words, an arc is always one-quarter of a circle or ellipse.

After you have drawn a line or arc, you can adjust it by clicking it and then dragging either of the love handles that appear.

Sorry, WinWord doesn't include powerful tools for drawing precise curves. If you need better curves than the arc button can provide, get yourself a real drawing program.

Drawing rectangles, squares, and circles

To draw a rectangle, follow these steps:

1. **Click the Rectangle tool.**

2. **Point to where you want one corner of the rectangle to be.**

3. **Press the mouse button and drag to where you want the opposite corner of the rectangle to be.**

4. **Release the mouse button.**

The procedure for drawing a circle or ellipse is the same as drawing a rectangle except that you click the Ellipse button rather than the Rectangle tool.

You can use the Format⇨Drawing Object command to change the fill color or the line style for a rectangle or circle. You can also use the buttons on the Drawing toolbar to change the color and line style. See the section "Setting the Fill Color, Line Style, and Shadow" later in this chapter.

To create an even square or a perfectly round circle, hold down the Shift key while you draw.

You can adjust the size or shape of a rectangle or circle by clicking it and dragging any of its love handles.

Drawing a polygon or freeform shape

A *polygon* is a shape that has many sides and has nothing to do with having more than one spouse (one is certainly enough for most of us). Triangles, squares, and rectangles are polygons, but so are hexagons and pentagons, as is any unusual shape whose sides all consist of straight lines. (Politicians are continually inventing new polygons when they revise the boundaries of congressional districts.)

WinWord's Freeform button is designed to create polygons, with a twist: not all the sides have to be straight lines. The Freeform button lets you build a shape whose sides are a mixture of straight lines and freeform curves. Figure 14-2 shows three examples of shapes I created with the Freeform tool.

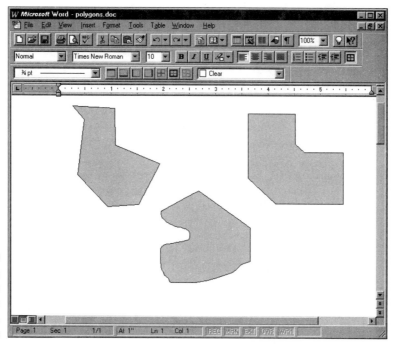

Figure 14-2:
Three
freeform
shapes.

Follow these steps to create a polygon or freeform shape:

1. **Click the Freeform tool.**

2. **Click where you want the first corner of the object to be.**

3. **Click where you want the second corner of the object to be.**

4. **Keep clicking wherever you want a corner to be.**

5. **To finish the shape, click near the first corner (the one you created in Step 2).**

You don't have to be exact; if you click anywhere near the first corner you put down, WinWord assumes that the shape is finished.

You're finished!

To draw a freeform side on the shape, keep holding down the mouse button when you click at a corner and then draw the freeform shape with the mouse. When you get to the end of the freeform side, release the mouse button. Then you can click again to add more corners. The second shape in Figure 14-2 includes one freeform side.

You can reshape a polygon or freeform shape by selecting it and clicking the Reshape button on the Drawing toolbar and then dragging any of the love handles that appear on the corners.

If you hold down the Shift key while you draw a polygon, the sides are constrained to 30- and 45-degree angles. The third shape in Figure 14-2 was drawn in this way.

How about a constitutional amendment requiring Congress to use the Shift key when they redraw congressional boundaries?

You can also use the Freeform button to draw a multisegmented line, called an *open shape.* In an open shape, the beginning point does not connect to the ending point. To draw an open shape, follow the procedure just described, but skip step 5. Instead, double-click or press the Esc key when the line is finished.

Drawing a text box

A *text box* is similar to a frame in that it contains text and you can move it around the page to place the text precisely where you want it. The primary differences between a text box and a frame are that text boxes don't adjust their size automatically based on how much text you type in them, and you can't add a text box by using a style. Text boxes don't usually stand by themselves, but they typically are used in combination with shapes drawn with the other drawing tools.

Drawing a text box is pretty much the same as drawing a rectangle. Follow these steps:

1. **Click the Text button.**

2. **Point to where you want one corner of the text box to be.**

3. **Press the mouse button and drag to where you want the opposite corner of the text box to be.**

4. **Release the mouse button.**

5. **Type some text.**

Drawing a callout

A *callout* is a special kind of text box that has a line attached to some other object, as shown in Figure 14-3. In the figure, I used callouts to label the various parts of a picture.

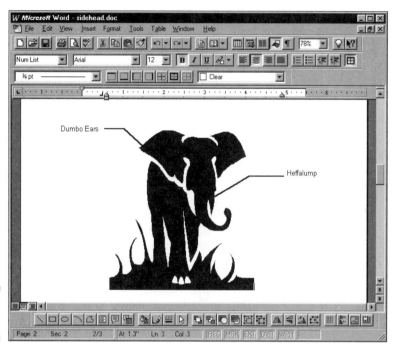

Figure 14-3:
Callouts.

Follow this procedure to create callouts while maintaining your sanity:

1. **Click the Callout tool.**

2. **Click where you want the callout line to be attached.**

3. **Drag the mouse to where you want the callout text to appear.**

    When you release the mouse, a big one-inch-square callout box appears.

4. **Type some callout text.**

    The text is inserted in the callout box.

5. **Adjust the size of the callout box.**

    It is probably way too big. Click its border and then drag any of the box's love handles to reshape the box.

Presto! You're finished. Keep the following points in mind when you work with callouts:

✔ Notice that as you drag a callout box around the screen, the callout line automatically adjusts itself so that it always points at the object to which you attached it. Cool!

✔ You can use the Line Style button to add an arrowhead to the callout line. See the section, "Setting the Fill Color, Line Style and Shadow" later in this chapter.

✔ You can change the callout format by clicking the Format Callout button. This step pops up the dialog box shown in Figure 14-4, where you can choose from four different callout styles and customize the size and shape of the callout line. If you select a callout before you click the Format Callout button, the format applies to the callout you selected. If you do not select a callout before you click the button, the format becomes the default for all callouts you subsequently create.

Figure 14-4:
The Callout
Defaults
dialog box.

Selecting Drawing Objects

Once you've added drawing objects to a document, you need to know how to select those objects so that you can move them, resize them, fill them with color, or delete them without remorse. Here are the tricks to successfully selecting objects d' art:

✔ You can usually select an object by moving the mouse pointer over the object and clicking it. As a visual clue, the mouse pointer changes from the normal I-beam pointer to an arrow when clicking will select a drawing object.

✔ If an object is hiding stubbornly behind text and the mouse pointer won't change to the arrow, click the Select Drawing Objects button on the Drawing toolbar to change the mouse pointer to an arrow, which can *only* select drawing objects. Click the Select Drawing Objects button again to return the mouse pointer to normal.

✔ To select more than one object at a time, hold down the shift key while clicking the objects.

✔ If you've selected several objects and you want to deselect one of them, click the unwanted object again while holding down the Shift key.

✔ Don't forget that drawing objects are not visible unless you're in Page Layout view. Switch to Page Layout view before attempting to select them.

Setting the Fill Color, Line Style, and Shadow

WinWord drawing objects have various attributes you can change:

✔ **Fill color:** The interior color of an object

✔ **Line color:** The color of the lines that outline the object (or, in the case of a line or arc, the color of the line or arc itself); if the object has no line color, the lines are not visible

✔ **Line style:** The thickness and style of the lines that outline the object, including dashed lines and arrowheads

To change any of these object attributes, follow these steps:

1. Select the object or objects you want to change.

2. Use the appropriate button to change the color or style.

Table 14-3 summarizes the toolbar buttons you can use for this purpose.

Table 14-3	Tools for Setting Colors and Line Styles	
Drawing Tool		*What It Does*
🖌	Fill-color	Sets the fill color
✏	Line-color	Sets the line color
▤	Line-style	Sets the line width and style

When you use these buttons to change the color or style, the selected object is changed. In addition, any new objects you create assume the new color or style.

If you have a dialog box fetish, you can use the Format⊃Drawing Object command to change colors and line styles. This command pops up a dialog box that has three tabs. Figures 14-5 and 14-6 show the Fill and Line tabs; the Size and Position tab is left for real computer nerds to explore.

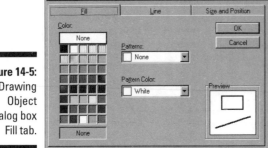

Figure 14-5:
The Drawing
Object
dialog box
Fill tab.

Figure 14-6:
The Drawing
Object
dialog box
Line tab.

Flipping and Rotating Objects

To *flip* an object means to create a mirror image of it. To *rotate* an object means to turn it about its center. WinWord lets you flip objects horizontally or vertically and rotate objects in 90-degree increments.

Flipping an object

WinWord lets you flip an object horizontally or vertically to create a mirror image of the object. To flip an object, follow these steps:

1. Select the object you want to flip.

2. Click the Flip Horizontal or Flip Vertical button on the Drawing toolbar.

Rotating an object 90 degrees

You can rotate an object in 90-degree increments by following these steps:

1. **Select the object you want to rotate.**

2. **Click the Rotate Right button on the Drawing toolbar.**

3. **To rotate the object 180 degrees, click the Rotate button again.**

4. **To rotate the object 270 degrees (the same as rotating it 90 degrees to the *left*), click the Rotate button again.**

Drawing a Complicated Picture

After you add more than one object to a page, several problems come up. What happens when the objects overlap? How do you line up objects so that they don't look like they were thrown at the page from a moving car? And how do you keep together objects that belong together?

The following sections show how to use WinWord features to handle over-lapped objects, align objects, and group objects. If you're interested in a description of how these WinWord features are used together to draw a picture, check out the sidebar, "Don't let me tell you how I drew that funny face."

Changing layers

Whenever you have more than one object on a page, the potential exists for objects to overlap one another. Like most drawing programs, WinWord handles this problem by layering objects like a stack of plates. The first object you draw is at the bottom of the stack, the second object is on top of the first, the third is atop the second, and so on. If two objects overlap, the one that's at the highest layer is the one that wins; objects below it are partially covered.

So far, so good. But what if you don't remember to draw the objects in the correct order? What if you draw a shape you want to tuck behind a shape you've already drawn, or what if you want to bring an existing shape to the top of the pecking order? No problem. WinWord lets you change the stack order, moving objects to the front or back so that they overlap just the way you want.

To complicate matters even more, WinWord has two distinct layers in which objects can be drawn: one in front of the text, and the other behind the text. Objects in front of the text obscure any text that happens to fall behind it. Objects behind the text are obscured by text that happens to overlap it.

WinWord provides four toolbar buttons for changing the stacking order. They are summarized in Table 14-4.

Table 14-4	Toolbar Buttons for Layering Objects	
Drawing Tool		*What It Does*
	Front	Brings an object to the front of other objects at the same layer
	Back	Sends an object behind other objects at the same layer
	F-text	Brings an object to the layer in front of the text
	B-text	Sends an object to the layer behind the text

Layering problems are most obvious when objects have a fill color. If an object has no fill color, any objects behind it are allowed to show through. In this case, the layering doesn't matter much.

Line 'em up

Nothing looks more amateurish than objects dropped randomly on the page with no apparent concern for how the objects line up with one another. WinWord provides several features that let you line up objects as you draw them:

 Snap to Grid: When this mode is on, the entire page is overlaid by an invisible grid to which objects are aligned. Whenever you create a new object or move an existing object, it automatically sticks to the nearest grid line. To turn Snap to Grid mode on or off, click the Snap to Grid button on the Drawing toolbar.

In case you're interested, the default grid spacing is ten lines per inch.

You can't see the grid, but trust me — it's there. Increase the zoom setting enough and you'll see the effects of objects snapping to it.

 Align Drawing Objects button: Lets you select several objects and then line them up. You can align the objects horizontally to the top, bottom, or center of the objects, or vertically to the left edges, right edges, or centers.

To align objects, simply select all the objects you want to align (hold down the Shift key while clicking each object) and then click the Align Drawing Objects button. The Align dialog box appears, as shown in Figure 14-7. Click the type of alignment you want and then click OK.

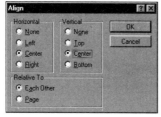

Figure 14-7:
The Align
dialog box.

Figure 14-8 shows how the alignments offered by the Align dialog box work. The top part of the figure shows three objects as they were originally drawn. The bottom part shows the result of selecting all three objects and using the various alignment options.

To center two or more objects, select the objects, click the Align Drawing Objects button, and choose Center for both horizontal and vertical alignment.

To align objects to the page rather than to each other, check the Page button.

Keep your fingers poised over Ctrl+Z at all times. Aligning often doesn't work the way you want, but pressing Ctrl+Z lets you quickly reverse a boo-boo before anyone notices.

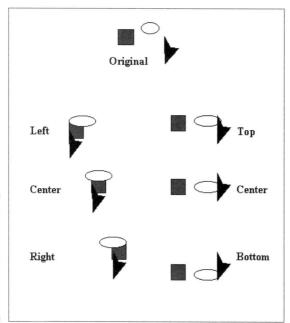

Figure 14-8:
Putting the
Align
Drawing
Objects
button
to work.

Group therapy

A *group* is a collection of objects that WinWord treats as though they were one object. Using groups properly is one of the keys to putting simple shapes together to make complex pictures without becoming so frustrated that you have to join a therapy group. ("Hello, my name is Doug, and WinWord drives me crazy.")

To create a group, follow these steps:

1. Select all the objects you want included in the group.

2. Click the Group button on the Drawing toolbar.

To take a group apart so that WinWord treats the objects as individuals again, follow this procedure:

1. Select all the objects you want included in the group.

2. Click the Ungroup button on the Drawing toolbar.

WinWord lets you create groups of groups. This capability is useful for complex pictures because it lets you work on one part of the picture, group it, and then work on the next part of the picture without worrying about accidentally disturbing the part you have already grouped. After you have several such groups, select them and group them. You can create groups of groups of groups, and so on, ad nauseam.

Part III
Making WinWord Work the Way You Do

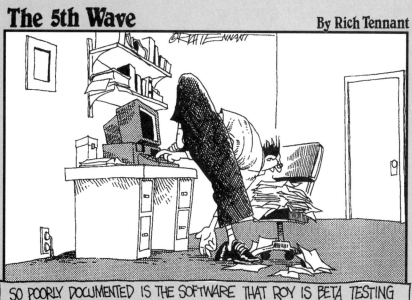

The 5th Wave

By Rich Tennant

SO POORLY DOCUMENTED IS THE SOFTWARE THAT ROY IS BETA TESTING THAT HE FAILS TO NOTICE THAT THE GAME RULES TO "TWISTER" HAVE ACCIDENTALLY BEEN INCLUDED.

In this part . . .

*E*ver wondered why there's a shortcut key for Bold and a shortcut key for Italic, but no shortcut key for Bold-Italic? If so, you'll love the chapters in this part. They show you how to customize WinWord so that it works the way you want it to. You learn how to set WinWord's many options; how to create your own toolbar buttons, menus, and shortcut keys; and how to create simple macros to automate routine chores.

This is definitely pocket-protector stuff, so be prepared to roll up your sleeves.

Chapter 15

Opting for Options

. . . .

In This Chapter

▶ What's with all the options?

▶ General options

▶ View options

▶ Edit options

▶ Print options

▶ File location options

▶ Save options

. . . .

Sometimes I long for the old pre-Windows days, when my favorite word processor was WordPerfect 4.2 and the only real options I had to contend with were to toil a little more with WordPerfect's screen colors or take the afternoon off and catch a quick round of golf. My golf game fell all to pieces after I began using Word for Windows. I spend so much of my time trying to figure out what all those options on the Tools⇨Options command are for that I don't have any time left over for such luxuries as golf.

You should read this chapter when you finally decide to give in to the Tools⇨Options command and you want to know what all those options do. It describes the most useful options but, more important, tells you which options can be safely ignored so that you (unlike some people I know — me, for example) can catch up on your golf.

I am aware, of course, that for many people, golf is a more frustrating game than playing with WinWord. And for some, golf is more boring than reading WinWord's on-line help. If you're one of those poor, unenlightened souls, feel free to substitute your favorite nongolf pastime.

What's with All the Options?

When you call up the <u>T</u>ools⇨<u>O</u>ptions command, you are presented with one of the most heavy-laden dialog boxes of all time. This dialog box has so many options that it earned Microsoft a Lifetime Achievement Award from the American Society of Windows Programmers.

Like many other dialog boxes in WinWord, the Options dialog box organizes its settings into tabs. Each tab has its own set of option controls. To switch from one tab to another, just click the tab label at the top of the dialog box.

Most WinWord dialog boxes that use tab labels have two or three tab labels, but the Options dialog box has 12 — count 'em — *12* tabs:

View: Contains options that control the way your document is displayed on-screen.

General: Contains a hodgepodge of miscellaneous options that the Microsoft programmers couldn't fit on any of the other tabs.

Edit: Contains options that affect the way WinWord's basic text-editing features work.

Print: Contains options that affect the way the <u>F</u>ile⇨<u>P</u>rint command works.

Re<u>v</u>isions: Contains options used in conjunction with the <u>T</u>ools⇨Re<u>v</u>isions command, which you can learn about in Chapter 23.

User Info: Stores your name and address.

Compatibility: Used if you think that you know more about older versions of Microsoft Word than the good folks at Microsoft do.

File Locations: Tells WinWord where to look for files.

Save: Has important options that control the way WinWord saves your documents.

Spelling: Used to get the spell checker to lighten up and turn off that annoying on-the-fly spell checker

Grammar: Doesn't make the grammar checker (the <u>T</u>ools⇨<u>G</u>rammar command) any better at turning you into a great writer.

AutoFormat: May be used if you like the AutoFormat thing.

To set options in WinWord, follow these steps:

1. **Call up the <u>T</u>ools⇨<u>O</u>ptions command.**

   The Options dialog box appears.

2. **Click the tab that contains an option you want to change.**

   If you're not sure which tab contains the option you're looking for, just cycle through them until you find the option.

3. **Set the option however you want.**

Most of the options are simple check boxes you click to check or uncheck. Some require that you select a choice from a drop-down list, and some have the audacity to require that you type a filename or otherwise demonstrate your keyboard proficiency.

4. **Repeat Step 3 until you have exhausted your options or until you're just plain exhausted.**

You can set more than one option with a single use of the Tools⇨Options command.

5. **Click OK.**

You're done!

As you fritter away your day playing with these tabs, keep the following points in mind:

✔ Several of the Options tabs have more than one road that leads to them. You can reach the Print options tab, for example, by using the File⇨Print command and then clicking the Options button.

✔ To move to a tab, just click the tab label. You can also move from tab to tab by using the keyboard's arrow keys. To move from the General tab to the Edit tab, for example, press the right-arrow key.

Many settings that a normal person would consider *options* are located elsewhere in WinWord's sinuous menu structure. You use the View⇨Toolbars command, for example, to display or hide toolbars.

Vying with the View Options

The options on the View tab, shown in Figure 15-1, let you customize the appearance of WinWord's humble display. The View tab options are arranged in three groups: Show, Window, and Nonprinting Characters.

The Show options

The View options grouped under the Show heading control the amount of detail displayed in the document window.

Some of the Show options appear on the View tab only when you are in Page Layout view. To set those options, you must switch to Page Layout view before using the Tools⇨Options command.

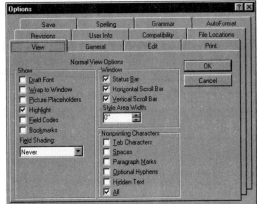

Figure 15-1:
The View
options tab.

This list gives you the lowdown on each of the options you can set from this tab:

Draft Font: This option displays all text in an ugly sans serif bold typeface and underlines any text that has special formatting, such as boldface or italics. Useful for improving performance when you're running WinWord on computers that are so slow they have no business running WinWord. (This option is available only in Normal view.)

Wrap to Window: An often useful option, this keeps text within the document window by breaking lines that are too wide to fit in the window. When you use this option, the line endings you see on-screen are different from the line endings that are printed. (This option is available only in Normal view.)

Picture Placeholders: If you insert a picture into a document, you probably will notice that WinWord hesitates a little when you scroll the picture into the document window. If you add 20 pictures to a document, the hesitations may come so often that you want to scream. Checking the Picture Placeholders option causes WinWord to display a simple rectangle where the picture should go. This eliminates the hesitation. (The pictures are still printed when you print the document.)

Highlight: Disable this option if you don't want to see highlighting made by Word's new Highlight feature.

Field Codes: Use this option when you're struggling with a maniacal mail merge and you want to see the codes inserted for each field rather than the results of the field.

Bookmarks: Check this option when you want any text referred to in a bookmark to be sandwiched between gray brackets.

Field Shading: Lets you draw attention to field results by shading them. This option can be set to Never (which never shades field results), Always (which always shades field results), and When Selected (which shades field results only when some or all of the field is selected).

Drawings: Displays a rectangle for each drawing object rather than the object itself. This option is available only in Page Layout view. (That's why it's not shown in Figure 15-1.)

Object Anchors: Displays anchors for frames and drawing objects. Available only in Page Layout view.

Text Boundaries: Displays lines around columns and margins so that you can quickly see the page layout. Available only in Page Layout view.

The Window options

The View options grouped under the Window heading let you tweak the appearance of WinWord document windows. This list shows the details:

Status Bar: WinWord's dashboard. It tells you what page you're on, where you are on the page, whether you pressed the Insert key to switch to Overtype mode, and so on. If all this stuff just takes up space, you can remove it by unchecking the Status Bar option. This action leaves more room for your document.

Horizontal Scroll Bar: The one at the bottom of the screen. If you discover one day that you have been using WinWord for two years and didn't know that a horizontal scroll bar was available, uncheck this option to free up more space to display your document. Be aware, though, that in addition to removing the horizontal scroll bar, unchecking this option also removes the view buttons next to it. With these buttons removed, you have to use the View menu commands to switch views.

Vertical Scroll Bar: At the right edge of the window. If your text is just a wee bit wide for the screen, consider unchecking the Vertical Scroll Bar option to remove the scroll bar. This action frees up a little space, and you can still press the Page Up and Page Down keys to scroll through your document.

Style Area Width: If you want to see the names of styles you have assigned to your paragraphs all lined up in a neat row down the left side of the window, increase the setting of this option from 0 inches to about 0.6 inches. To remove the Style Area, return this setting to 0.

Vertical Ruler: Places a ruler at the left edge of the window. Available only in Page Layout view.

The Nonprinting Characters options

The View options grouped under the Nonprinting Characters heading let you control which special characters, shown in the following list, are displayed in the document window:

Tab Characters: Displays tab characters as an arrow. I usually leave this option checked so that I can keep track of tabs.

Spaces: Displays spaces as little dots. I usually leave this option unchecked.

Paragraph Marks: Displays paragraph marks. I usually leave this option checked so that I can quickly find extraneous paragraphs.

Optional Hyphens: Displays optional hyphens. They are used when you want precise control over hyphenation (see Chapter 11).

Hidden Text: *Hidden text* is text that is in your document but not printed. To display hidden text, you must check the Hidden Text box.

All: Displays all hidden characters. Choosing this option is the same as clicking the Show/Hide Paragraph button on the Standard toolbar.

When the Show/Hide Paragraph button on the Standard toolbar is depressed, all nonprinting characters are displayed. When the button is not depressed, only those nonprinting characters specified on the View options tab are displayed. You should set the options on the View tab so that only those nonprinting characters you *always* want displayed — such as Tab characters and paragraph marks — are checked. You can display the other nonprinting characters at any time by simply clicking the Show/Hide Paragraph tool.

Saluting the General Options

Back in the days of Microsoft Word Version 1.0, the options on the General options tab were lowly Private Options. But they re-upped for version 2 and eventually decided to become career options. Now they've made it all the way to the rank of General. You had better snap-to whenever you call up these options (see Figure 15-2).

This list gives you the lowdown on what the General options do:

Background Repagination: Ever notice that when you take a breather from your sustained typing rate of 90 words per minute, WinWord sometimes causes page breaks to dance about? This dance is WinWord's *Background Repagination* feature at work, constantly surveying the length

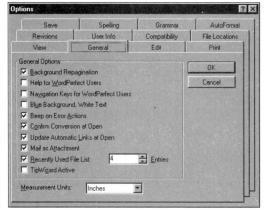

Figure 15-2:
The General
options tab.

of your document and inserting page breaks where they rightfully belong. If you uncheck this box, WinWord repaginates the document only when you print it; create a table of contents, index, or other table; or work in Page Layout or Print Preview view.

Turning Background Repagination off might make your computer run a little faster, but you'll always be wondering whether you're at the top or bottom of the page. I don't recommend it. (You can't turn off Background Repagination when in Page Layout view, because Page Layout view requires that page breaks always be up-to-date.)

Help for WordPerfect Users: An option that is little more than wishful thinking on behalf of the billions and billions of WordPerfect users switching to WinWord. If you momentarily forget that you're using WinWord and press a WordPerfect function key, such as Shift-F7, you receive a minor electric shock as a gentle reinforcement to use the correct WinWord command instead.

Navigation Keys for WordPerfect Users: Another futile attempt to help WordPerfect users who have been forced at gunpoint to switch to WinWord, this time by making the Page Up, Page Down, Home, End, and Esc keys behave in the same brain-damaged manner as they do in WordPerfect.

Blue Background, White Text: Makes WinWord *really* look like WordPerfect.

Beep on Error Actions: When this option is checked, your neighbors are alerted to the fact that you haven't yet mastered WinWord.

Confirm Conversion at Open: This is not some kind of option for a religious awakening, but rather, it instructs Word to ask for your consent before opening a non-Word document.

Update Automatic Links at Open: Automatically updates any files that are linked to a document when you open the document. It's usually best to leave this one on.

Mail as Attachment: Relevant only if your computer is attached to a network and you want to zap documents around by using e-mail.

Recently Used File List: Tells WinWord how many files to list at the bottom of the File menu. You can list as many as nine files.

TipWizard Active: If the Tip Wizard makes you nauseous, you can disable it by unchecking this box.

Measurement Units: In case you don't like inches, you can change WinWord's measurements to centimeters, points, picas, fathoms, leagues, cubits, or parsecs.

Enumerating the Edit Options

The Edit tab options, shown in Figure 15-3 and in the following list, affect the way WinWord's basic editing operations work:

Typing Replaces Selection: If you highlight text by dragging the mouse over it or holding down the Shift key while moving the cursor and then type something, the whatever-it-was-you-typed obliterates the whatever-it-was-you-highlighted. If this behavior drives you bonkers, you can turn it off by unchecking the Typing Replaces Selection box.

Drag-and-Drop Text Editing: More commonly known as dragon dropping; lets you move text by selecting it and then dragging it with the mouse. If it annoys you, turn it off by unchecking this field.

Automatic Word Selection: One of the niftiest features in WinWord. It causes WinWord to assume that you meant to select an entire word when, for example, you place the cursor in the middle of a word and press Ctrl+I, making the entire word italicized. It can be disconcerting at first, though. If it's against your religion, you can turn it off by unchecking the Automatic Word Selection option.

Use the INS Key for Paste: Makes the Insert key double as a shortcut for the Edit⇨Paste command.

Overtype Mode: Puts WinWord into Overtype mode, in which any text you type obliterates text on-screen. Whether you check this option or not, you can press the Insert key to switch between Insert and Overtype modes (unless you checked the Use the INS Key for Paste option).

Use Smart Cut and Paste: Adjusts spaces before and after text you cut and paste so that you don't end up with two spaces between some words and no spaces between others. Leave this option checked; it's too good to turn off.

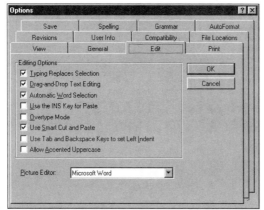

Figure 15-3:
The Edit
options tab.

Use Tab and Backspace Keys to Set Left Indent: If this option is enabled, the tab key behaves funny if you use it at the beginning of an existing paragraph: Rather than insert a tab character, it actually increases the paragraph's first line indent setting found in the Format⇨Font command. Similarly, the Backspace key, when used at the beginning of a paragraph, decreases the left indent. This feature drives me crazy, so I usually disable this option.

Allow Accented Uppercase: Lets you put accents on capital letters when text is formatted as French.

Picture Editor: Lets you use a graphics program other than WinWord to edit imported graphics.

Parading the Print Options

Figure 15-4 shows the options that are available from the Print options tab. You can reach this tab by using the Tools⇨Options command, or you can access it from the File⇨Print command by clicking the Options button.

The Printing Options group

The Printing Options group includes general printing options:

Draft Output: If you check this option, WinWord may omit complicated formatting to speed printing. Which type of formatting gets axed depends on the printer type.

Reverse Print Order: Prints pages in reverse order. This option lets you read the end of the document first, sort of like the way I read mystery novels.

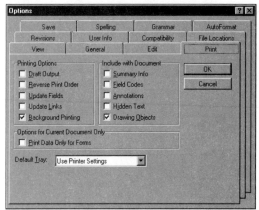

Figure 15-4:
The Print
options tab.

Update Fields: Updates the contents of fields before printing.

Update Links: Updates information linked into WinWord from other files before printing. This option is necessary only if you link files on a network and you want to be abso-posolutely sure that you print the most current data.

Background Printing: With this option checked, you can print a document and continue working while the document is being printed. If you uncheck this option, WinWord makes you wait, arms folded, while it prints the file. The plus is that printing is faster when this option is unchecked.

The Include with Document options

The next set of Print options tell WinWord what to print along with the document itself:

Summary Info: All that information displayed by the File⇨Summary Info command is printed on a separate page if you check this option.

Field Codes: Check this option if you want to print field codes (such as { SEQ Tables * MERGEFORMAT }) rather than the calculated value of each field.

Annotations: If annotations have been added to the document, check this option to print them on a separate page. See Chapter 24 for more information about annotations.

Hidden Text: If the document has any hidden text and you want it printed, check this option.

Drawing Objects: Prints stuff you have drawn with WinWord's drawing tools. See Chapter 14 if you don't know about WinWord's drawing tools.

Other options

The Print options tab has two other options:

> **Print Data Only for Forms:** If you used the forms feature (see Chapter 26) to print on preprinted forms (such as invoices and purchase orders), check this box to tell WinWord to print the data in a form but not print the form itself.

> **Default Tray:** Tells WinWord which paper tray the printer should suck up paper from. Usually the default paper tray set from Control Panel is used.

Futzing with the File Locations Options

The File Locations tab of the Tools⇨Options command lets you customize WinWord by changing the locations of various files that are used. Figure 15-5 shows the File Locations tab.

The File Locations dialog box consists of a list of files used by WinWord and a Modify button. To change the location of one of these file types, choose it in the File Types list and then click Modify. You are greeted with a dialog box you can use to choose the drive and directory in which the files are located.

This list gives you the lowdown on the File Types listed in the File Locations dialog box:

> **Documents:** Changes the default folder for the File⇨Open and File⇨Save As commands.

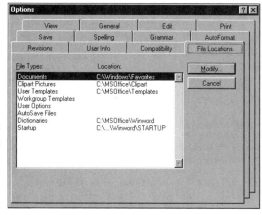

Figure 15-5:
The File
Locations
options tab.

Clipart Pictures: If you have your own collection of clip art, you might want to modify this file type to make your clip art easier to find.

User Templates: You probably should leave this one alone. It tells WinWord where to create templates.

Workgroup Templates: This option lets you set up a secondary location for template files.

All the rest: Leave the rest of the options alone.

Salivating over the Save Options

The options on the Save tab, shown in Figure 15-6, come into play when you save a document. Like the Print options, this option tab can be reached from the Tools⇨Options command or from the Save As command.

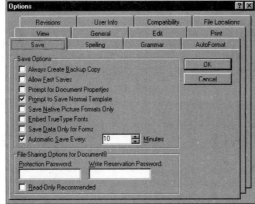

Figure 15-6:
The Save
options tab.

Pay attention to what these options do:

Always Create Backup Copy: If this option is checked, WinWord uses the extension BAK to save a backup copy of your file before it saves any changes you have made. That way, if you annihilate your document, you can open the backup document and count your blessings.

Allow Fast Saves: This option lets WinWord save files quickly by saving only the changes you have made to a file instead of saving the entire file.

You can't have your cake and eat it too: You can choose Always Create Backup Copy or Allow Fast Saves, but not both.

Prompt for Document Properties: If you want to store summary information with your documents, check this option. Then WinWord asks for summary information whenever you save a new document.

Prompt to Save Normal.dot: If you're obsessed about preserving the chastity of NORMAL.DOT, check this option. It pops up a friendly note whenever NORMAL.DOT is about to be changed.

Save Native Picture Formats Only: This option is weird. If you import some kind of foreign picture file (from a Macintosh, for example), WinWord must convert the picture to a suitable Windows format. If you want WinWord to then discard the foreign format and save only the Windows version of the picture with the document, check this option. It saves disk space.

Embed TrueType Fonts: This one is weird, too. If you used a weird font, like Grumpy Old Style or Gastric Antiqua, and you want to give the document to a friend who doesn't have those fonts, check this option before saving the file. WinWord saves the fonts along with the document. Then, when you give the document to your friend, the fonts are a part of the package.

Embedding TrueType fonts is different from copying the fonts to a disk and giving them to a friend. The latter is illegal (unless the fonts are free, public-domain fonts). When you embed fonts, the user can access the fonts only from within WinWord, but only for the document in which the fonts are embedded. It's perfectly legal.

Save Data Only for Forms: This option lets you tie forms to a database. See Chapter 26 for more info about forms.

Automatic Save Every: Set this option to ten Minutes or so to cause WinWord to automatically save your documents periodically. Then you don't have to worry about a lightning bolt, twister, or comet ruining your document.

File-Sharing Options: The remaining three options on the Save options tab let you limit other users' access to your document. If you supply a Protection Password, other users must know the password to access the document. If you type a Write Reservation Password, other users must know the password to update the document. Without the password, a user can open the document but cannot save changes.

If you check Read-Only Recommended, WinWord suggests to any user who opens the file that the file should be opened as read-only. It's only a suggestion, so the user can do whatever she pleases. But at least the user was warned.

Chapter 16

Rolling Your Own Toolbars, Menus, and Keyboard Shortcuts

• •

In This Chapter

▶ Making toolbars appear (and disappear!)

▶ Adding buttons to a toolbar

▶ Creating a new toolbar

• •

*H*iding down at the bottom of the <u>T</u>ools menu is a potent little command called <u>C</u>ustomize. Lurking within the dialog box that appears when you conjure up this command is the ability to improve the toolbars, menus, and keyboard shortcuts that come with WinWord. If you routinely apply a style named Limerick to samples of fine poetry within your documents, for example, you can add a Limerick button to one of WinWord's templates. Or you can add a Limerick command to the Format menu or define Ctrl+L as a keyboard shortcut for applying the Limerick style. This chapter shows you how.

Please feel free to skip this chapter if you already think that WinWord is the world's perfect word processor, beyond need for refinement.

Customized toolbars, menus, and keyboard shortcuts are stored along with styles, AutoText, and macros in document templates. Unless you specify otherwise, any customizations you create are stored in the NORMAL.DOT template so that they are available to all documents. If you want, you can store customizations in other templates so that they are available only when you're editing documents attached to those templates. For the complete scoop on templates, see Chapter 4.

Toying with Toolbars

Martin Luther said, "If you must sin, sin boldly!" The people who designed WinWord's toolbar buttons were apparently students of Luther, because they didn't just throw in a few buttons here and there — they threw in nine separate toolbars, with something like 98 buttons. Kind of inspires a song:

> *Ninety-eight buttons appear on the screen,*
> *Ninety-eight buttons appear,*
> *Tools⇨Customize is one button's demise,*
> *Ninety-seven buttons appear on the screen.*

If 98 buttons aren't enough for you, WinWord keeps a few unused buttons in reserve. You can add these buttons to any of the existing button bars, or you can create new button bars altogether. And if that's *still* not enough, you can even design your own buttons!

Although WinWord's toolbar buttons might be just a little excessive, they are one of the best ways to tailor WinWord to the way you work. I hardly ever use right-justified text, for example, but I frequently use strikethrough. So I replaced the Align Right button on the formatting toolbar with a Strikethrough button. It took about two minutes, and it saves me from wading through the Format⇨Font command to find the Strikethrough check box.

This section sums up the procedures for calling up WinWord's hidden toolbars and creating custom toolbars that suit your fancy.

Making toolbars appear (and disappear!)

If your favorite toolbar is missing, you or someone else may have inadvertently sent it to toolbar exile. To get the toolbar back, follow these steps:

1. Call up the View⇨Toolbars command.

The Toolbars dialog box appears, as shown in Figure 16-1.

2. Click the little box next to the toolbar that you want displayed.

A check mark appears in the box. To remove a toolbar, click its box to make the check mark disappear.

3. Click OK.

The toolbars you chose are displayed.

Figure 16-1:
The
Toolbars
dialog box.

Here are a few points to ponder when you display toolbars:

- ✔ Some toolbars cling to the top of the document window, whereas others are free spirits that wander about the window.

- ✔ If you don't like the position of a toolbar on-screen, you can move it. Just point to any part of the toolbar between buttons and drag. You can also change the shape of a floating toolbar by dragging one of its edges or corners.

- ✔ If you drag a toolbar to the top of the document window, it clings to the top like the Standard and Formatting toolbars do. If you drag a toolbar far enough away from the top of the window, the toolbar becomes a floater again.

To make a floating toolbar go away, click the close button in its top-right corner.

Removing toolbar buttons

In case you don't like the buttons that appear on WinWord's toolbars, you can remove buttons you don't use. You often have to do this before you add new buttons to a toolbar because the toolbars that come with WinWord are stuffed to the gills with buttons.

Follow these steps to remove a button:

1. Call up the Tools⇨Customize command.

A dialog box appears, which you can ignore for now. You don't have to use it to remove toolbar buttons. (If the dialog box obscures the button you want to remove, relocate the dialog box by dragging it by the title bar.)

2. Click the Toolbars tab if it is not already chosen.

This step brings to the forefront the options for customizing toolbars.

3. **Click the button you want to remove and drag it off the toolbar.**

It doesn't matter where you drag the button; just drag it well clear of the toolbar.

4. **Release the mouse button, and the toolbar button is removed.**

The other buttons on the toolbar adjust.

Keep these important points in mind when you remove a button:

✔ The Undo command (Ctrl+Z) doesn't cover modifications you make to a toolbar. If you inadvertently delete a toolbar button, however, you can quickly restore the entire toolbar to its pristine condition by using the View⇨Toolbars command and clicking the Reset button.

✔ You can quickly call up the Tools⇨Customize command's Toolbars tab by pointing the mouse to one of the spaces within a toolbar between buttons or above or below a button, pressing the right mouse button, and choosing the Customize command from the menu that appears.

Adding a new button to a toolbar

Although WinWord comes with nine toolbars capable of showing millions of buttons, that's not enough. If you want to add an extra button to a toolbar, follow these steps:

1. **Call up the Tools⇨Customize command.**

The dialog box shown in Figure 16-2 appears. If the Toolbars tab is not on the top, click it to bring it front and center.

2. **If necessary, make way for the new button by removing a button you don't use.**

This is the hard part. If there isn't any room on any of the toolbars that are visible, you have to make room by deleting a button or two that you don't use. To delete a button, just drag it off the toolbar. See the preceding section, "Removing toolbar buttons," for more information.

3. **Choose the Category of button you want to add.**

As you scroll through the Categories list, the buttons shown in the Buttons section of the dialog box change to indicate which buttons are available for the category. As you examine the categories, you see familiar buttons, such as the New, Open, and Save buttons, plus unfamiliar buttons, such as binoculars and the padlock.

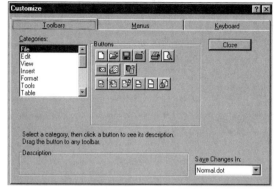

Figure 16-2:
The
Customize
dialog box.

If you're patient enough, you can scroll through the entire Categories list and find four interesting categories hiding out at the bottom of the list: Macros, Fonts, AutoText, and Styles. These options don't present a bunch of predefined buttons you can use. Instead, they let you assign buttons to the specific macros, fonts, AutoText entries, or styles that are available.

Just above the Macros, Fonts, AutoText, and Style categories is the All Commands category. It lists all the commands available in WinWord, in alphabetic order.

4. Choose the button you want to add and drag it to the toolbar at the location where you want the button added.

As soon as you release the mouse button, the toolbar button is added to the toolbar right where you clicked.

5. If you used the Macros, Fonts, Autotext, or Styles categories, choose a button from the Custom Button dialog box.

Figure 16-3 shows the Custom Button dialog box, which is displayed if you drag a macro, font, AutoText, or style name to a toolbar. You can choose one of the 37 predefined button pictures or you can click the Text Button to create a button that contains text. If you do that, type in the Text Button Name field the text that you want to appear on the button. Click Assign to add the new button.

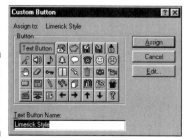

Figure 16-3:
The Custom
Button
dialog box.

6. **Click Close to dismiss the Customize Toolbars dialog box.**

   You're finished!

If none of the 37 predefined custom buttons suits your fancy, click the Edit button to create your own button design. The dialog box shown in Figure 16-4 appears. Paint the button by clicking in the Picture area and picking whichever color you want to paint with from the Colors area of the dialog box. When you're finished, click OK. To erase the button and start over from scratch, click Clear.

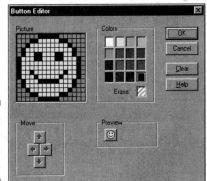

Figure 16-4:
Creating
your own
button.

Creating a new toolbar

If you can't find room for a few extra tools in one of the existing toolbars, you can create a new toolbar. Just follow these steps:

1. **Call up the View⇨Toolbars command.**

   The Toolbars dialog box appears. If you must look, a picture of it is shown in Figure 16-1. That's quite a few pages back, though, and you don't really need to see it to continue to the next step.

2. **Click New.**

   A dialog box appears, asking you to type a name for the new toolbar.

3. **Type a name for the toolbar and then click OK.**

   Use whatever name you want.

4. **When WinWord creates an empty toolbar and pops up the Customize Toolbar dialog box, drag whatever buttons you want to the new toolbar.**

5. Click Close.

The Customize dialog box vanishes.

6. Move the new toolbar to its final resting place.

Drag it by the edge to wherever you want it to appear on-screen.

7. You're finished.

To delete a toolbar you have created, use the View⇨Toolbars command, choose the toolbar you want to delete, and click the Delete button.

Messing with Menus

In addition to customizing WinWord's toolbars, you can customize its menus. You can add or delete individual commands in WinWord's existing menus or you can add new menus to WinWord's menu bar.

There are several reasons you might want to mess with WinWord's menus. If you have created a macro you use frequently, you might want to add it to a menu to make it easier to use. Or if you use a template that has dozens of styles, you might want to add to a menu the five or six styles you use most often so that you don't have to continually scroll through the entire list to apply those styles.

To modify WinWord's menus, follow these steps:

1. Call up the Tools⇨Customize command.

Figure 16-5 shows the Menus tab of the Customize dialog box. If these options are not visible when you use the Tools⇨Customize command, click the Menus tab.

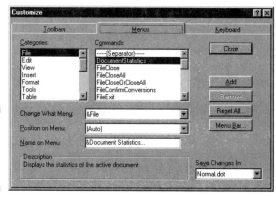

Figure 16-5: Changing WinWord's menus.

2. Play with the menu options.

To add a menu item, first choose the menu from the Change What Menu list. Then pick the command you want to add to the menu by choosing a category from the Categories list and the command from the Commands list. Use the Position on Menu list to tell WinWord where to place the new menu item on the menu. Then click Add to add the menu item.

To delete a menu item, choose the menu from the Change What Menu list, choose the menu item from the Position on Menu list, and then click Remove.

To create an altogether new menu, click the Menu Bar button. The Menu Bar dialog box appears (see Figure 16-6); type the name of the new menu, click Add, and then click Close.

3. Click Close.

You're finished.

Figure 16-6:
The Menu
Bar dialog
box.

The following are some random thoughts to keep in mind as you mess with menus.

✔ Mess up? Pressing Ctrl+Z doesn't work for the Tools⇨Customize command. You can reset the menus to their undefiled state, however, by clicking the Reset All button.

✔ When you type the menu name in the Name on Menu box, type an ampersand (&) immediately in front of the letter you want to be the menu command's hot key. If *y* is the hot key for a menu item named Slay Dragon, for example, type **Sla&y Dragon** in the Name on Menu box.

✔ If you scroll through the Categories list, you find various categories for WinWord commands plus categories for macros, fonts, AutoText entries, and styles.

✔ To add a menu command you use frequently and for many different kinds of documents, set the Save Changes In field to Normal. If you plan to use the custom menu only for documents created with a particular template, save the changes in the current document's template.

Creating Custom Keyboard Shortcuts

WinWord lets you assign your own keyboard shortcuts to styles, macros, fonts, AutoText entries, commands, and symbols.

Follow these steps to assign a new keyboard shortcut:

1. **Call up the Tools⇨Customize command.**

   The Customize dialog box appears. Figure 16-7 shows the options on its Keyboard tab. If these options aren't visible, click the Keyboard tab to bring them into view.

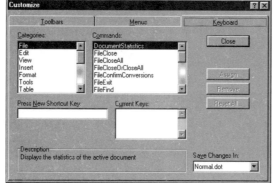

Figure 16-7:
Changing
keyboard
shortcuts.

2. **Choose the command, style, macro, font, or other item for which you want to create a keyboard shortcut by using the Categories and Commands lists.**

   Spend some time exploring these lists. Lots of useful commands are buried amongst a bunch of foreign-looking gobbledygook, such as FileConfirmConversions and TableUpdateAutoFormat.

3. **Click in the Press New Shortcut Key field and then type the new keyboard shortcut.**

   When you type the shortcut, WinWord lets you know whether the key is already assigned to some other command.

4. **Click Assign to assign the keyboard shortcut. Then choose Close.**

   You're finished! Try the shortcut to see whether it work.

This list presents some key points to remember about keyboard shortcuts:

✔ You can also assign keyboard shortcuts by clicking the Shortcut Key from the Insert Symbol command or the Format⇨Style, Modify command.

✔ A quick way to assign a shortcut to a menu command, font, or style is to press Ctrl+Alt++ (the plus sign on the numeric keyboard). When the keyboard changes to a pretzel, choose the menu, style, or font to which you want to assign the shortcut key. The Customize dialog box pops up, waiting for you to type the shortcut key.

✔ To reset all keyboard shortcuts to their WinWord defaults, call up the Tools⇨Customize command, choose the Keyboard tab, and click the Reset All button.

Chapter 17
Messing with Macros

. . . .

. . . .

A *macro* is a sequence of commands or keystrokes that WinWord records and lets you play back at any time. It's a way to create your own customized shortcuts for things you do over and over again. For example, WinWord comes with built-in keyboard shortcuts to make text bold (Ctrl+B) and to make text italic (Ctrl+I), but no built-in shortcut exists to make text bold and italic all at the same time. To do that, you have to press Ctrl+B and then Ctrl+I. If you do that a million times a day, pretty soon that extra keystroke becomes bothersome. Wouldn't it be nice if you had a shortcut for Bold-Italic? With WinWord's macro recorder, you can create one.

This chapter shows you how to record and play back simple macros. It doesn't show you how to create complex macros by using WinWord's macro programming language, WordBasic. That's the subject for an entirely separate, six-pound, 900-page book that comes with a pocket protector and thick glasses stapled to the back cover. I skip that subject entirely.

Macros are stored in a document template along with styles, keyboard shortcuts, customized menus and button bars, AutoText, the spare tire, and a two-year supply of Windex (this is Word for *Windows,* after all). Unless you specify otherwise, any macros you create are stored in the NORMAL.DOT template so that they are available to all documents. If you want, you can store macros in other templates so that the macros are available only when you're editing a document attached to the template that contains the macros. For more information about templates, refer to Chapter 4.

A Twelve-Step Program for Recording a Macro

To record a macro, follow these 12 steps:

1. **Try to talk yourself out of it.**

   Fiddling around with macros can be a bit of a time-waster. Ask yourself whether you think that you will really use the macro after you have gone to the trouble of recording it. If not, go directly to step 12.

2. **Think about what you're going to do. Rehearse it if necessary.**

   Think through all the steps you have to follow to accomplish whatever task it is want to automate with a macro. To create a macro that makes text bold and italic, for example, all you have to do is press Ctrl+B and then press Ctrl+I. That's a pretty simple macro, but other macros might be much more complex, involving dozens of steps. If necessary, rehearse the steps before you record them as a macro.

3. **Call up the Tools⇨Macro command.**

   The Macro dialog box appears, as shown in Figure 17-1.

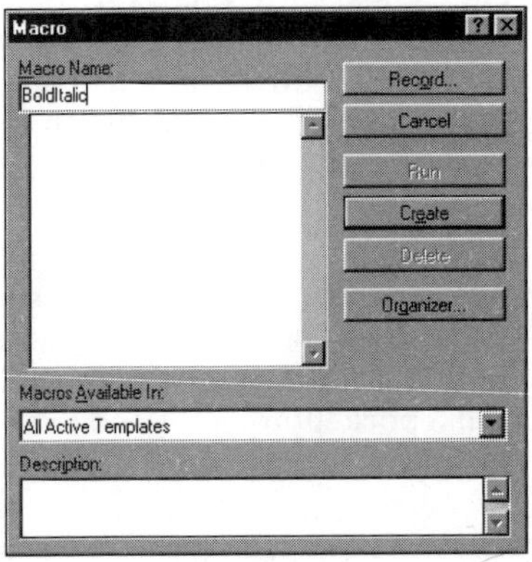

Figure 17-1:
The Macro dialog box.

4. **Type the name of the macro you want to create.**

   The name can be anything you want, but it cannot include spaces, commas, or periods. In Figure 17-1, I typed BoldItalic for the name.

5. **Click the Record button.**

   The Record Macro dialog box appears, as shown in Figure 17-2.

Figure 17-2:
The Record
Macro
dialog box.

6. **If you want to make your macro accessible from a toolbar, a menu, or the keyboard, click the Toolbars, Menus, or Keyboard button. Click Close when you're finished.**

   This step calls up the Customize dialog box, all set to add your macro to a toolbar, menu, or keyboard shortcut. Figure 17-3 shows the Customize dialog box that is displayed if you click the Keyboard button. All you have to do is press the shortcut key combination you want to assign to the macro (in this case, I pressed Ctrl+Shift+B), click Assign, and then click Close.

   For more information about customizing toolbars, menus, or the keyboard, refer to Chapter 16.

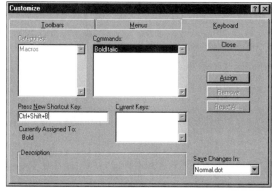

Figure 17-3:
The
Customize
dialog
box for
assigning a
macro to a
keyboard
shortcut.

7. **Click OK to begin recording the macro.**

   The Record Macro dialog box disappears, and a little macro recorder toolbar appears, as shown in Figure 17-4. You use this toolbar to stop recording the macro.

Figure 17-4:
The Macro
Record
toolbar.

8. **Type the keystrokes and menu commands you want recorded in the macro.**

To record the BoldItalic macro, for example, press Ctrl+B and then press Ctrl+I.

For more complicated macros, you may have to access menu commands. You can do that by using either the keyboard or the mouse.

 9. **If you have to stop recording temporarily, click the Pause button. Click it again to resume recording.**

You might forget how to do something, for example, especially if you skipped Step 2. If you click the Pause button, you can call up WinWord's Help command, look up the procedure for whatever it is you forgot, dismiss Help, and click the Pause button again to resume recording.

 10. **When you're finished, click the Stop button.**

The macro is added to the template. You're almost finished.

11. **Test the macro.**

If you assigned the macro to a keyboard shortcut, use the shortcut now to see whether the macro works.

12. **You're finished.**

Congratulate yourself.

Here are a few pointers to keep at the forefront of your mind as you record macros:

✔ You can call up the Record Macro dialog box directly by double-clicking the word REC on the status bar at the bottom of the screen. This action saves you from wading through the Tools menu and the Macro dialog box. WinWord proposes a boring name for the macro, such as Macro1, so you have to type your preferred name in the Record Macro dialog box rather than in the Macro dialog box.

✔ If the macro doesn't work, you may have made a mistake while recording it. If the macro is short enough, the best thing to do is to record the macro again. If the macro is long and you don't have anything important to do, try editing the macro to expunge the problem. See the section "Editing a Macro" later in this chapter.

✔ Macros are normally stored in the global NORMAL.DOT template. To store a macro in the template attached to the current document, change the setting of the Record Macro dialog box's Make Macro Available To field.

If the function of the macro isn't obvious from the macro name, type a more elaborate description of the macro in the Record Macro dialog box's Description field. You will thank yourself later on, when you forget what the macro does.

I hate to tell you about unexpected side effects

Sometimes a macro has unexpected side effects. Suppose that rather than record the keystrokes Ctrl+B and Ctrl+I for the BoldItalic macro, you decide to record these steps instead:

1. Call up the Format⇨Font command.

2. Choose Bold Italic as the Font Style.

3. Click OK.

The macro would seem to work, but sooner or later, you would discover that in addition to recording the Bold Italic font style, the macro recorded other character attributes — such as font, size, and effects. If the text to which you applied the Format⇨Font command when you recorded the macro used the Times New Roman font, any text you apply the macro to is switched to Times New Roman.

You can avoid these side effects in two ways:

✔ Avoid recording dialog boxes in macros whenever a keyboard shortcut or toolbar button will do the trick. Whenever you record a dialog box in a macro, you record all the dialog box's settings.

✔ Fix the macro later by editing it and removing the extraneous information. See the section "Editing a Macro" later in this chapter.

Running a Macro

There's more than one way to run a macro after you have recorded it. If you assigned the macro to a toolbar button, menu, or keyboard shortcut, you can quickly run the macro by clicking its button, choosing its menu command, or typing its keyboard shortcut.

If you didn't assign a button, menu, or keyboard shortcut to a macro, you have to run it from the Tools⇨Macro command. Follow the bouncing ball through these steps:

1. **Call up the Tools⇨Macro command.**

    The Macro dialog box appears.

2. **Choose the macro you want to run from the Macro Name list.**

3. **Click Run.**

If the macro you want to run doesn't show up in the list, try checking the Macros Available In setting. The macro might be in a different template.

Editing a Macro

If you make a minor mistake while recording a long macro, you can abandon the recording and start all over again. Or you can finish the recording and then edit the macro to correct the mistake. When you edit a macro, the macro's commands appear in their own document window, and most of WinWord's editing features are available to you. So you can correct a misspelled word, delete an unnecessary command, or otherwise fiddle with the macro.

The macros you edit may contain WordBasic programming commands not suitable for viewing by noncomputer nerds. Parental discretion is advised.

Follow these steps to edit a macro:

1. **Call up the Tools⇨Macro command.**

    The Macro dialog box appears.

2. **Choose the macro you want to run from the list of macros that are available.**

3. **Click Edit.**

    The macro appears in its own document window, and a special toolbar for editing macros appears also (see Figure 17-5).

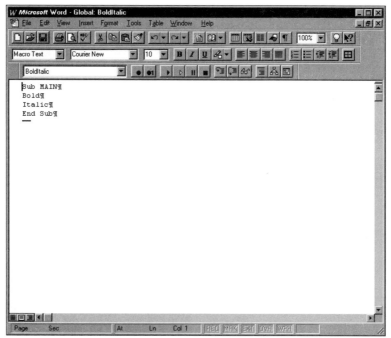

Figure 17-5:
Editing a
macro.

4. **Edit the macro!**

   Make whatever changes you want to make. If you misspelled a word, find it and correct it. If you added an unnecessary command, find it and remove it.

5. **Use the File⇨Save Template command (or press Ctrl+S) to save your macro.**

   The Save Template command saves the template that contains the macro you're editing. Any other changes you have made to the template — such as customized menus or keyboard shortcuts — are saved also.

6. **Use the Window command to return to the document window or use the File⇨Close command to close the macro window and return to your document window.**

   Either way works. Use the Window command if you plan to return to the macro window to edit the macro some more. If you're finished editing the macro, close it by using the File⇨Close command.

Here are some points to keep in mind for safe macro editing:

- ✔ Ignore the Macro toolbar. It has no buttons that are of interest to novice macro editors. The buttons on the Macro toolbar should be used only by licensed WinWord programmers.

- ✔ Don't be shocked if a macro turns out to be more complicated than you expect. Sometimes even the simplest macros can appear complex when you edit them. For example, Figure 17-6 shows what the BoldItalic macro looks like if you record the Format⇨Font command to set the Bold Italic font style rather than record the simpler Ctrl+B and Ctrl+I keystrokes.

- ✔ If you must know more about macro programming, consult the on-line help. It has complete information about WinWord's macro programming language, WordBasic.

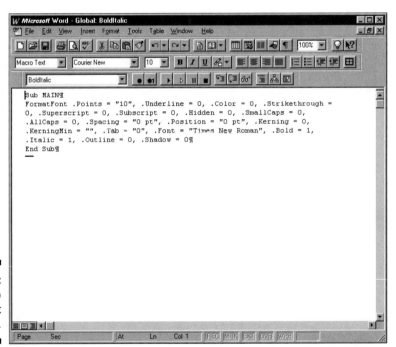

Figure 17-6:
A macro
that got out
of hand.

Using WinWord's Hidden Macros

WinWord comes with a bevy of prewritten macros that most people don't know about because they're hidden away in lost templates (the macros, not the people). To liberate these macros, you first must attach the templates that contain them as global templates. The macros are contained in four templates that live in the \MSOffice\Winword\Macros folder.

MACRO7.DOT: Contains a hodgepodge of useful macros

CONVERT7.DOT: Contains macros useful for converting files to different formats

LAYOUT7.DOT: Contains a bunch of macros that help you lay out your documents

TABLES7.DOT: Contains macros for working with tables

PRESENT7.DOT: Contains macros for using Word together with PowerPoint

Table 17-1 lists the hidden macros in the MACRO7.DOT template that I like best. You have to search the other templates for macros you like.

Table 17-1 The Best of the Hidden Macros in MACRO7.DOT

Macro	What It Does
ExitAll	Displays a dialog box that lists all open documents, enabling you to check the documents you want to save before exiting
FindSymbol	Searches for and optionally replaces symbols
FontSampleGenerator	Generates a sample of every font on your computer
InsertFootnote	Runs the Footnote Wizard, which automatically creates bibliographic footnotes that can satisfy even the snootiest college professors
MindBender	A memory game
SuperDocStatistics	Combines a bunch of interesting document information into one dialog box
WordPuzzler	A game

To enable the hidden macros, follow these steps:

1. **Call up the File⇨Templates command.**

2. **Click the Add button.**

3. **Locate the \MSOffice\Winword\Macros folder.**

4. **Choose the template you want to activate and click OK.**

5. **Repeat Steps 3 and 4 for other templates you want to activate.**

Here are a few interesting things to note about the supplied macros:

✔ Far and away the most fun macro is MindBender. It's a memory game, sort of like the old Concentration card game where you flip over pairs of cards, keep them if they match, or otherwise turn them back over and try to remember what they were. MindBender gives you an idea of how potent the WordBasic programming language is. Figure 17-7 shows the MindBender game's screen. As you can see, the computer can pretty much whip me, even when the game is set to its lowest skill level.

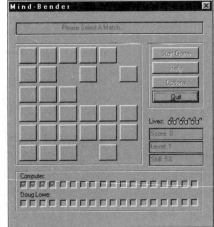

Figure 17-7: MindBender lets you enjoy life just a little.

✔ The WordPuzzler macro, new to Word for Windows 95, is like those silly puzzles that your parents made you play to keep you quiet while you drove to the Grand Canyon. As Figure 17-8 shows, WordPuzzler should bring back lots of memories.

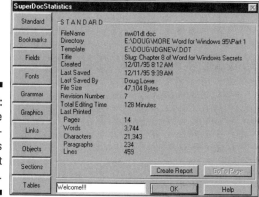

Figure 17-8:
The
WordPuzzler
game.

✔ After you've had your fun, don't forget to remove the macro templates from the Global Templates and Add-ins list under the File➪Templates command.

✔ One of my favorite macros is SuperDocStatistics, which gathers up a bunch of information about your document and presents it all in one dialog box, as shown in Figure 17-9. Notice the column of buttons running down the left edge of the dialog box. You can click any of these buttons to display additional information about the current document. I don't like this macro enough to buy the company, but I do like it enough to add a button for it on my Standard toolbar.

✔ If you want to see how these macros work, open the template as a document. To do that, call up the File➪Open command and change the Files of type field to Document Templates (*.dot). Then find the template in the MSOffice\Winword\Macros folder and open it. Next call up the Tools➪Macro command and change the Macros Available In field to the template you just opened. Then choose the macro you want to examine and click the Edit button.

Figure 17-9:
The
SuperDoc-
Statistics
macro at
work.

If you find that you want one of the supplied macros to be available at all times, use the organizer to copy the macro to Normal. Call up the Tools⇨ Macro command and click the Organizer button. Close the Normal template with the Close File button if it appears on the left side of the Organizer dialog box and open the template that contains the macro you want to copy in its place. Make sure that Normal is the template open on the right side of the dialog box. Choose the macro and then click the Copy button to copy it to Normal.

Almost Ten Easy but Useful Macros

Here are ten (well, five, but who's counting?) moderately easy but often useful macros you can create yourself. Although you can create most of these macros by recording keystrokes, I decided to spice things up a little and let you type the macro commands directly into a macro editing window. You don't have to invest in a pointy cap or a pocket protector to do this; just follow the bouncing ball, and all should go well.

Follow these steps to create each macro:

1. **Call up the Tools⇨Macro command.**

   The Macro dialog box appears.

2. **Type the name of the macro you want to create.**

   A suggested name is provided for each of the macros, but you can use any name you want.

3. **Click Create.**

   You are sent to a macro editing window with macro containing only these three lines:

   ```
   Sub MAIN

   End Sub
   ```

4. **Type the text of the macro between the Sub MAIN and End Sub lines.**

   The text for each macro is provided with the macro description. Type carefully and check your work.

5. **Use the Window command to return to your document.**

   Many of the macros cannot be run while the macro editing window is active.

6. **Run the macro by calling up the Tools⇨Macro command, choosing the macro, and clicking Run.**

7. **If you like the macro, use the Tools⇨Customize command to assign a keyboard shortcut to the macro.**

The following sections provide a brief description of each macro along with the text to type between the Sub MAIN and End Sub lines. For macros that can easily be recorded from keystrokes, you will also find a step-by-step procedure for recording the macro.

PrintCurrentPage

WinWord places a Print button on the Standard toolbar for printing an entire document, but I frequently want to print just the current page. Rather than go through the Print dialog box, I've created a PrintCurrentPage macro and assigned a toolbar button to it, right next to the Print button on the Standard toolbar. This macro is simple, but I use it all the time.

To create this macro, call up the Tools⇨Macro command, click Create, and type the following line between the Sub MAIN and End Sub lines:

```
FilePrint .Range = "2"
```

To create this macro by recording it, double-click the REC indicator on the status bar, type the macro name, and follow these steps:

1. **Call up the File⇨Print command.**

2. **Click Current Page.**

3. **Click OK.**

4. **Click the Stop recording button.**

SwapWords

This macro provides a quick way to swap words. It works by selecting the word, cutting it to the Clipboard, moving the cursor one word to the left, and then pasting the Clipboard contents to the new location. To use the macro, you first place the cursor in the word you want moved in front of the preceding word. In other words, place the cursor in the second of the two words you want to transpose.

To create the SwapWords macro, call up the Tools⇨Macro command, click Create, and type the following lines between the Sub MAIN and End Sub lines:

```
ExtendSelection
ExtendSelection
EditCut
WordLeft 1
EditPaste
```

If you prefer to record this macro, start recording and then follow these steps:

1. **Press F8.**

2. **Press F8 again. This step selects the current word.**

3. **Press Ctrl+X to cut the selection.**

4. **Press Ctrl+left arrow to move the cursor back one word.**

5. **Press Ctrl+V to paste the Clipboard contents.**

SwapSentences

This macro resembles the SwapWords macro, but it swaps entire sentences. Like SwapWords, it works by selecting an entire sentence, cutting it to the Clipboard, moving the cursor to a point in front of the preceding sentence, and pasting from the Clipboard. To use this macro, first place the cursor somewhere in the second of the two sentences you want to transpose.

To create the SwapSentences macro, call up the Tools⇨Macro command, click Create, and type the following lines between the Sub MAIN and End Sub lines:

```
ExtendSelection
ExtendSelection
ExtendSelection
EditCut
WordLeft 1
ExtendSelection
ExtendSelection
ExtendSelection
Cancel
CharLeft 1
EditPaste
```

If you prefer to record this macro, start recording and then follow these steps:

1. **Press F8.**

2. **Press F8 again. This step selects the current word.**

3. **Press F8 a third time to select the entire sentence.**

4. Press Ctrl+X to cut the selection.

5. Press Ctrl+left arrow to move the cursor back one word.

6. Press F8 three times to select the sentence.

7. Press Escape to deactivate Extend mode.

8. Press the left-arrow key to move the cursor to the left of the sentence.

9. Press Ctrl+V to paste the Clipboard contents.

ShowToolbars

If you want to work with an uncluttered window to see as much text as possible but be able to quickly call up your favorite toolbars, try this macro. It alternately shows and hides the Standard toolbar and the Formatting toolbar. You may want to customize it to show and hide other toolbars also.

To create the ShowToolbars macro, call up the Tools⇨Macro command, click Create, and type the following lines between the Sub MAIN and End Sub lines:

```
If ToolbarState("Standard") Then
  ViewToolbars .Toolbar = "Standard", .Hide
Else
  ViewToolbars .Toolbar = "Standard", .Show
End If

If ToolbarState("Formatting") Then
  ViewToolbars .Toolbar = "Formatting", .Hide
Else
  ViewToolbars .Toolbar = "Formatting", .Show
End If
```

Because this macro involves programming commands, there's no way you can record it from keystrokes. The only way to create it is to type these commands.

InsertFigureLegend

The InsertFigureLegend macro inserts a figure *legend,* which consists of a figure number and text for the legend. The figure number is created by using a SEQ field, so the numbering is automatic; the text for the legend is obtained from the user by using a WordBasic command (InputBox$) that accepts input from the user. The resulting figure legend appears something like this:

Figure 3. Incidence of heart attack during bowling matches, 1984-1994.

To create the InsertFigureLegend macro, call up the Tools⇨Macro command, click Create, and type the following lines between the Sub MAIN and End Sub lines:

```
Bold
Insert "Figure "
InsertField .Field = "SEQ Figure \* MERGEFORMAT"
Insert ". "
Bold
Text$ = InputBox$("Type the text for the figure legend.")
Insert Text$ + "."
InsertPara
```

Because this macro involves programming commands, there's no way you can record it from keystrokes. The only way to create it is to type these commands.

Part IV

I Always Wondered How to DoThat

The 5th Wave   **By Rich Tennant**

IF BOB DYLAN HAD PURSUED A CAREER IN COMPUTERS.

@RICHTENNANT

"PUT HIM IN FRONT OF A TERMINAL AND HE'S A GENIUS, BUT OTHER-WISE THE GUY IS SUCH A BROODING, GLOOMY GUS HE'LL NEVER BREAK INTO MANAGEMENT."

In this part . . .

Remember the old TV show, *You Asked For It*? People would write in about things they had always wondered about, and, well, you asked for it, you got it.

The chapters in this part are like that. All those WinWord features you read about on the back of the box or in a magazine review but never really learned how they work are here, just waiting for you to ask.

Chapter 18
The Magic of Master Documents

In This Chapter

▶ Understanding master documents

▶ Creating a master document from scratch

▶ Inserting existing files into a master document

▶ Breaking down an existing document into smaller subdocuments

▶ Cool things to do after you've made a master document

Suppose you have been bestowed upon by a great honor: serving as the moderator of this year's Village Idiot Convention. As moderator, one of your jobs is assembling a little 1,200-page book titled *Village Idiot '96: Proceedings of the Annual Village Idiot Trade Show and Conference*. Notable Village Idiots from all across the globe will present papers, and your job is to assemble all of these documents into one huge book. Fortunately for you, the Village Idiot Association (VIA) has adopted Word for Windows 95 as its standard word processor, so each idiot of note will send you a document on disk. All you have to do is combine the files into a single document and print them.

This is definitely a job for WinWord's Master Document feature. It lets you create long documents by piecing them together from small documents. It's all very confusing and worth figuring out only if you have to do this sort of thing often. If you find yourself needing to read this chapter, I offer my sincerest condolences.

You probably shouldn't tackle master documents until you have a pretty good understanding of WinWord's Outline view, because the master document feature is sort of an advanced form of outlining. If you haven't yet read Chapter 6, I would read it first, if I were you.

Understanding Master Documents

A *master document* contains special links to other documents, which are called *subdocuments.* If you were putting together a book that consists of 30 chapters, for example, you probably wouldn't want to put the entire book into one document. Instead, you would create a separate document for each chapter. That's all well and good, but what happens when you want to print the whole thing with page numbers that begin at page one and run through the end of the book rather than restart at page one at the beginning of each chapter? Or what if you want to print a table of contents for the book or create an index?

That's where master documents come in. With a master document, you create each chapter as a separate document. Then you create a master document for the entire book. In this master document, you create links to each of the chapter subdocuments. Then you can print the entire book, and WinWord takes care of numbering the pages for you. You can also create a table of contents or index in the master document, and the page numbers are all correct.

WinWord has a whole separate view for working with master documents, called — drum roll, please — *Master Document view.* Master Document view is a variation of Outline view, except that the portions of the master document that are subdocuments are indicated by little icons. You can double-click one of these icons to open a subdocument in a separate window to edit it.

Master Document view is used mostly when you want to create a new master document, when you want to change the order in which individual subdocuments appear in the master document, or when you want to add or remove subdocuments. If all you want to do is edit one of the individual chapters in your book, you just open the chapter document as you normally would, without even worrying about its being a subdocument in a master document.

If you open a master document and switch to Normal view or Page Layout view, WinWord treats the master document and all the subdocuments as though they were a part of one large document. You can scroll through the master document all the way to Chapter 12 and begin typing, for example, or you can use the File⇨Print command to print the entire book, or you can use the Edit⇨Replace command to replace all occurrences of *WordPerfect* with *Word for Windows* throughout the entire document.

You can assemble a master document in three ways:

> ✔ If you know that you need a master document beforehand, you can create the master document and all the subdocuments from scratch. This technique results in a master document and a collection of empty subdocuments, which you can then call up and edit as you see fit. See the section "Creating a Master Document from Scratch" later in this chapter.

✔ If you get part of the way into a project and realize, "Hey! This document is way too long! I should have used a master document," it's not too late. You can bust a big document into several smaller subdocuments. See the section "Breaking an Existing Document into Smaller Subdocuments" later in this chapter.

✔ If you already have a bunch of WinWord documents you want to assemble into a master document, you can create a master document by using these existing documents as the subdocuments. See the section "Inserting Existing Files into a Master Document," also later in this chapter.

All this stuff about master documents is confusing, I'm sure, but it makes more sense when you begin to use them. (I promise.) Just to muddy the waters a little more, the following list shows you some additional things you need to know about master documents before I jump into the procedures for creating and using them:

✔ In the master document, each subdocument is contained within its own section. Each subdocument, therefore, can have its own page layout, column arrangement, and all the other niceties that go along with being in your own section.

✔ When you work in Master Document view, a small toolbar of specialized master document buttons appears. The function of each of these buttons is summarized in Table 18-1.

It's best to base the master document and all the subdocuments on the same templates. Otherwise, you will have nightmares trying to figure out which styles, macros, and other template goodies are available.

Table 18-1   Buttons on the Master Document Toolbar

Button	What It Does
🗎	Breaks the selected text into subdocuments, using heading styles to determine where to begin each subdocument
🗎	Copies the contents of a subdocument into the master document and breaks the link to the subdocument file
🗎	Inserts an existing file as a subdocument
🗎	Combines two subdocument files into one subdocument file
🗎	Splits a subdocument into two subdocuments
🗎	Locks or unlocks a subdocument

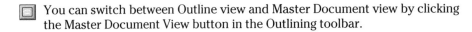

You can switch between Outline view and Master Document view by clicking the Master Document View button in the Outlining toolbar.

You can open a subdocument in two ways. You can first open the master document and then double-click the subdocument icon. WinWord opens the subdocument in a separate window. Alternatively, you can ignore the master document and open the subdocument file the way you would open any other WinWord document: by using the File⇨Open command or clicking the Open button in the Standard toolbar.

If you have a network and more than one person is involved with the creation of your documents, WinWord keeps track of who owns which subdocument, based on the Author Name field of the subdocuments. Before you can edit a subdocument that someone else created, you must unlock it by clicking the Lock/Unlock button in the Master Document toolbar.

The master document and its subdocuments can be spread out across different directories and can even live on different computers if you have a network. Life is much easier, however, if you create a separate directory for just the master document and all its subdocuments. Trust me.

Creating a Master Document from Scratch

If none of the documents you want to combine by using a master document has been created yet, the best way to begin is to create the master document and all its subdocuments at one time. Then you can call up each subdocument individually to fill in the missing chapters of your book.

These steps show you the procedure for creating a master document and its subdocuments from scratch:

1. **Choose the File⇨New command.**

   Or just click the New button.

2. **Use the View⇨Master Document command.**

   You are switched into Master Document view. Because you're working with a new document, the only immediate change is that the Outlining and Master Document toolbars appear.

3. **Create a Heading 1 paragraph for the title of the master document.**

   If you're creating a book, for example, type the book's title as a Heading 1 paragraph.

4. Create a Heading 2 paragraph for each subdocument you want to create.

If each subdocument represents a chapter, type the chapter titles as Heading 2 paragraphs.

Figure 18-1 shows an example of a master document with a Heading 1 paragraph for the master document title and a Heading 2 paragraph for each subdocument title.

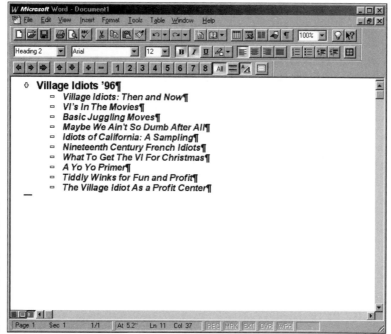

Figure 18-1:
A master document, ready to be busted up into sub-documents.

5. Select the Heading 2 paragraphs.

Drag the mouse or hold down the Shift key while moving the cursor with the arrow keys. Each Heading 2 paragraph you select is converted to a separate subdocument in the next step.

6. Click the Create Subdocument button in the Master Document toolbar.

Clicking this button tells WinWord to bust up the selected heading para-graphs into smaller subdocuments, sort of like the Justice Department would like to do to Microsoft.

7. Admire your handiwork.

Figure 18-2 shows a document that's been busted up. Notice how WinWord draws a box around each subdocument and adds a little subdocument icon in the top left corner of the box.

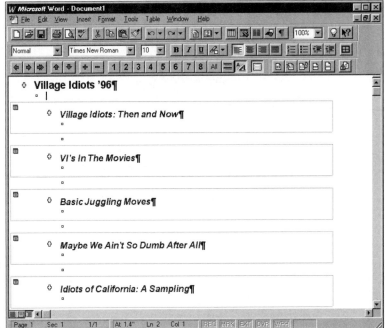

Figure 18-2:
You're
busted.

8. Use the File⇨Save command to save the files.

You have to provide the name and location of the master document. WinWord makes up names for all the subdocuments, using the first eight characters of the heading paragraph if possible.

9. You're finished.

Well, not quite. All you have is the outline of a book with a bunch of empty subdocuments. You still have to write the chapters!

Here are a few thoughts to keep in mind when you're creating a master document from scratch:

✔ You don't *have* to use the Heading 1 style for the master document title and Heading 2 for the subdocument titles. But it makes sense. WinWord examines the text you selected before clicking the Create Subdocuments button to find the first Heading paragraph. Then it creates a separate subdocument for each paragraph in the selected text that's formatted with the same heading style as the first heading. If the first heading paragraph is formatted with the Heading 3 style, WinWord creates a separate subdocument for each Heading 3 paragraph. Most of the time, it makes sense to use Heading 1 for the master document title and Heading 2 for each subdocument title.

✔ The subdocuments aren't saved until you use the File⇨Save command to save the master document. Then all the subdocuments are automatically saved in the same directory as the master document.

✔ After you've created subdocuments, you can edit a subdocument by double-clicking the little subdocument icon next to the subdocument heading. This action opens the subdocument in a separate document window and leaves the master document open in its own window, too. When you're finished editing the subdocument, save it and close the window to return to the master document window.

Inserting Existing Files into a Master Document

If you (or your buddies) have already created a bunch of smaller files that you want to combine into one larger publication, you can plug each file into a master document as a subdocument. Then you can create a table of contents or an index for the whole publication or print the publication with uninterrupted page numbers.

Follow these steps to create a master document and insert existing documents into it as subdocuments:

1. **Using the My Computer window, copy the various files you need into a single folder.**

   This step isn't strictly necessary, as it is acceptable to create a master document from subdocuments spread out all across your hard drive. But life is simpler all the way around if the master document and all its subdocucments all live together in a single folder.

2. **Run the File⇨New command.**

   Or just click the New button.

3. **Use the View⇨Master Document command.**

   You are switched into Master Document view. Because you're working with a new document, the only immediate change is that the Outlining and Master Document toolbars appear.

 4. **Click the Insert Subdocument button in the Master Document toolbar.**

   An Insert Subdocument dialog box appears. This dialog box is identical to the Open dialog box except for name.

5. **Find the file you want to insert as a subdocument, choose it, and click Open.**

   The file is inserted into the master document as a subdocument. Section breaks are created before and after it.

6. **Repeat Steps 4 and 5 for any other subdocuments you want to insert.**

7. **Use the Save command to save the master document.**

8. **You're finished.**

Here are a few points to ponder when you insert subdocuments into a master document:

- Inserting a subdocument doesn't change the subdocument file's filename or folder location.

- When you click the Insert Subdocument button, the subdocument is inserted at the position of the insertion point. Make sure that the insertion point is either at the beginning or end of the master document or between two previously inserted subdocuments. If the insertion point is within a subdocument when you click the Insert Subdocument button, the subdocument you select is inserted within the subdocument, not within the master document. If you're not careful, you can end up with subdocuments within subdocuments within subdocuments, kind of like those fancy Russian nesting dolls.

The contents of the subdocument file are not copied into the master document. Instead, a link to the subdocument file is created so that whenever you open the master document, the subdocument file is accessed also. You can still open the subdocument file separately, apart from the master document.

Breaking an Existing Document into Smaller Subdocuments

Sometimes a project just gets out of hand. It starts out as a half-page memo about where to keep spare pencils and ends up being a 300-page office-procedures manual. You obviously wouldn't use a master document for the half-page memo (unless you're really bored), but somewhere around page 100 you might wish that you had. No problem! Just bust up the big document into two or more subdocuments.

Follow these steps to break a large document into smaller subdocuments:

1. **Open the document.**

2. **Choose View⇨Master Document to switch to Master Document view.**

3. **Play with the headings to make each section of text you want to become a subdocument begin with a Heading 2 style.**

   The most logical thing is to format the document title as a Heading 1 and each subdocument as a Heading 2. You may have to use the promote and demote buttons to accomplish this. Bother.

4. **Select the range of text you want converted into subdocuments, beginning with the heading for the first subdocument and ending with the last paragraph of the last subdocument.**

 5. **Click the Create Subdocument button.**

   WinWord breaks up the document into smaller subdocuments based on the heading paragraphs. Section breaks are inserted before and after each subdocument.

6. **Call up the File⇨Save command to save your work.**

   The master document is saved, as is each of the subdocuments. WinWord retains the name of the original file for the master document and makes up names for the subdocuments, using the first eight characters of each subdocument's heading, if possible.

7. **You're finished!**

   Celebrate by taking the rest of the day off.

You can promote or demote all the headings in a document by selecting the entire document (press Ctrl+A) and clicking the promote or demote buttons in Master Document View.

You don't have to format the document title as a Heading 1 and the title of each subdocument as a Heading 2. The first paragraph of the first subdocument must be formatted with one of the heading styles, however, and the first paragraph of each subsequent subdocument must be formatted with the same heading style. Microsoft suggests using Heading 1 for the master document title and Heading 2 for each subdocument title, and although arguing with Microsoft can be fun, I see no reason to do so in this case.

Numbering Subdocument Pages Consecutively

When you use a master document, you can number all the pages of your publication consecutively. In other words, the first page of a subdocument is one greater than the last page of the subdocument that precedes it.

These steps show you the procedure:

1. Open the master document.

You can work in Normal view or Master Document view, but you have to be working with the master document, not with an individual subdocument.

 2. Call up the View⊅Header and Footer command.

WinWord temporarily throws you into Page Layout view, confines you to the header area of the page, and throws the Headers and Footers toolbar up on the screen. To add a footer rather than a header, click the Switch Between Header and Footer button.

 3. Format the header or footer to include a page number.

Type whatever text you want to include in the header or footer. To add a page number, click the Page Numbers button.

4. Click the Close button when you're happy with the header or footer.

You are returned to Normal or Master Document view.

5. Print the master document and check the page numbers.

Pretty cool, eh?

If you want each subdocument to begin on a new page, add the Page Break Before option to the Heading 2 style's Paragraph format (or whatever style you use for the title of each subdocument). The Page Break Before option is found on the Text Flow tab of the Format⊅Paragraph command.

Chapter 19

Table of Contents? Table of Figures? No Problemo!

- -

In This Chapter

▶ Formatting your document to make a table of contents easy to create

▶ Creating a table of contents

▶ Using other styles to create a table of contents

▶ Creating a table of figures or other similar table

▶ Updating tables of contents or tables of figures

- -

*1*n the old days, creating a table of contents for a book, manual, or other long document was a two-step affair. First you created the table of contents, leaving blanks or Xs where the page numbers eventually went. Then, after the pages of the document were in their final form, you browsed through the entire document, made a list of the page numbers for each chapter, and added the page numbers to the table of contents.

Now, assuming that you format your document properly, creating a table of contents is a matter of clicking the mouse a few times. WinWord takes care of the drudgery of counting pages and even adjusts the table of contents for you if you make changes to the document that affect page numbers in the table.

This chapter shows you all the ins and outs of making a table of contents. It also shows you how to create a table of figures or other type of similar table.

The term *table of contents* is a little cumbersome to use over and over again throughout this chapter. Being a bit of a computer nerd myself, I kind of like using TLAs (*t*hree-*l*etter *a*cronyms). So I frequently use the TLA *TOC* to stand for table of contents in this chapter, if for no other reason than to save paper.

Formatting Your Document to Make a Table of Contents Easy to Create

The Table of Contents feature is one of several WinWord features that depend on the proper use of styles for trouble-free operation. When you create a table of contents, WinWord searches through your document and looks for heading paragraphs to include in the table. How on earth does WinWord know which paragraphs are headings? By looking at the style you assigned to each paragraph: the heading paragraphs all should be formatted with heading styles, such as Heading 1, Heading 2, and so on.

If you plan to create a table of contents, make sure that you use heading styles to format your document's headings, especially those headings that you want to appear in the TOC. You should do this anyway, of course: it helps you to format all your headings consistently, and it lets you take advantage of WinWord's Outline view.

WinWord provides three shortcut keys for applying heading styles:

Ctrl+Alt+1	Heading 1
Ctrl+Alt+2	Heading 2
Ctrl+Alt+3	Heading 3

If you routinely use additional heading styles for additional heading levels, you can assign those styles to keyboard shortcuts, such as Ctrl+Alt+4, Ctrl+Alt+5, and so on, by using the Tools⇨Customize command (Chapter 16) or the Format⇨Style command (Chapter 2).

If you want, you can tell WinWord to use different styles to create a TOC. If you format your chapter titles with a style named Chapter Title, for example, you can tell WinWord to include paragraphs formatted with the Chapter Title style in the TOC. For more information, see the section "Using Other Styles to Create a Table of Contents" later in this chapter.

Creating a Table of Contents

If you assign heading styles to your document's headings, creating a table of contents is easy. Just follow these simple steps:

1. **Move the insertion point to the place where you want the table of contents to appear.**

   The TOC generally appears on its own page near the beginning of a document. Press Ctrl+Enter to create a new page if necessary, and click the mouse to position the insertion pointer in the empty page.

You may want to add a heading, such as Contents or Table of Contents, at the top of the page. Format this heading however you want, but don't use one of the heading styles unless you want the TOC to include the page number of the table of contents.

2. **Call up the Insert⇨Index and Tables command and click the Table of Contents tab.**

   The dialog box shown in Figure 19-1 appears.

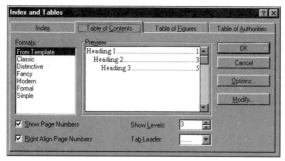

Figure 19-1: The Index and Tables: Table of Contents dialog box.

3. **Choose the Table of Contents style you want from the Formats list.**

   As you click the various formats, the Preview window shows how the resulting TOC will appear.

4. **Play with the other controls to fine-tune the table of contents.**

   Uncheck the Show Page Numbers box if you want the TOC to show the document's outline but not page numbers.

   Uncheck the Right Align Page Numbers if you want the page numbers to be placed right next to the corresponding text rather than at the right margin.

   Change the Show Levels field to include more or less detail in the table.

   Change the Tab Leader field to change or remove the dotted line that connects each TOC entry to its page number.

5. **Click OK.**

   The TOC is inserted into the document.

This list shows some things to remember when you compile a TOC:

✔ If the table of contents looks like {TOC \o "1-3" \p " "}, call up the Tools⇨Options command, click the View tab, and uncheck the Field Codes check box. When you click OK, the table ought to appear as it should.

✔ You can make changes directly to a TOC by clicking in the table and typing, but that's a bad idea because any changes you make are lost the next time you regenerate the table of contents. See the section "Updating Tables of Contents or Figures" for more information.

✔ Unfortunately, WinWord doesn't add "Chapter 1" in front of the TOC entry for Chapter 1. If you want chapter numbers to appear in your TOC, you must include them in the paragraphs formatted with a style that is included in the TOC (such as Heading 1).

✔ To delete a TOC, select the entire table and then press the Delete key. Or press Ctrl+Z immediately after creating the table.

✔ The entries in a TOC are formatted with a set of standard styles named TOC 1, TOC 2, TOC 3, and so on. If you don't like any of the predefined formats listed in the Formats list in the Index and Tables Dialog Box (see Figure 19-1), choose Custom Style from the Formats list and click the Modify button. This step takes you to a special version of the Style dialog box, in which only the standard TOC styles are shown. You can then change the appearance of the Custom Style Table of Contents format by modifying the various TOC styles.

Using Other Styles to Create a Table of Contents

Using the standard heading styles to create a table of contents is convenient but not always exactly what you want to do. What if you have created a document that consists of several chapters and you have marked the title of each chapter with a style named Chapter Title? Fortunately, WinWord lets you create a table of contents based on paragraphs formatted with any style you want, not just the standard heading styles.

To create a table of contents by using styles other than the standard heading styles, follow this procedure:

1. **Call up the Insert⇨Index and Tables command and click the Table of Contents tab.**

   The Table of Contents dialog box appears.

2. **Click the Options button.**

   The Table of Contents Options dialog box appears, as shown in Figure 19-2. This dialog box lists all the styles available in the document and lets you assign a Table of Contents level to each style.

Figure 19-2:
The Table
of Contents
Options
dialog box.

Table of Contents Options

Build Table of Contents From:
☑ Styles

Available Styles:	TOC Level
✓ Heading 1	1
✓ Heading 2	2
✓ Heading 3	3
Heading 4	
Heading 5	
Heading 6	

☐ Table Entry Fields

OK
Cancel
Reset

3. Adjust the TOC Level fields to reflect the styles you want to include in your table of contents.

The TOC Level fields initially are set to include standard heading styles, but that's easy to change. To exclude a style from the table of contents, select the style's TOC Level field and delete the number in the field. To add a style to the table of contents, choose the style's TOC Level field and type a number.

4. Click OK to return to the Table of Contents dialog box.

5. Click OK again to insert the table of contents.

Voilà! You're finished.

Keep in mind the following when using styles other than the standard style to create a table of contents:

✔ The initial settings for the TOC Level fields reflect the Show Levels setting on the Table of Contents dialog box. If you plan to exclude the standard heading levels from your table of contents, set the Show Levels field to 1 before calling up the Table of Contents Options dialog box. Then you only have to clear the TOC Level field for the Heading 1 style.

✔ If you really mess up the Table of Contents options, you can click the Reset button to return everything to normal.

✔ There's no rule that says that the styles you include in the table of contents all have to appear at different levels. Suppose that you want paragraphs formatted with the Chapter Title, Preface Title, Foreword Title, and Appendix Title styles all included in the table of contents at the top level. No problem. Just type **1** in the TOC Level field for each of these styles in the Table of Contents Options dialog box.

Only a crazy person would use fields to create a table of contents

Because of styles, compiling a table of contents in WinWord is as easy pie — as easy as popping a frozen pie in the oven, that is. The table of contents equivalent of baking a pie from scratch is using fields rather than styles to create the TOC. The only real reason to do this is if you want the text that appears in the TOC to vary slightly from the document text on which the TOC is based. You might want to add "Chapter 1" in front of the title for Chapter 1, for example.

To create a TOC from fields rather than from styles, you first must insert special TC fields throughout your document wherever you want a TOC entry created. Here are the painful steps for inserting these fields:

1. Place the Insertion Pointer where you want the TC field to be inserted.

2. Call up the Insert⇨Field command. The Field dialog box appears.

3. Choose Index and Tables from the Categories list.

4. Choose TC from the Field Names list.

5. In the Field Codes field, type the text that you want included in the TOC in quotation marks immediately after the TC field code, as shown in this example:

   TC "Chapter 1 I Am Born"

6. Click OK or press Enter.

The field is inserted in the document at the cursor location. It should look something like this:

{ TC "Chapter 1 I Am Born" }

It is formatted as hidden text, so you may not be able to see it. If you can't, call up the Tools⇨Options command, click the View tab, check the Hidden Text check box, and then click OK.

After you get all the TC fields inserted, you create the TOC by using the Insert⇨Index and Tables command, the same as when you base the TOC on styles. Click the Options button and then check the Table Entry Fields check box in the Table of Contents Options dialog box. Click OK to return to the Table of Contents dialog box, and then click OK again to compile the table.

Creating a Table of Figures or Other Similar Tables

Tables of contents aren't the only kind of tables you can create with the Insert⇨Index and Tables command. You can also use this command to compile tables of figures, tables, equations, or other similar collectibles. Chapter 20 shows how to use this command to create an index.

These steps show you how to create tables of figures or other similar tables:

1. **Use the Insert➪Caption command to create a caption for each item you want to include in the table.**

   Figure 19-3 shows the Caption dialog box. Choose the type of caption you want to create (Figure, Table, or Equation) in the Label field. Then type the caption in the Caption field. When you're finished, click OK.

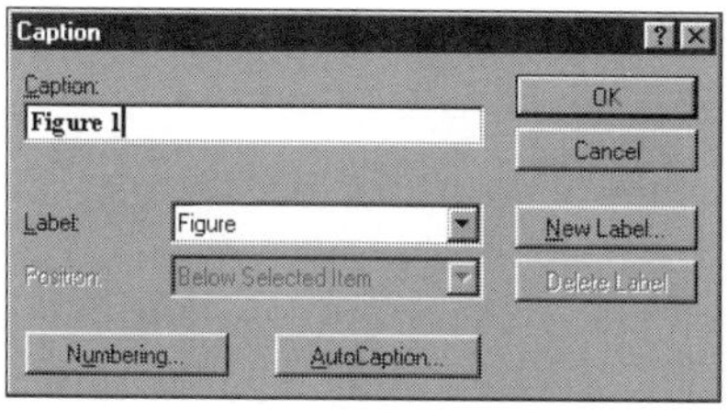

Figure 19-3:
The Caption dialog box.

2. **Move the insertion pointer to where you want the table inserted.**

3. **Call up the Insert➪Index and Tables command and click the Table of Figures tab.**

   Figure 19-4 shows the resulting dialog box.

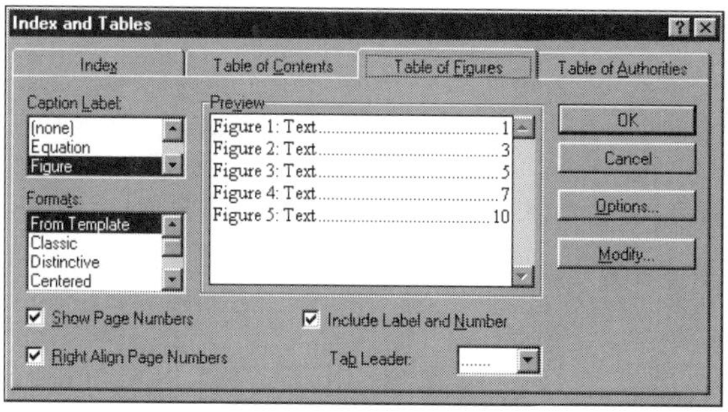

Figure 19-4:
The Index and Tables: Table of Figures dialog box.

4. Choose the type of table you want to create from the Caption Label list.

This setting corresponds to the Label setting in the Caption dialog box. To create a table of all figure captions, for example, choose Figure for the Caption Label field.

5. Choose the style you want from the Formats list.

As you click the various formats, the Preview window shows how the resulting table appears.

6. Fiddle with the other controls to fine-tune the table's appearance.

Uncheck the Show Page Numbers box if you want the table to list the captions but not page numbers.

Uncheck the Right Align Page Numbers if you want the page numbers to be placed right next to the corresponding text rather than at the right margin.

Uncheck the Include Label and Number check box if you want the table to include the caption text (for example, "A Heffalump and a Woozle" or "Ratio of Red M&Ms") but not the number (for example, Figure 1 or Table 3).

Change the Tab Leader field to add or remove the dotted line that connects each table entry with its page number.

7. Click OK.

The table is inserted into the document.

Here are some things to remember when you compile a table of figures or other similar table:

✔ If the table looks like { TOC \c "Figure" }, call up the Tools⇨Options command, click the View button, and uncheck the Field Codes check box. When you click OK, the table should appear correctly.

✔ WinWord is set up to create captions and tables for equations, figures, and tables. If you want to create other types of captions and tables — for limericks or cartoons, for example — you can add items to the list of labels that appears in the Caption and Table of Figures dialog boxes. Call up the Insert⇨Caption command and click the New Label button. Then type a new label (such as Limerick or Cartoon) and click OK. Type the caption text and click OK to insert the first caption of the new type. Later, when you call up the Insert⇨Index and Tables command and click the Table of Figures tab, the label you created appears in the Caption Label list.

✔ For more information about captions, see Chapter 13.

If you detest the Insert⇨Caption command, type your captions as separate paragraphs and create a style for them. Then call up the Insert⇨Index and Tables command, click the Table of Figures tab, and click the Options button. Check the Style check box, and choose the style you used to format the captions.

To delete a table of figures, select the entire table and then press the Delete key. Or press Ctrl+Z immediately after you create the table.

The entries in a table of figures are formatted with a standard style named Table of Figures. If you don't like any of the predefined formats listed in the Formats list in the Index and Tables dialog box, choose Custom Style and click the Modify button. This action takes you to a special version of the Style dialog box, in which only the standard Table of Figures style is shown. You can then change the appearance of the Custom Style format by modifying the Table of Figures style.

Updating Tables of Contents or Figures

As you edit your document, it's likely that a table of contents or table of figures you've created will become out of date. The page numbers might change, you might delete headings or captions, or you might insert headings or captions.

When you print your document, you can make sure that your tables are up to date in several ways:

✔ Call up the Tools⇨Options command, click the Print tab, check the Update Fields check box, and then click OK. Then tables (and other fields in the document) are automatically updated every time you print your document.

✔ To update a table without printing the document, select the table and press F9. A dialog box appears, asking whether you want to just refresh the table's page numbers or completely rebuild the table. Just refreshing the page numbers is faster, but it doesn't account for items you have added or deleted since you created the table.

✔ If you point to a table and click the right mouse button, the shortcut menu that appears includes an Update Field command. Using this command works the same as pressing F9.

✔ To update all tables in your document, press Ctrl+A to select the entire document and then press F9.

✔ Another way to update a table is to select the table and then use the Insert⇨Index and Tables command to replace the table.

Don't forget to save your file after you update the table of contents.

Chapter 20

Indexing for Fun and Profit

● ●

In This Chapter

▶ Marking index entries

▶ Creating an index

▶ Marking a range of pages

▶ Building an index from a list of words

▶ Creating subentries

▶ Creating cross-references

▶ Updating an index

● ●

*I*f all you ever use Word for is to create one- and two-page memos on mundane subjects such as how to clean the coffee maker, you can skip this chapter. After all, you don't need to index a two page memo on coffee maker cleaning unless you work for the Pentagon. If, on the other hand, your memo turns into a 200-page policy manual on appliance maintenance, an index may well be in order.

As luck would have it, Word just happens to have an indexing feature that can help you with this tedious task. It doesn't create the index for you automatically, but it does help you identify which words to include in the index, and Word compiles and formats the index from the words you mark without too much complaining.

Creating an index is a three-stage affair. First, you must mark (one at a time) all the words and phrases within your document that you want to appear in the index. Second, you call on the Insert⇨Index and Tables command to create the index. This command takes all the words and phrases you marked, sorts them in alphabetical order, and combines identical entries. Third, you carefully review the index, lament that WinWord didn't do a better job, and fix what you can.

I've indexed quite a few books in my day, and I have yet to find a word processor with an indexing feature that really does the trick. WinWord is no exception. It does a better job than any other word processors I've had the pleasure of working with, but you should still be prepared to do a ton of work yourself.

There are two ways to mark the words you want included in an index: manually, marking each word one by one, or automatically, giving WinWord a list of words you want in the index and letting it mark the words in the document.

Marking Index Entries Manually

The first — and most important — task in creating an index is to mark the words or phrases you want included in the index. The most common way to do that is to insert an index marker in the document at each occurrence of each item you want to appear in the index.

To mark index entries, follow these steps as long as you can stay awake:

1. **Open the document you want to index.**

   Use the File➪Open command.

2. **Select a word or phrase you want to put in the index.**

   Start at the beginning of the document and begin reading until you come across something worthy of an entry in the index. Then highlight it by using the mouse or keyboard.

3. **Press the keyboard shortcut Alt+Shift+X.**

   This is one of WinWord's more memorable keyboard shortcuts, to be sure. It pops up the Mark Index Entry dialog box, shown in Figure 20-1.

Figure 20-1:
The Mark
Index Entry
dialog box.

Mark Index Entry	? ✕
Main Entry: mangy mutt	Mark
Subentry:	Cancel
Options	
○ Cross-reference: See	Mark All
● Current Page	
○ Page Range	
Bookmark:	
Page Number Format: ☐ Bold ☐ Italic	
This dialog box stays open so that you can mark multiple index entries.	

4. **Double-check the contents of the Main Entry field. If it is correct, click the Mark button. Otherwise, correct it and click Mark.**

   The text does not have to appear in the index exactly as it appears in the document. You might highlight an abbreviation to include in the index, for example, but then edit the Main Entry field so that the full spelling of the word, rather than the abbreviation, appears in the index.

5. **If you want to index this entry under a different word, type the alternative entry in the Main Entry field and click the Mark button again.**

   For example, you might want to create an entry for "mutt, mangy" in addition to "mangy mutt."

6. **The Mark Index Entry dialog box remains on-screen. You can mark additional index entries by highlighting them in the document and clicking the Mark button.**

   The Mark Index Entry dialog box works somewhat like the Spelling dialog box in the way it stays on-screen so that you can efficiently mark additional index entries.

7. **When you've marked each of the index entries you want to mark, click the Close button.**

The index entries are marked with special codes formatted as hidden text so that you can't normally see them and they don't print. They are there, however, waiting to be counted when you create the index.

- ✔ The most efficient way to create an index is after you've written and edited your document. Set aside some time to work through the document with the Mark Index Entry dialog box. Don't bother to create index entries as you write your document; it just slows you down and distracts you from your primary task: writing.

- ✔ Another way to summon the Mark Index Entry dialog box is to call up the Insert⇨Index and Tables command, click the Index tab, and then click the Mark Entry button.

- ✔ If you come across a word or phrase while marking index entries that you know occurs elsewhere in your document, click the Mark All button. This action creates an index entry not only for the selected text, but also for any other occurrence of the selected text within the document.

- ✔ Each time you mark an index entry, WinWord activates the All check box of the Tools⇨Options command's View tab. This action reveals not only the hidden text used to mark index entries, but also other characters normally hidden from view, such as field codes, tab characters, optional hyphens, and so on. This behavior is normal, so don't be surprised when it happens. To return your display to normal, just click the Show/Hide button on the Standard toolbar.

- ✔ Index entries look something like this: { XE "mangy mutt" }, formatted as hidden text. You can edit the index entry text (the part between quotation marks) if you want to change an index entry after you create it.

Creating an Index

After you have marked the index entries, the process of generating the index is relatively easy. Here are the steps:

1. **Move the insertion point to the place where you want the index to appear.**

   The index generally begins on a new page near the end of the document. Press Ctrl+Enter to create a new page if necessary, and click the mouse to position the insertion pointer on the empty page. You may want to add a heading, such as Index, at the top of the page.

2. **Call up the Insert⇨Index and Tables command and click the Index tab.**

   The Index and Tables dialog box appears, as shown in Figure 20-2.

Figure 20-2:
The Index
and Tables
dialog box
(Index tab).

3. **Choose the Index style that you want from the Formats list.**

   As you click the various formats, the Preview window shows how the resulting index will appear.

4. **Play with the other controls to fine-tune the index.**

   The Type options let you place index subentries on separate indented lines (Indented) or run together (Run-in).

   Check the Right Align Page Numbers if you want the page numbers to be placed at the right edge of the index.

   Set the Columns field to the number of columns to include in the index. Two is the norm.

Change the Ta<u>b</u> Leader field to change or remove the dotted line that connects each index entry to its page number. This option is allowed only when the <u>R</u>ight Align Page Numbers option is checked.

5. Click OK.

The index is inserted into the document.

If the index looks like { INDEX \r \h "A" \c "2" }, call up the <u>T</u>ools⇨<u>O</u>ptions command, click the View button, and uncheck the <u>F</u>ield Codes check box. Click OK, and the index should appear as it should.

To delete an index, select the entire index and then press the Delete key. Or press Ctrl+Z immediately after creating the index.

The entries in an index are formatted with a set of standard styles named Index 1, Index 2, Index 3, and so on. If you don't like any of the predefined formats listed in the Forma<u>t</u>s list in the Index and Styles dialog box, choose Custom Style and click the <u>M</u>odify button. This step takes you to a special version of the Style dialog box in which only the standard Index styles are shown. You can then change the appearance of the Custom Style Index format by modifying the various Index styles.

Marking a Range of Pages

If a particular topic is discussed for several pages in your document, you might want to create an index entry that marks a range of pages (for example, *26-29*) rather than each page individually (*26, 27, 28, 29*).

Unfortunately, the procedure for marking page ranges isn't as slick as it could be. You have to mess around with a WinWord doohickey called a *bookmark*. A bookmark is a name you can assign to a selection of text. Bookmarks are usually used to mark locations in your document so that you can get to them later, but they have all sorts of more interesting uses. This is just one.

Hang on to your hat:

1. Highlight the entire range of text you want included in the index entry's page range.

For a long discussion of a single topic, this selection could go on for pages.

2. Call up the <u>E</u>dit⇨<u>B</u>ookmark command.

3. **Type a bookmark name to identify the bookmark.**

   Bookmark names can be as long as 40 characters and can be made up of any combination of letters and numbers. Spaces aren't allowed, but you can use an underscore to double as a space.

4. **Click _A_dd to create the bookmark.**

5. **Position the cursor at the beginning of the bookmark and press Alt+Shift+X.**

   This step summons the Mark Index Entry dialog box.

6. **Type the text you want to appear in the index in the Main _E_ntry text box.**

7. **Click the Current _P_age option button.**

8. **Choose the bookmark you just created from the list of bookmark names in the Bookmark drop-down list box.**

9. **Click the _M_ark button to create the index entry.**

After the bookmark and an index entry naming the bookmark have been created, the index includes the range of page numbers for the entry.

The location of various bookmarks in your document are indicated by large brackets in the text. These brackets appear only if you check the Boo_k_marks option in the _T_ools⇨_O_ptions command (View tab).

Make the bookmark name as close to identical to the index entry text as you can. Use underscore characters rather than spaces: "master_document" for "master document," for example.

Marking Index Entries Automatically from a Word List

Yet another way to create index entries is to use a word list. You just type a list of words that you want WinWord to include in the index. WinWord then creates an index entry for each occurrence of each word in the list. Sounds like a great time-saver, eh? It is, sometimes.

Here's the step-by-step procedure.

1. **Create a new document for the word list.**

2. **Type the list of words you want indexed, each on its own line.**

For example:

> Kirk
>
> Spock
>
> McCoy
>
> Scotty

3. **If you want the text in the index to be different from the text in the document, press the Tab key and then type the text exactly as you want it to appear in the index.**

For example:

> Kirk   Kirk, James T.
>
> Spock   Spock, Mr.
>
> McCoy   McCoy, Leonard H.
>
> Scotty   Scott, Montgomery

4. **Save the word list document (choose File⇨Save).**

5. **Close the word list document (choose File⇨Close).**

6. **Open the document you want indexed (choose File⇨Open).**

7. **Call up the Insert⇨Index and Tables command and click the Index tab.**

   The Index and Tables dialog box pushes its way to the front. If the Index tab isn't on top, click it to bring the indexing options into view.

8. **Click the AutoMark button.**

   A dialog box similar to the File Open dialog box appears.

9. **Find the file you saved in Step 4, choose it, and click Open.**

10. **Hold your breath while WinWord adds the index entries.**

    If your word list or the document is long, this process may take awhile. Be patient.

11. **Now select the index and press F9 to update your index with the marks added in Step 10.**

    It's done.

After the automatic index entries have been created, you probably will want to work your way through the document by creating additional index entries.

Unfortunately, the AutoMark option doesn't account for running discussions of a single topic that span several pages. It results in index entries such as "Vogons, 14, 15, 16, 17, 18" that should read "Vogons, 14-18."

When you use tabs to separate the keywords used to locate items to be indexed and the actual text you want inserted in the index for those items, keep in mind that the tab-stop positions in the word list document don't matter. I usually create a tab stop at about 1½ inches so that the two columns of information line up, but this step isn't necessary.

If you want, you can use WinWord's Table feature to create the word list. Create a two-column table and use the first column for the text to find in the document and the second column for the text to include in the index.

WinWord refers to the word list as a *concordance.* Just thought you'd want to know.

Creating Subentries

A subentry is what happens when a word is used for two different meanings or when a word serves as a category organizer for several related words. For example, you might want to create an index entry that looks like this:

crew

> Kirk, James T., 15
>
> McCoy, Leonard H., 16
>
> Scott, Montgomery, 16
>
> Spock, Mr., 17

Here, the index entries for Kirk, McCoy, Scott, and Spock are all *subentries* of the main entry, crew.

To create index subentries, you follow the normal procedure for marking index entries. You type text for both the main entry and the subentry, however, in the Mark Index Entry dialog box. Each of the index entries shown above, for example, would have "crew" for the Main Entry field and the individual crew member's name as the Subentry.

Creating Cross-References

A cross-reference is one of those annoying messages signaling that you're about to embark on a wild goose chase:

crew, *see* cast.

To create a cross-reference, begin marking an index entry as you normally would. On the Mark Index Entry dialog box, check the <u>C</u>ross-reference button and then type some text in the accompanying text box. WinWord automatically merges the cross-reference with other index entries for the same text.

Updating an Index

Whenever you edit your document, you run the risk of messing up the index. Even a slight change can push text from the bottom of one page to the top of the next and possibly invalidate the index. Fortunately, this section gives you several ways to keep your index up to date.

In the <u>T</u>ools⊄<u>O</u>ptions dialog box, click the Print tab, check the <u>U</u>pdate Fields check box, and then click OK. Then indexes are updated automatically every time you print your document.

To update an index without printing the document, select the index and press F9. If you point to the index and click the right mouse button, the shortcut menu that appears includes an Update Field command. Using this command works the same as pressing F9.

Chapter 21

I Object!
(To Tables of Authorities, That Is)

●●●

In This Chapter

▶ Marking citations

▶ Creating a table of authorities

▶ Adding your own categories

▶ Updating a table of authorities

▶ Disclaimer of warranties and limit of liability

●●●

*1*nasmuch as you, hereinafter referred to as the "Reader," has deemed it necessary, appropriate, and befitting to create, prepare, and otherwise compile a table, list, or enumeration of various and sundry citations, references, and quotations from legal authorities and other sources including but not limited to cases, statutes, rules, treatises, regulations, constitutional provisions, and other authorities occurring within and among documents, files, and other materials prepared with the word-processing software known as Word for Windows, hereinafter referred to as "WinWord," now therefore and thereupon I, hereinafter referred to as "I," agree to provide within this chapter a thorough and comprehensive description, discussion, and presentation of the techniques, methods, and procedures required to prepare such aforementioned tables, lists, or enumerations. In consideration hitherto, *e pluribus unum,* et cetera, et cetera, et cetera.

In other words, this chapter shows you how to use WinWord's Table of Authorities feature. If you're a lawyer or legal secretary, you already know what a Table of Authorities is. If you aren't, you should skip ahead to the next chapter before it's too late.

Creating a table of authorities is much like creating an index. First you mark the citations where they appear within the document. Then you use the Insert⇨Index and Tables command to compile the table of authorities based on the citations you marked. If necessary, you can then edit the table or adjust its formatting. You can also update the table to make sure that all the entries are up to date.

Marking Citations in the Document

The first step in creating a table of authorities is reviewing the entire document and marking any citations you want included in the table. Follow these steps:

1. Find a citation you want to mark.

It's best to start at the beginning of the document and work through the whole thing, marking citations as you go. You can simply read through the document to find citations or you can let WinWord find the citations for you.

2. When you find a citation you want to mark, highlight it and press Alt+Shift+I.

The Mark Citation dialog box appears, as shown in Figure 21-1.

Figure 21-1:
The Mark Citation dialog box.

3. Edit the Selected Text field so that it is exactly the way you want the citation to appear in the table of authorities.

This field initially contains the text that was selected when you pressed Alt+Shift+I. If the citation in the document is not as it should appear in the table of authorities, click in the Selected Text field and type away. If you want to split the citation into two lines, just position the cursor where you want the line to be split and press the Enter key.

4. Edit the Short Citation field so that it exactly matches the way the short version of the citation is used in subsequent references throughout the document.

The first time you cite an authority, you must provide a complete citation (such as "Kringle v. New York, 28 NY 2d 312 (1938)"), but thereafter you use the short form ("Kringle v. New York"). Edit the Short Citation field to match the short form of the citation. That way, WinWord can automatically locate subsequent citations and mark them.

5. Choose the type of authority being cited from the Category list box.

WinWord comes equipped with several common categories: Cases, Statutes, Other Authorities, Rules, Treatises, Regulations, and Constitutional Provisions. You can also create your own categories.

6. Click Mark to mark the citation.

WinWord inserts a hidden field code to mark the citation.

7. The Mark Citation dialog box stays on-screen so that you can mark additional citations. Click the Next Citation button to find the next citation.

The Next Citation button searches for text that is commonly found in citations, such as *v.*

8. Highlight the complete text of the citation found by the Next Citation button.

The Next Citation button doesn't highlight the complete citation — only the text it found that convinced it to stop because a citation is probably nearby. Use the mouse to highlight the citation in the document. (The Mark Citation dialog box patiently stays on-screen while you do this.)

9. Repeat Steps 3 through 8 until you have marked all the citations you can stand.

10. When you finish marking citations, click the Close button.

WinWord marks citations with field codes formatted as hidden text so that they are normally invisible. They jump to life, however, when you compile a table of authorities. See the next section, "Creating a Table of Authorities," for the procedure.

Another way to summon the Mark Citation dialog box is to call up the Insert⇨Index and Tables command, click the Table of Authorities tab, and then click the Mark Citation button.

If the screen suddenly changes to Print Preview mode when you try to mark a citation, the reason is that you pressed Ctrl+Alt+I rather than Alt+Shift+I. Ctrl+Alt+I is the keyboard shortcut for toggling Print Preview on and off. These two keyboard shortcuts are perilously close to one another, but don't panic if you hit the wrong one. Just press Ctrl+Alt+I again to return to Normal view and then start over.

If you stumble on a citation that you know occurs later in your document, click the Mark All button. This step creates a citation for not only the selected text, but also any subsequent occurrences of the citation.

¶ Each time you mark a citation, WinWord activates the Ⱥll check box of the
Tools⇨Ǫptions command's View tab. This step not only reveals the hidden text
used to mark citations, but also perverts the screen with dots for spaces,
paragraph and tab marks, and other obnoxious codes. To return your display
to normal, click the Show/Hide button (shown in the margin) on the Standard
toolbar.

The field codes for citations look like this:

```
{ TA \l "Kringle v. New York
28 NY 2d 312 (1938)" \s "Kringle v. New York" \c 1 }
```

These codes are formatted as hidden text, so you don't normally see them. You
can edit the long citation text (the part between quotes following \l) or the
short citation text (the quoted text that follows \s) if you want to change a
citation after you create it.

Creating a Table of Authorities

After you have marked all the citations in your document, you can follow these
steps to create the table of authorities:

1. **Move the insertion point to the place where you want the table of
   authorities to appear.**

   You can place the table of authorities at the front or back of the document.
   If you want the table to appear on its own page, press Ctrl+Enter to create
   a page break. You may also want to type a heading, such as *Table
   of Authorities*.

2. **Call up the Ịnsert⇨Indeẋ and Tables command and click the Table of
   Ⱥuthorities tab.**

   The Index and Tables dialog box appears with the table of authorities
   options in plain view, as shown in Figure 21-2.

3. **Pick the style you want from the Formaṯs list.**

   As you click the various formats, the Preⱴiew window shows how the
   resulting table of authorities appears.

4. **Play with the other controls to fine-tune the table of authorities.**

   Check the Use Ṗassim box if you want WinWord to use the word *Passim*
   when a citation occurs on five or more pages. (*Passim* is a Latin word that
   means "scattered throughout," not an ugly, overgrown, ratlike creature
   that hangs upside down by its tail.)

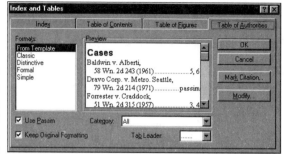

Check the Keep Original Formatting box if you want character formatting (such as underline and italics) applied to the citation as it appears in the document to be carried over into the table of authorities.

In the Category list box, choose the citation category you want compiled. Usually you leave this field set to the default, All. If you want to compile a table of one category (cases, rules, regulations, and so on), choose the category from the drop-down list.

Change the Tab Leader field to change or remove the dotted line that connects each citation to its page number.

5. Click OK.

The table of authorities is created.

The remainder of this section tells you some things to remember when you compile a table of authorities:

- ✔ If the table of authorities looks like { TOA \h \c "1" \p }, call up the Tools➪Options command, click the View button, and uncheck the Field Codes check box. Click OK and the table should appear as it should.

- ✔ To delete a table of authorities, select the entire table and then press the Delete key. Or press Ctrl+Z immediately after creating the table.

- ✔ The entries in a table of authorities are formatted with a standard style name (Table of Authorities), and the headings for categories are formatted by using a style named TOA Heading. If none of the predefined formats listed in the Formats list tickles your fancy, choose Custom Style and click the Modify button. This action takes you to a special version of the Style dialog box in which only the standard table of authorities styles are shown. You can customize the Custom Style format by modifying the Table of Authorities and TOA Heading styles.

Updating a Table of Authorities

If you edit a document after creating a table of authorities, the table may become out-of-date. To make sure that the table is up-to-date, use one of these techniques:

✔ In the Tools⇨Options command, click the Print tab, check the Update Fields check box, and then click OK. Then the table of authorities is automatically updated every time you print your document.

✔ To update a table of authorities without printing the document, select the table and press F9.

✔ If you point to a table of authorities and click the right mouse button, the shortcut menu that appears includes an Update Field command. Using this command works the same as pressing F9.

Disclaimer of Warranties and Limit of Liability

The author, Doug Lowe, and IDG Books Worldwide, Inc., make no representations or warranties with respect to the accuracy or completeness of the contents of this chapter and specifically disclaim any implied warranties or merchantability or fitness for any particular purpose and shall in no event be held liable for any loss of profit or any other commercial damage, including but not limited to such damages as losing a big case because of a key citation's being omitted from a pleading or a brief; tripping, falling, or stumbling over this book; or the cost of medical treatment and/or hospitalization, pain and suffering, lost wages, or emotional anguish due to stress inflicted or sustained while using or attempting to use the Table of Authorities feature in the Word for Windows 95 software program. So let it be written, so let it be done.

Chapter 22

Field of Dreams
(The Insert Field Command)

· ·

· ·

A *field* is a special placeholder code that tells WinWord to insert something — usually text of some sort — into the document. A date field, for example, tells WinWord to insert the current date into the document. No matter when you edit or print the document, the date field causes the document to contain the current date.

Fields are everywhere in WinWord. Many of the commands you have come to know and love rely on fields to do their business. Fields let you put the page number in a header or footer, create a table of contents or an index, and print mail-merged letters. These fields get inserted into your document by accident, as a result of your using some other command, such as Insert⇨Page Numbers or Tools⇨Mail Merge.

This chapter shows you what you need to know to insert fields on purpose, by using the Insert⇨Field command. WinWord provides mass quantities of different types of fields (more than 60). As an act of kindness, this chapter doesn't go into the boring details of all of them. It does conclude, however, by showing you how to use ten of the most popular fields.

Be warned that fields can be a source of severe mental anguish. I should have titled this chapter *Field of Nightmares*. Fortunately, you don't have to read this chapter if you don't what to. This stuff is all very optional.

Understanding Fields

A *field* is a code that WinWord translates into text, which is then inserted into the document. When you insert a date field, for example, you're really saying to WinWord, "Insert the current date right here, and make sure that you get the date right. When I print this document, I want to see today's date. If I print it tomorrow, I want to see tomorrow's date. Next week, I want to see next week's date. A year from now. . . ." You get the idea. A date field is like a placeholder for an actual date, which WinWord inserts automatically.

Other fields work in the same way. The text WinWord inserts in place of the field code is called the *result.* For a date field, the result is the current date. For a page-number field, the result is the current page number. Other field types produce more complicated results, such as a table of contents or an index. For some fields, the result isn't text at all, but a picture or a chart.

When you print a document, there's no way to distinguish between text you typed directly into the document and text that is a field result. Consider, for example, the following text you might use in a letter:

> As of today, Saturday, April 02, 1996, you have been banished from Remulak and sentenced to live out the remainder of your existence among the Blunt Skulls of Earth.

You can't tell that *Saturday, April 02, 1996* is a field result.

When you edit a document in WinWord, you must have some way to distinguish between regular text and field results. WinWord normally displays field results so that the document appears on-screen just as it does when you print it. If the result isn't quite what you expected, however, or if you want to make sure that you used the correct field to produce a result, you can switch the display to show field codes. WinWord also has an option that displays field results but shades them so that you can distinguish field results from ordinary text.

The preceding letter fragment with field codes displayed looks like this:

> As of today, { TIME \@ "dddd, MMMM dd, yyyy" }, you have been banished from Remulak and sentenced to live out the remainder of your existence among the Blunt Skulls of Earth.

The field is the stuff marked by the curly braces ({ }), which are called *field characters.* Their whole purpose in life is to tell WinWord that a field lives here. They look just like the curly braces you can type from the keyboard, but they're not. The only way you can create these field characters is by using the Insert⇨Field command or some other WinWord command that inserts a field.

Trapped between the field characters is the field itself. Each field begins with a *field type* that tells you what type of field you're dealing with. In the preceding example, you're looking at a TIME field, which provides the current date or time in any of about six million formats.

Following the field type are *instructions,* which tell the field what to do. The TIME field in the preceding example contains an instruction that tells WinWord how to format the time: *dddd, MMMM dd, yyyy.* The hard part about using fields is figuring out what to do with the instructions. Each field type has its own gang of instruction codes.

Inserting a Field

Many WinWord commands, such as Insert➪Date and Time and Insert➪Index and Tables, quietly insert fields into your document without boasting. But WinWord provides many other fields you can insert only by using the Insert➪Field command.

Follow this procedure to insert a field in your document:

1. Move the cursor to the point where you want the field to be inserted.

2. Call up the Insert➪Field command.

The Field dialog box appears, as shown in Figure 22-1.

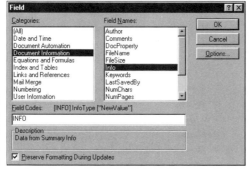

Figure 22-1:
The Field
dialog box.

3. Choose the field type you want by scrolling through the Categories and Field Names lists.

Because mass quantities of field types exist, WinWord breaks them down into categories to make them easier to find. When you choose a category from the Categories list, the Field Names list is updated to list only the field types in the chosen category. If you're not sure which category contains the field you want to insert, choose All as the category. This action lists all WinWord's field types in the Field Names list.

4. In the Field Codes box, add any additional instructions required by the field.

WinWord automatically adds the field type to the Field Codes text box. Then it gives you a hint about how to complete the field code by listing, just above the Field Codes box, which instructions the selected field type accepts. Look back at Figure 22-1. You can see that WinWord added the field type INFO to the Field Codes box and shows that you can include an InfoType (whatever that is) and a NewValue (huh?). This is very helpful, if you happen to know what an InfoType and NewValue are.

5. If you're stumped by Step 4, click the Options button.

A Field Options dialog box appears, which looks something like Figure 22-2. Now we're getting somewhere.

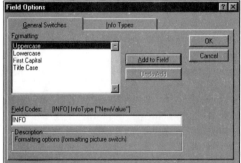

Figure 22-2:
The Field
Options
dialog box.

6. Add options to the field codes by choosing an option you want to add in the Name list and then clicking Add to Field.

The Field Options dialog box sort of resembles a salad bar. You get to peruse the day's offerings (they're different for each field) and add just the ones you want. Every time you click the Add to Field button, the selected option is added to the Field Codes box. Also, a concise description of each field option is at the bottom of the Field Options dialog box.

7. Click OK when you have added all the options you can carry in one trip.

You are returned to the Field dialog box.

8. Click OK to insert the field into the document.

The field is inserted into the document.

Here are some deep thoughts to consider as you meditate on the finer points of inserting fields:

✔ When you insert a field, either the field code or the result is displayed, depending on whether the Fields Codes view option is set. You can switch between field codes and field results by pressing Alt+F9.

✔ A whole bevy of specialized keyboard shortcuts are available for working with fields. They are summarized for your convenience in Table 22-1.

Table 22-1	Keyboard Shortcuts for Fields
Keyboard Shortcut	*What It Does*
F9	Updates the selected field or fields
Shift+F9	Switches the display between field codes and field results for the selected field or fields
Alt+F9	Switches the display between field codes and field results for all fields in the document
Ctrl+F9	Inserts a field into a document
Ctrl+Shift+F9	Converts a field to text (unlinks the field)
F11	Finds the next field in the document
Shift+F11	Finds the previous field in the document
Ctrl+F11	Locks a field so that it cannot be updated
Ctrl+Shift+F11	Unlocks a field

If you get something like `Error!Unknown switch argument` rather than the field result you expected, you made a mistake when you composed the field instructions. You have to edit the field directly by pressing Alt+F9 to reveal the field codes and then clicking in the field and typing your correction.

Formatting Field Results with Switches

WinWord provides a gaggle of switches that you can use on most any field to control the formatting applied to the field result. You don't have to use any of these fields if you don't want to. If you omit them, WinWord makes an educated guess about the format of the field result.

You can use three switches to format a field's result:

- ✔ The Format switch, *, tells WinWord whether to capitalize the results field and, for fields that produce numeric results, which type of numbers to create (Arabic or Roman numerals, for example).
- ✔ The Numeric Picture switch, \#, controls the format of numbers.
- ✔ The Date-Time Picture switch, \@, sets the format of dates and times.

Each of these switches has numerous options you can mix and match to format the field in just about any way you want. The various uses of these three switches are explained in the following sections.

The nerdy way to insert a field

If you have a fetish for typing complicated commands, you can insert a field by typing it directly in your document. Just follow these steps:

1. Position the cursor where you want the field to be inserted.

2. Type the field name and instructions for the field you want to insert. Don't worry about the curly braces for now.

3. Select the text you typed in Step 2.

4. Press Ctrl+F9.

Ctrl+F9 converts the selected text to a field by enclosing it in those curly little braces called field codes that look just like the curly braces you can type on the keyboard but aren't the same thing at all. If you prefer, you can reverse these steps: position the cursor where you want the field to be placed and press Ctrl+F9; an empty field appears, which you can select. Then you can type the field name and instructions within the braces.

Preserving formatting when you update fields: the * mergeformat switch

When you update a field, WinWord usually removes any formatting, such as bold or italics, that you have applied to a field result. If you want WinWord to keep this type of formatting, include the * mergeformat switch in the field. It's usually a good idea to preserve formatting, so I recommend using this switch.

You can tell WinWord to automatically add a * mergeformat switch to a field by checking the Preserve Formatting During Updates check box in the Field dialog box.

If you're not sure what I mean by "updating a field," skip ahead to the section, "Updating a Field."

I almost always use this switch. You see it in all the field examples in the rest of this chapter, so get used to it.

Capitalizing field results

Use the Format switch (*) options listed in Table 22-2 to control capitalization in a field result. The following field, for example, inserts the name of the current file in lowercase letters:

{ filename * lower * mergeformat }

Table 22-2	Capitalizing Field Results
Switch	**What It Means**
* caps	The First Letter Of Each Word Is Capitalized
* firstcap	The first letter of the first word is capitalized
* lower	all the letters are lowercase
* upper	ALL THE LETTERS ARE UPPERCASE

Using strange number formats

Numbers are usually displayed by using Arabic numerals. You can change the format of numbers in field results, however, by using the switches listed in Table 22-3. Consider this text, for example:

> This is the { page * ordtext * mergeformat } page.

This line produces a result like this:

> This is the thirty-third page.

In this case, the * ordtext switch caused the page number to be spelled out as a number.

Table 22-3	Using Strange Number Formats
Switch	**What It Means**
* alphabetic	Converts numbers to their corresponding letters of the alphabet (*1* becomes *A, 2* becomes *B,* and so on)
* arabic	The usual number format (nothing special here)
* cardtext	Spells out the number (for example, *1994* becomes *one thousand nine-hundred ninety-four*)
* dollartext	Spells out a dollar amount the way you would write it on a check (*289.95* becomes *two hundred eighty-nine and 95/100*)
* hex	A favorite of computer nerds, converts numbers from the normal earth dweller base 10 numbering system to base 16 (for example, *492* becomes *1EC*)
* ordinal	Adds *st, nd, rd,* or whatever is appropriate to the end of the number (for example, *307* becomes *307th*)
* ordtext	Spells out the number and adds *st, nd, rd,* or whatever is appropriate to the end (for example, *307* becomes *three hundred seventh*)
* roman	Converts the number to Roman numerals; used by film directors to mark copyright dates (for example, *1953* becomes *mcmliii*)

Creating custom number formats

If you don't like the way WinWord displays numbers, you can create your own custom number formats by using the Numeric Picture switch (\#). Numeric pictures are created by stringing together a bunch of pound signs, zeros, commas, decimal points, plus or minus signs, dollar signs, and other characters to show how you want numbers to appear. Rather than show you the individual characters you can use, Table 22-4 lists the numeric picture switches you're most likely to use.

You can automatically add the numeric pictures listed in Table 22-4 to formulas if you use the Table⇨Formula command rather than the Insert⇨Field command to create the formula. The Table⇨Formula command provides a drop-down list box that lists these pictures; you just choose the number format you want, and WinWord inserts the appropriate switch into the field. For more information about the Table⇨Formula command, see Chapter 9.

Table 22-4	Sample Numeric Picture Switches
Picture Switch	*Description*
\# #,##0	Prints whole numbers with commas to separate groups of thousands (for example, 1,024 and 1,244,212)
\# #,##0.00	Prints numbers with commas to separate groups of thousands and two decimal positions; both decimal positions are printed even if one or both of them is zero (for example, 1,024.00 and 8.47)
\# $#,##0.00;($#,##0.00)	Prints numbers as money: commas to separate groups of thousands, two decimal positions, and a leading dollar sign; negative numbers are enclosed in parentheses — for example, $1,024.00 and ($97.38)
\# 0	Prints whole numbers without commas (for example, 38 and 124873345)
\# 0%	Prints whole numbers without commas, followed by a percent sign (for example, 98%)
\# 0.00	Prints numbers without commas but with two decimal positions (for example, 1024.00 or 3.14)
\# 0.00%	Prints numbers without commas, with two decimal positions, and followed by a percent sign (for example, 97.99%)

Creating custom date and time formats

When you use the Insert⇨Field command to insert a date field, you can click the Options button and choose from one of 14 different formats. If you don't like any of the 14 formats, you can compose your own custom date format by using the Date-Time Picture switch (\@). You just string together the various components of the date or time by using combinations of characters, such as MMM to stand for the three-letter month abbreviation, and dddd to stand for the day of the week, spelled out.

Frankly, creating custom date and time formats by using the \@ is a bit off the deep end. If none of the 14 date formats listed in the Field Options dialog box for date fields doesn't satisfy you, you have to learn to be less picky.

Updating a Field

When you first insert a field, WinWord calculates the field's result. Thereafter, the field result may become out of date. To recalculate a field result to make sure that it is up to date, follow one of these procedures:

- ✔ Call up the Tools⇨Options command and choose the Print tab. Check the Update Fields check box and then click OK. This action tells WinWord to automatically update all fields every time it prints the document.

- ✔ To update a specific field, select the field and press F9. If you select several fields, pressing F9 updates all of them. You can quickly update all the fields in a document by pressing Ctrl+A to select the entire document and then pressing F9 to update the fields.

- ✔ If you point to a field and click the right mouse button, a shortcut menu appears. Choose the Update Field command from this menu to update the field.

Preventing a Field from Being Updated

If you do *not* want a field to be updated, you can either lock the field or unlink the field. If you lock the field, WinWord prevents it from being updated until you *unlock* the field. If you *unlink* the field, WinWord deletes the field code and replaces it with the result text. Locking a field prevents it temporarily from being updated; unlinking the field is permanent.

To lock, unlock, or unlink a field, first select it. Then use the keyboard shortcuts found in Table 22-5.

Table 22-5 Keyboard Shortcuts for Locking, Unlocking, or Unlinking a Field

Keyboard Shortcut	What It Does
Ctrl+F11	Locks the field
Ctrl+Shift+F11	Unlocks the field
Ctrl+Shift+F9	Converts the field to results text (unlinks the field)

Chapter 23

Revisionist History (The Politician's Favorite WinWord Feature)

- -

In This Chapter

▶ Tracking revisions as you make them

▶ Accepting revisions

▶ Comparing document versions

- -

*W*ouldn't it be great if you could quickly see what changes have been made to a document? It would be a great help to anyone in charge of maintaining corporate bylaws, legal documents, records about investments in failed savings and loans, congressional testimony, and so on.

With WinWord's revision marks, you can! Revision marks let you indicate what changes have been made to a document. Any text that is deleted is shown with a line running through it (*strikethrough*). Text that has been inserted is underlined. And any line that contains a change is marked with a vertical line in the margin, so you can quickly scan through a document to find changes. Figure 23-1 shows an example of a document with revision marks. This chapter shows you how to create revision marks like these.

 WinWord displays revision marks in a different color, generally blue. I tried to convince IDG Books to print this book in color so that Figure 23-1 would show how stunning the revision marks appear on-screen. They said that they would be happy to, but that the additional cost of color printing would be deducted from my royalty check. Given the choice between blue revision marks or groceries, I opted for groceries. Sorry.

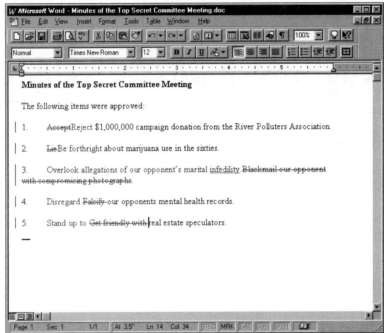

Figure 23-1:
A document
with revision
marks.

Tracking Revisions as You Make Them

The easiest way to create revision marks is to turn on the revision-marking feature before you begin editing your document. Then WinWord keeps track of revisions as you make them. You can then print the document with or without the revision marks, and you can later accept or reject the revisions.

Follow these steps to begin marking revisions:

1. Call up the Tools⇨Revisions command.

The Revisions dialog box appears, as shown in Figure 23-2.

Figure 23-2:
The
Revisions
dialog box.

2. Check the Mark Revisions While Editing check box.

This step causes WinWord to keep track of the revisions you make while editing the document.

3. If you do not want the revisions to appear on-screen while you edit the document, uncheck the Show Revisions on Screen check box.

The revision marks normally appear on the screen as you type. This can be annoying, so you may want to uncheck this box. As long as the Mark Revisions While Editing check box is checked, WinWord tracks revisions whether or not the revision marks are shown on-screen.

4. If you do not want the revision marks to be printed, uncheck the Show Revisions in Printed Document check box.

Revision marks are usually printed when you print the document. Uncheck this box to omit the revision marks when the document is printed. You can always check this box later to print the document with revision marks.

5. Click Open.

The Revisions dialog box is whisked away. The letters MRK are highlighted in the status bar at the bottom of the screen to remind you that revisions are being tracked.

To disable revision marking, call up the Tools⇨Revisions command again, uncheck the Mark Revisions While Editing check box, and click OK. I sometimes do this to correct a simple and obvious typographical error that doesn't need to be highlighted by a revision mark. Then I turn revision marking back on again.

You can quickly call up the Revisions dialog box by double-clicking the letters MRK in the status bar.

What are all those other buttons on the Revisions dialog box? I'll get to them later.

The three check boxes in the Revisions dialog box work independently of one another. Mark Revisions While Editing tells WinWord whether to keep track of revisions while you edit your document. The other two control whether revisions marks are displayed or printed.

If you click the Options button in the Revisions dialog box, WinWord lets you customize the highlighting and colors used to mark inserted text, deleted text, and changed lines.

Accepting or Rejecting Revisions

When you have accumulated a bunch of revision marks, sooner or later you will want to accept or reject the revisions. If you accept the revisions, the changes are permanently incorporated into the document, and the revision marks are removed. If you reject the changes, the document reverts to its previous state and the revisions are deleted along with the revision marks.

To accept or reject revisions, follow these steps:

1. Call up the Tools⇨Revisions command.

Or double-click MRK on the status bar. Either way, the Revisions dialog box appears.

2. Click Accept All to accept all revisions, or Reject All to reject all revisions.

Either way, WinWord asks you a confirming question, such as "Are you nuts?" Click Yes to continue.

3. Click the Close button.

You are returned to your document.

Skim through your document to confirm that revisions have indeed been accepted or rejected as you intended. It should be obvious.

If you have second thoughts, press Ctrl+Z. The revision marks are restored.

Revision marks accumulate in a document until you either accept or reject them. You can therefore collect a set of revision marks over a period of days or weeks and then deal with them all by accepting or rejecting them.

If you would rather accept or reject revision marks one by one, click the Review button. This action calls up the Review Revisions dialog box, shown in Figure 23-3. From this dialog box, you can click one of the Find buttons to find the next or previous revision mark and then click Accept or Reject to dispense with the revision. To streamline the search even more, check the Find Next After Accept/Reject check box. Then WinWord automatically moves to the next revision mark after you click Accept or Reject.

Figure 23-3:
The Review
Revisions
dialog box.

Review Revisions	? X
Description	Hide Marks Cancel
Replaced By: Doug Lowe	
Date: 12/26/95 9:12 AM	Undo Last
← Find Find → Accept Reject ☐ Find Next After Accept/Reject	

Comparing Document Versions

WinWord tracks revisions only when you activate revision marks with the Tools⊅Revisions command. If you forget to activate revision marking, you can still re-create revision marks by comparing a document with an earlier version of the same document. WinWord does its best to mark text that has been inserted or deleted from the older version of the document.

Follow these steps to compare documents:

1. **Open the newer version of the two documents you want to compare.**

2. **Call up the Tools⊅Revisions command.**

    The Revisions dialog box appears.

3. **Click the Compare Versions button.**

    The Compare Versions dialog box appears, which looks almost like the Open File dialog box.

4. **Choose the file to which you want to compare the current file.**

    In other words, choose the older version of the file you opened in Step 1.

5. **Click OK.**

WinWord compares the files and automatically inserts revision marks in the newer document.

Don't expect WinWord to insert revision marks perfectly when it compares documents. WinWord is good at marking minor revisions, but some revisions may confuse WinWord and cause it to insert wacky revision marks. It's better to mark revisions as you make them, if possible.

You can call up the Tools⊅Revisions command and click the Review button to selectively accept or reject revisions after comparing the documents.

Chapter 24

Say, AI, What Do You Think of This? (Using the Annotation Feature)

*T*he annotation feature lets other people add commentary to your document, which you can later say that you reviewed and carefully considered before rejecting their suggestions as ludicrous. It's a great feature to use if you want people to think that you're a team player or if you want to foster the appearance of cooperative work. Heck, it's also a good feature to use if you really do want to be a team player or if you want to work cooperatively with your cohorts.

Inserting Annotations

An *annotation* is a way of commenting on a part of a document without modifying the document. When you insert an annotation, WinWord adds a hidden annotation mark to the text at the location of the annotation and then adds your comments to a separate *Annotation Pane,* which is keyed to the annotation marks in much the same way as footnotes are keyed to footnote marks. You can then come back later and view each of the comments.

To insert an annotation, follow these steps:

1. Select the text you want to comment on.

If the text is really long, just move the cursor to the end of the text. If you select the text before creating the annotation, WinWord highlights the text later when you display the annotation.

2. Use the <u>I</u>nsert⇨<u>A</u>nnotation command.

Or just press Ctrl+Alt+A. Either way, an annotation mark is inserted as hidden text following the text you selected. Then the screen is split in two, revealing the annotations in the bottom portion of the screen. WinWord refers to this as the Annotation Pane, and it's right. Figure 24-1 shows a WinWord screen with the Annotation Pane visible.

3. Type your comments.

They are added to the Annotation Pane at the correct position.

4. Click the <u>C</u>lose button to dismiss the Annotation Pane and return to the document.

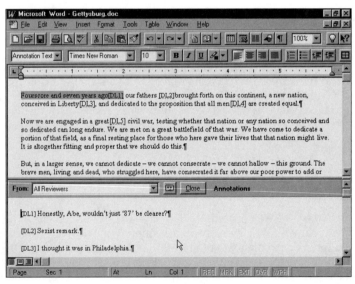

Figure 24-1:
The
Annotation
pane.

This list that follows shows some things to keep in mind when you insert annotations:

- ✔ Notice how the annotation marks in the document are keyed to annotations in the Annotation Pane. WinWord uses your initials (it gets them from the User Info options), followed by a sequence number. For example, the first annotation I created in Figure 24-1 is identified as DL1; the second is DL2; and so on. Under this scheme, several people can add annotations to a document, and you can easily determine which comment came from each person.

- ✔ If you're going to insert a bunch of annotations, you can leave the annotation pane open. After typing an annotation, just click the mouse anywhere in the document. Both the Document Pane and the Annotation Pane remain visible. Find the next bit of text you want to comment on, select it, and press Ctrl+Alt+A to insert another annotation.

- ✔ If you have a sound card, a microphone, and more disk space than you know what to do with, you can add a voice annotation by clicking the cassette-tape button in the Annotation Pane.

- ✔ If you can't say something nice, don't say nothin' at all.

Viewing Annotations

To view annotations that have been added to a document, open the Annotation Pane by using the View⇨Annotations command. You can then scroll through the Document Pane or the Annotation Pane to look at annotations along with the corresponding document text. Notice that as you scroll through either pane, the other pane is scrolled in sync. When you select an annotation by clicking it in the Annotation Pane, the Document Pane is scrolled to the text to which the annotation refers, and the referenced text is highlighted.

If the document contains annotations created by more than one user, you can restrict the Annotation Pane so that it shows just that user's comments by choosing that user from the From drop-down list. To display all annotations regardless of who inserted them, select All Reviewers.

If you want to copy an annotation directly into the document, select the annotation text you want to copy. Press Ctrl+C, click in the document at the location where you want the text inserted, and then press Ctrl+I.

If the Annotation Pane is too big or too small, you can change its size. Hold the mouse steady over the top edge of the Annotation Pane for a moment, and the mouse cursor changes to a double arrow. Then you can hold down the left mouse button and drag the Annotation Pane up or down to increase or decrease its size.

There is no keyboard shortcut to go to the next annotation. WinWord does have a GoToNextAnnotation command, however, which you can assign to a keyboard shortcut if you are brave enough to tackle the Tools➪Customize command. (See Chapter 16 if you have the nerve.) WinWord also has a GoToPreviousAnnotation command.

You can print annotations by calling up the Tools➪Options command, clicking the Print tab, and checking the Annotations check box. Then when you print the document, the hidden text that marks the annotation locations is printed along with the document, and the annotations are printed on a separate page after the document has been printed. In addition, the annotations page includes the page number to which each annotation refers. (If you want to print just the annotations page without printing the document, call up the File➪Print command and select Annotations for the Print What field.)

Removing Annotations

To remove an annotation, highlight the hidden annotation mark in the document text and press the Delete key. If the annotation marks aren't displayed, click the Show/Hide Paragraph button on the Standard toolbar. Believe it or not, WinWord doesn't provide a quick way to wipe out all annotations in a document. To delete all annotations, you have to delete each one individually.

It's a route!

If you have a network and the right electronic-mail software, you can use WinWord's routing feature to send a document to other network users so that they can add their comments. To route a document to other users, open the document and use the File➪Add Routing Slip command to select the names of the users to which you want the document sent. Click Route to send the document.

WinWord gives you the option of sending the document to several users one at a time or all at one time. If you send the document to one user at a time, the first user on the list receives the document first. When that user is finished with the document, the document is forwarded to the second user, and then the third, and so on.

In this way, each user can add annotations or revisions to the document.

If you send the document to all users at one time, you can request that each user return the annotated or revised document to you. Then WinWord merges the revisions and annotations from each copy of the document. When you send a document to several users at a time, you should select the Protect for Annotations option so that the users are allowed to add annotations but not revise the document. Allowing more than one user at a time to revise a document is not a good idea. It's too much like that episode of "Gilligan's Island" in which each of the castaways puts a sleeping pill in Gilligan's tea, unaware that the others have done the same thing.

Chapter 25

Move Over, Einstein (Creating Equations)

. . . .

In This Chapter

▶ Creating an equation

▶ Editing an equation

▶ Adding text to an equation

. . . .

Steven Hawking wrote in the preface to his book, *A Brief History of Time,* that his editor warned him that every mathematical equation he included in the book would cut the book's sales in half. So he included just one: the classic *e=mc²*. See how easy that equation was to type? The only trick was remembering how to format the little two as a superscript.

My editor promised me that every equation I included in this book would double its sales, but I didn't believe her, not even for a nanosecond. Just in case, Figure 25-1 shows some examples of the equations you can create by using WinWord's handy-dandy Equation Editor program. You wouldn't even consider trying to create these equations by using ordinary text, but they took me only a few minutes to create by using Equation Editor. Aren't they cool? Tell all your friends about the cool equations you saw in this book so that they'll all rush out and buy copies for themselves. Or better yet, read this chapter to learn how to create your own knock-'em-dead equations, and then try to convince your friends that you understand what they mean.

Introducing Equation Editor

Equation Editor is a special version of a gee-whiz math program called MathType, from Design Science. Equation Editor also comes with Microsoft PowerPoint for Windows 95. If you have PowerPoint and already know how to use its Equation Editor, you're in luck — they're identical.

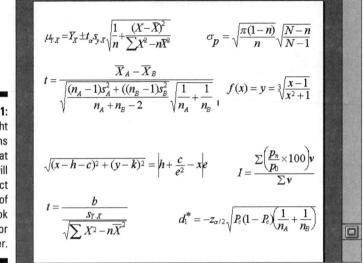

Figure 25-1:
Eight equations that probably will not affect the sales of this book one way or another.

If you've read my book, *PowerPoint For Windows 95 For Dummies,* you've already read this chapter. So you can skip it here.

You don't have to know anything about math to use Equation Editor. I don't have a clue what any of the equations in Figure 25-1 do, but they sure look great, don't they?

Don't forget to tell your friends how great the equations in Figure 25-1 are. They alone are worth the price of the book.

Equation Editor has its own, complete help system. After you're in Equation Editor, press F1 or use the Help command to call up complete information about using it.

Creating an Equation

To add an equation to a document, follow these steps:

1. **Use the Insert⇨Object command.**

   The Object dialog box appears, as shown in Figure 25-2.

2. **Choose Microsoft Equation 2.0 from the Object Type list and then click OK.**

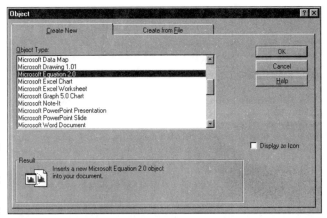

Figure 25-2:
The Object
dialog box.

This step summons Equation Editor, which argues with WinWord for a few
moments about who's really in charge. Then it replaces WinWord's menus
with its own and pops up a floating toolbar that's chock-full of mathematical doohickies (see Figure 25-3).

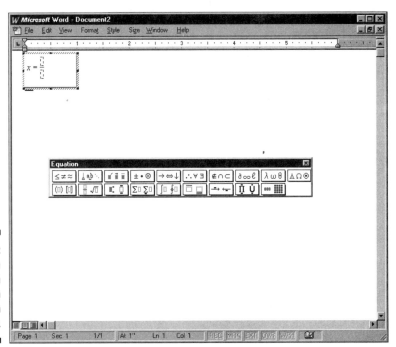

Figure 25-3:
Creating an
equation
with
Equation
Editor.

A *floating toolbar* is nothing more than a window jammed full of toolbar buttons. Floating toolbars have a nasty habit of getting in the way, but you can move them by dragging them by their title bars.

3. **Start typing your equation.**

The variables and basic operators, such as plus and minus signs, are easy enough. But how do you get those fancy symbols, like square root and summation? The answer lies in the floating Equation toolbar.

4. **To add a symbol that's not on the keyboard, use one of the buttons in the top row of the Equation toolbar.**

Each button yields a menu of symbols, most of which only Robert Oppenheimer could understand. There's nothing special about the tools in the top row of the Equation toolbar; they simply insert special characters into your equation. The magic of Equation Editor lies in the bottom row on the toolbar, which lets you build the parts of the equation that have elements stacked on top of one another, such as fractions, superscripts, and roots.

5. **To add a stacked symbol, use one of the buttons in the bottom row of the Equation toolbar.**

Each button in the bottom row of the toolbar is attached to a menu of *templates,* which you use to create stacked symbols (not to be confused with document templates, which are altogether different). Most templates include a symbol and one or more *slots,* in which you type text or insert other symbols. Back in Figure 25-3, for example, I used a template to create a fraction. You can see that the fraction template consists of a horizontal stroke with a slot for the numerator above and the denominator below.

To complete this fraction, I can type a number in each slot. Or I can add another symbol or template to make the equation more interesting. Most equations consist of templates nestled within the slots of other templates. The beauty of it is that Equation Editor adjusts the equation on the fly as you add text or other templates to fill a slot. If you type something like ax^2+bx+c in the top slot, for example, Equation Editor stretches the fraction bar accordingly.

To move from one template slot to the next, press the Tab key.

6. **When you're finished, click anywhere outside the equation.**

Equation Editor bows out, enabling WinWord to restore its menus and toolbars. You can now drag the equation object to change its size or location.

Confused? I don't blame you. After you latch on to the idea behind templates and slots, you can slap together even the most complex equations in no time. But the learning curve here is steep. Stick with it.

- The *denominator* is the bottom part of a fraction, not an Arnold Schwarzenegger movie.

- Sometimes Equation Editor leaves droppings behind and obscures the clean appearance of the equation. When that happens, use the View➪Redraw command to clean up the equation.

- Spend some time exploring the symbols and templates available on the toolbar. There's enough stuff here to write an entire book about building your own atomic bomb. (*Note:* None of the equations in Figure 25-1 has anything to do with atomic bombs. Honest. I stole them all from a statistics book.)

Editing an Equation

To edit an equation, follow these steps:

1. **Double-click the equation.**

   This step summons Equation Editor. If double-clicking doesn't work, select the equation and choose Edit➪Equation Object.

2. **Make your changes.**

   Add stuff, delete stuff, move stuff around. Indulge yourself.

3. **Click outside the equation when you're finished.**

All the standard Windows editing tricks work in Equation Editor, including the Ctrl+X, Ctrl+C, and Ctrl+V shortcuts for cutting, copying, and pasting text.

Adding Text to an Equation

Equation Editor watches any text you type in an equation and does its level best to figure out how the text should be formatted. If you type the letter *x,* for example, Equation Editor assumes that you intend for the *x* to be a variable, so the *x* is displayed in italics. If you type **cos**, Equation Editor assumes that you mean the Cosine function, so the text is not italicized.

You can assign several different text styles to text in an equation:

- **Math:** The normal equation style. When you use the Math style, Equation Editor examines text as you type it and formats it accordingly by using the remaining style types.

- **Text:** Text that is not a mathematical symbol, function, variable, or number.

- ✔ **Function:** A mathematical function, such as *sin*, *cos*, or *log*.

- ✔ **Variable:** Letter that represents an equation variable, such as *a, b,* or *x*. Normally formatted as italic.

- ✔ **Greek:** Letters from the Greek alphabet that use the Symbol font.

- ✔ **Symbol:** Mathematical symbols such as +, =, summation, integral, and so on. Based on the Symbol font.

- ✔ **Matrix-Vector:** Characters used in matrices or vectors.

You can change the text style by using the <u>S</u>tyle commands, but you should normally leave it set to Math. That way, Equation Editor can decide how each element of your equation should be formatted.

On occasion, Equation Editor's automatic formatting doesn't work. Type the word **cosmic**, for example, and Equation Editor assumes that you want to calculate the cosine of the product of the variables *m, i,* and *c*. When that happens, highlight the text that was incorrectly formatted and use the <u>S</u>tyle⇨<u>T</u>ext command.

Don't use the spacebar to separate elements in an equation — let Equation Editor worry about how much space to leave between the variables and the plus signs. The only time you should use the spacebar is when you're typing two or more words of text formatted with the Text style.

The Enter key has an interesting behavior in Equation Editor: It adds a new equation slot, immediately beneath the current slot. This key is sometimes a good way to create stacked items, but it's best to use an appropriate template instead.

Chapter 26

Form Follows Function (How to Set Up and Use Forms)

*M*y guess is that Microsoft had a big contract with the government — probably the military — to sell a million copies of Word for Windows to the government if the program provided a feature for creating and filling in forms, preferably in triplicate. So here I am, at the last chapter in this section. I'd really rather call it a day and maybe catch a quick round of golf, but who knows — maybe the government will buy a truckload of copies of this book at $913 each if I throw in a chapter about creating and filling in forms. So what the heck.

You may not realize it, but creating a form that can be filled out later by you or someone else qualifies as a type of programming. As such, you must adopt a bit of a programmer's mentality, distasteful as that may seem. In this chapter, I'll use the word *user* to refer to the person — you or someone else — who fills out a form that you create, just to keep you alert.

Understanding Forms

A *form* is a special type of document in which parts of the document are protected from being modified by the user. The user is allowed to enter information only in predefined fill-in-the-blank portions of the document, which are called *form fields*.

Figure 26-1 shows an example of a form that I created with WinWord. Most of the text you see in the document is protected. The only parts of the document that the user can modify are the shaded parts: the name and address fields, the answers to the two questions, and the check boxes.

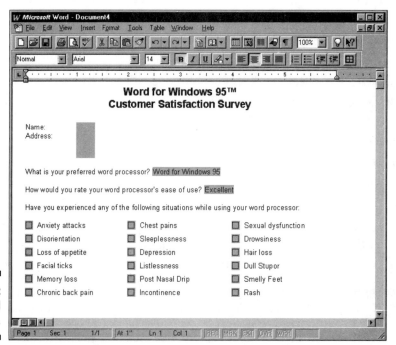

Figure 26-1:
A WinWord
form.

The exact steps for creating and filling out a blank form are provided later in this chapter, but the general idea goes something like this: first, you must create a new template. Then you add any text that you want to appear in the form to the template and you add the form fields using the Insert⇨Form Field command. When the blank form is finished, you use the Tools⇨Protect Document command to prevent the user from modifying any part of the document other than the form fields, and finally, you save the template.

To fill in a blank form, you have to create a new document based on the form template. Then fill in the blanks. WinWord doesn't allow you to move the insertion point anywhere outside the form fields, so you don't have to worry about accidentally messing up the form.

✔ Think of the template as a pile of blank forms. To fill out a form, first you have to grab a form off the pile by opening the template. Once you fill out the form (the template), you can save it as a normal document. The saved document contains the form itself that's copied from the template, plus whatever information you typed into the form fields.

✔ Although it's not apparent from Figure 26-1, the form fields for the first two questions are actually drop-down list boxes. Instead of typing in a response to the question, the user selects one of several permissible responses. If, for example, the user clicks the mouse in the form field for the first question ("What is your preferred word processor?"), the drop-down list shown in Figure 26-2 appears.

Figure 26-2:
A drop-down form field.

✔ WinWord comes with three pre-built form templates: an invoice (Invoice.dot), a purchase order (Purchase Order.dot), and a weekly time sheet (Weekly Time Sheet.dot). To see what you can do with forms, try creating a new document based on one of these templates and start exploring.

Creating a Form Template

Before you can fill out a form, you must create a template. The template contains any text and graphics that appear on the blank form as well as the form fields, into which the user enters information.

To create a form template, follow these steps:

1. Call up the File⇨New command to access the New dialog box.

Clicking the New button in the Standard toolbar is insufficient, because this action bypasses the New dialog box.

2. **Check the Template button.**

This action tells WinWord that you are creating a new template rather than a new document.

3. **Select the template that you want to base the new template on.**

Usually, Normal works fine. If the new form is similar to a form you've previously created or one of the forms that comes with WinWord, select the appropriate template.

4. **Click OK.**

A document window for the new template opens.

5. **Create your form.**

Type text where you want text to appear, insert graphics where you want graphics to appear, and insert form fields where you want form fields to appear.

There are three basic types of fields that you can insert into a form: text fields, list box fields, and check box fields. To create any of these, call up the Insert⇨Form Field command. Then check whichever field type you want to create and click OK. If you're creating a check box field, set the default value; if you're creating a list box field, add as many items to the drop-down list as you want. For more specific information on creating these fields, see the following three sections.

6. **Call up the Tools⇨Protect document command.**

The Protect Document dialog box appears, as shown in Figure 26-3.

Figure 26-3:
The Protect
Document
dialog box.

7. **Check the Forms option and click OK.**

This action protects the document so that the user can enter data only into the form fields.

8. **Use the File⇨Save command to save the template.**

Assign a meaningful name to the template file and store it in the same directory with your other templates.

9. **That's all.**

You're done.

Here are some suggestions for creating forms:

✔ If you're converting a paper form to WinWord, create the WinWord form so it looks as much like the current paper form as possible. Work in Page Layout view so you can see how things line up.

✔ If you want the form to be laid out on a grid with ruled lines and boxes, use tables, frames, borders, shading, and whatever other WinWord features you can muster. See Chapter 9 for more information about working with tables and Chapter 12 for information about working with frames.

✔ If this is your first time creating a template, you may want to refer back to Chapter 4 to make sure you know the ins and outs of working with templates.

✔ Creating a form is tedious work. You may not want to wait until the very end to save the template. In fact, you should probably press Ctrl+S to save your work every few minutes or activate the AutoSave feature so that the template is automatically saved at regular intervals.

✔ WinWord provides a Forms toolbar, which includes the buttons listed in Table 26-1. To activate this toolbar, call up the View➪Toolbars command, check the Forms check box, and click OK.

✔ If you protect the template using the Tools➪Protect Document command, you'll have to unprotect the template if you need to change the layout of the form later on. Call up the Tools➪Unprotect document. Don't forget to protect the form again when you're finished!

Table 26-1	Buttons on the Forms Toolbar
Button	*What It Does*
[ab] Text	Inserts a text field
[⊠] Check	Inserts a check box field
[▦] Drop	Inserts a drop-down field
[▦] Options	Calls up the Form Field Options dialog box for a field
[▦] Table	Inserts a table
[▦] Frame	Inserts a frame
[▦] Shading	Turns field shading on or off
[🔒] Lock	Protects or unprotects a form

Creating a Text Field

A *text field* is a form field that the user can type information into. You use text fields to provide a space on the form where the user can enter information like a name or address. The form shown in Figure 26-1 uses four text fields: one for the name and three for the address lines.

To create, or insert, a text field in a form, follow these steps:

1. **Position the insertion point on the template where you want the text field to appear.**

2. **Call up the Insert⇨Form Field command.**

   The Form Field dialog box appears, as shown in Figure 26-4.

Figure 26-4:
The Form
Field dialog
box.

3. **Select the Text option.**

4. **Click OK.**

   The text field is inserted on the template.

It's a good idea to type some sort of text in the template next to the field to tell the user what to type into the field. For example, in Figure 26-1, I typed "Name:" next to the text field that is supposed to contain the name.

If you want to provide a *default value* for the text field — that is, a value that the field assumes if the user doesn't type anything into the field — select the Text option and then click the Options button. The Text Form Field Options dialog box appears, as shown in Figure 26-5. Type a default value for the field in the Default Text box and then click OK.

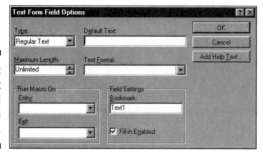

Figure 26-5:
The Text
Form Field
Options
dialog box.

The Text Form Field Options dialog box also lets you set the field type. WinWord lets you create six different types of text fields, as summarized in Table 26-2.

Table 26-2	The Six Types of Text Fields
Text Field Type	*What It Does*
Regular Text	This field consists of ordinary text, like a name or address. The user can type anything into the field.
Number	The user must type a number into the field.
Date	The user must type a date into the field. The date must be in the usual date format (for example, *05/31/94* or *6-24-94*) or may include the month spelled out (as in *March 28, 1994*).
Current Date	WinWord automatically inserts the current date into the field. The user can't type anything in the field.
Current Time	WinWord automatically inserts the current time into the field. The user can't type anything in the field.
Calculation	The field contains a formula field (=) to calculate a result value, usually based on the value of one or more number fields. The user also can't type anything into this field.

If you uncheck the Fill-in Enabled check box in the Text Form Field Options dialog box, WinWord displays the text field, but the user won't be able to modify it. Use this field only if you plan on doing some fancy macro programming, in which a macro enables or disables the field at will. This kind of macro programming requires programming knowledge that is way beyond the realm of reasonableness.

After you've created a text field, you can call up the Text Form Field Options dialog box by double-clicking the field or right-clicking the field (that is, pointing to the field and clicking the right mouse button) and selecting the Form Field Options command from the shortcut menu that appears.

Creating a Check Box Field

A *check box field* is a field that the user can check or uncheck to provide a yes or no answer. Check box fields work just like regular check boxes in dialog boxes: you click them with the mouse to check or uncheck them.

Follow these steps to create or insert a check box field:

1. **Position the insertion point in the template where you want the check box field to appear.**

2. **Call up the Insert⇨Form Field command.**

   The Form Field dialog appears.

3. **Check the Check Box check box.**

   Sounds like a scene from *Airplane,* doesn't it?

   Roger: "Check the Check Box check box, Chuck."

   Chuck: "Roger, Roger. Checking the Check Box check box now. Chuck out."

   Roger: "Check, Chuck."

4. **Click the Options button.**

   The Check Box Form Field Options dialog box appears, as shown in Figure 26-6.

Figure 26-6:
The Check
Box Form
Field
Options
dialog box.

Check Box Form Field Options	? X

OK
Cancel
Add Help Text...

Check Box Size
○ Auto
○ Exactly: 10 pt

Default Value
○ Not Checked
○ Checked

Run Macro On
Entry:

Exit:

Field Settings
Bookmark:
Check1

☑ Check Box Enabled

5. **Set the Default Value by checking Checked or Not Checked.**

   To check, or not to check. That is the question.

6. **Click OK.**

The check box is now inserted in the document.

Here are some pointers for creating a check box field:

- ✔ Obviously, a check box by itself is of little worth. You'll want to place some text in the template right next to the check box so that you'll know what the check box field means.

- ✔ Unless you're into writing macros, the only thing you can do with a check box is check it or uncheck it. If you want to roll up your sleeves and do some heavy-duty macro programming, you can come up with all sorts of exotic uses for check box fields.

- ✔ If you want to change the default size of the check box field, check Exactly and type the size of the check box in points.

- ✔ If you uncheck the Check Box Enabled check box, WinWord displays the check box field, but the user won't be able to modify it. Use this field only if you plan to do some fancy macro programming, in which a macro enables the field if the user enters a certain value into another field.

- ✔ You can call up the Check Box Form Field Options box after you've inserted a check box field by double-clicking the field or right-clicking the field (that is, pointing to it and clicking the right mouse button) and selecting the Form Field Options command from the shortcut menu that appears.

Creating a Drop-Down Field

A *drop-down field* is like a text field, except that the user isn't allowed to type text directly into the field. Instead, the user must select from a list of preset choices that are given in a list box. List boxes are great for fields like marital status, shipping instructions, or gender. In other words, fields that have only a limited set of correct answers.

Follow these steps to create, or insert, a drop-down field:

1. **Position the insertion point where you want the text field to appear.**

2. **Call up the Insert⇨Form Field command.**

   The Form Field dialog box appears.

3. **Check the Drop-Down option button and click the Options button.**

   The Drop-Down Form Field Options dialog box appears, as shown in Figure 26-7.

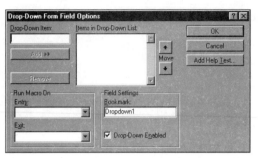

Figure 26-7:
The Drop-
Down Form
Field Option
dialog box.

4. **To add an item to the drop-down list, type text in the D̲rop-Down Item box and then click the A̲dd button.**

The text is added to the Items in Drop-Down List field.

Repeat this step for each item you want to include in the drop-down list.

5. **When you've added all the items you want in the list, click OK.**

The drop-down field is added to the document.

If you're going to go to the trouble of creating drop-down list fields, you should keep the following hot tips in mind:

✐ The first item in the drop-down list is the default selection — that is, the item that is initially selected for the field.

✐ To rearrange items in the drop-down list, call up the Drop-Down Form Field Options dialog box, select the item that you want to move to another position in the list, and click the up or down Move buttons.

✐ To delete an item from the list, select the item and click the R̲emove button.

✐ To correct a mistake in a list item, delete the incorrect item. WinWord copies the deleted item to the D̲rop-Down Item field, where you can correct the mistake and click the A̲dd button to reinsert the item.

✐ If you uncheck the Drop-Down E̲nabled check box, WinWord displays the drop-down list field, but the user won't be able to modify it. Use this field only if you plan to do some fancy macro programming, in which a macro enables or disables the field on the fly. Better con a computer nerd friend into doing this for you.

✐ You can call up the Drop-Down Form Field Options dialog box after you've inserted a drop-down field by double-clicking the field or right-clicking (that is, pointing to the field and clicking the right mouse button) the field and selecting the Form Field Options command from the shortcut menu that appears.

Filling Out a Form

Once you have created a form template and protected it, it's time to put it to good use collecting the vital information it was so carefully designed to record. In other words, it's time to fill out the form.

To fill out a form using a form template you or someone else created, follow these steps:

1. **Call up the File⇨New command.**

   The New dialog box appears, listing all the available templates.

2. **Select the correct form template from the Template list.**

3. **Click OK.**

4. **Fill in the form fields.**

   When you fill in the form fields, you can use any of the keyboard actions listed in Table 26-3.

5. **Print the document.**

   Use the File⇨Print command or click the Print button in the Standard toolbar.

6. **Save the file, if you want.**

   Use the File⇨Save command or click the Save button in the Standard toolbar. WinWord asks for a filename.

Table 26-3   Keys You Can Use When Filling Out a Form

Key	What It Does
Enter, Tab, or down arrow	Moves the insertion point to the next field
Shift+Tab, or up arrow	Moves the insertion point to the previous field
Alt+down arrow, or F4	Displays a drop-down list
Up arrow or down arrow	Moves up or down in a drop-down list
Space or X	Checks or unchecks a check box field
F1	Displays the help text for a field
Ctrl+Tab	Inserts a tab character into a text field

Adding Help to a Form Field

WinWord lets you add your own help text to form fields. Then if you forget what a field is for when you're filling out a form, the help text reminds you.

You can create two types of help text for each field. The status bar help is a single line of text that appears in the status bar whenever the insertion point moves into the field. WinWord limits this help text to 138 characters so it can fit in the space provided on the status bar. If the status bar help isn't enough, you can supply help text, which the user can summon by pressing F1. You can provide up to 256 characters for help text. Figure 26-8 shows an example of help text.

Figure 26-8:
Help text for
a form field.

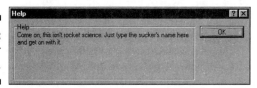

To create help text for a field, follow these steps:

1. **Select the field you want to add help text to.**

   Make sure the form is unprotected. You can't add help text to a field while the form is protected.

2. **Double-click the field to call up the Form Field Options dialog box.**

3. **Click the Add Help Text button.**

   The Form Field Help Text dialog box appears, as shown in Figure 26-9.

4. **Type the Status Bar help text in the Status Bar tab and the help text in the Help Key (F1) tab.**

5. **Click OK.**

   The help text is now attached to the field. The user can display it by pressing F1.

Figure 26-9:
Adding help
text to a
form field.

Part V

Shortcuts and Tips Galore

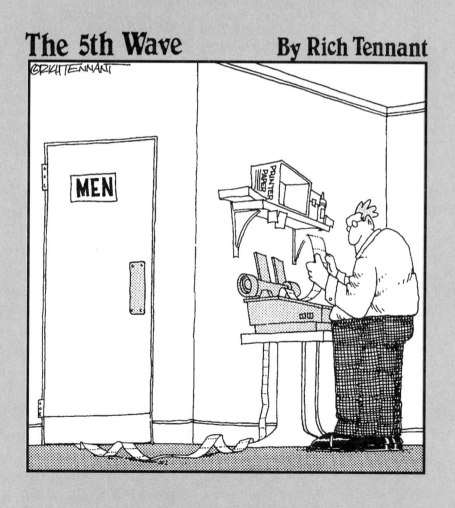

The 5th Wave   By Rich Tennant

In this part . . .

My favorite store in the good ol' Silicon Valley is Weird Stuff. It's the place to go for used, unusual, and often unidentifiable computer stuff. You can find just about any type of computer and any other electronic gizmo ever invented in there.

I can easily kill a few hours perusing the shelves at Weird Stuff, wondering what this doo-hickey is or what that thingamabob does. But what's even more fun than looking at the weird stuff on the shelves is watching the weird people who shop there — people who know *exactly* what this doo-hickey is and what that thingamabob does.

This part is kind of like that Weird Stuff store. Its chapters are filled with doo-hickeys and thingamabobs you probably didn't know existed, or if you did, maybe you didn't know what they were for. Weird stuff like using the spelling checker to cheat at crossword puzzles, secret places to click with the mouse, and best of all, the top-secret hidden credits screen.

Enjoy!

Chapter 27
Cool New Features in Word 7

* *

In This Chapter

▶ Word 7's improved file handling features

▶ File properties

▶ The new and improved Find command

▶ On-the-fly spell checking

▶ Internet Assistant

* *

*T*his chapter briefly describes the more important new features that Microsoft has introduced with Word version 7. Most of these new features are merely accommodations of the Windows 95 way of doing things. But some of the new features represent genuine innovations, and some are even moderately useful.

Better File Handling

Back in the dark ages of Windows 3.1 and Word 6, filenames were limited to eight characters plus a three-character extension. The extension indicated whether the file was a document (DOC) or a template (DOT), so users had to cram as much identifying information as possible into the eight-character filename.

Users have long grumbled about the eight-character filename limit of MS-DOS, so this limitation was one of the first problems Microsoft addressed in Windows 95. With Windows 95, you can now use filenames as long as 255 characters. You can say good-bye to filenames like JRNL0595.DOC and LTRBOBAB.DOC and hello to filenames like "Journal for May 1995" and "Letter to Bob Abbott."

To accommodate these longer filenames, Microsoft has thoroughly revamped the standard File dialog boxes for the File⇨Open, File⇨Save As, and File⇨New commands. Figure 27-1 shows the appearance of the new File Open dialog box.

Here are some of the File Open dialog box's more notable new features:

- Long filenames, which can include spaces, are supported.

- The familiar Drive and Directories controls have been replaced with a Look in control, which enables you to rummage through your drives and directories (oops, I mean *folders,* the new Windows 95 term for directory).

- Get used to the new format for displaying files and folders. An icon is displayed next to each file to indicate the file type. Because the File Open dialog box displays only Word Documents, the Word icon appears next to all of the files.

- You can use various buttons to display file details, properties, or a preview of each file's contents.

- You can quickly search for documents that contain specific text by typing the text in the Text or property field.

Figure 27-2 shows the Save As dialog box, which is similar to the Open dialog box. The Save As dialog box also supports long filenames, and it lets you create a new folder. Word 7 automatically suggests a filename for you based on the contents of the first line of the document. If this first line contains a document title, you can accept the suggested filename as is. Otherwise, you can replace it with a more pertinent filename of your own choosing.

You can create a new directory (er, folder) from the Save As dialog box by clicking the Create New Folder button (a welcome new feature). Back in the days of Windows 3.1, you'd have to switch to File Manager (yuck!) just to create a new directory.

The File⇨New command has also been improved to provide more flexibility in the way templates are assigned to documents. In Word 6, the File⇨New command displayed a list of templates that were present in the template directory

Figure 27-2:
The Save As
dialog box
has been
revamped
also.

specified in the Tools⇨Options⇨File Locations dialog box (usually
\WINWORD\TEMPLATE). All document templates had to be stored in this directory, and as a result, the list of templates could easily become unmanageable.

Word 7 lets you organize your templates into folders beneath the default
template folder. These folders show up in the File New dialog box as tabs, as
you can see in Figure 27-3. When you click a tab, Word 7 displays icons for the
templates in the corresponding folder. The tab labeled General is the template
folder itself, which usually contains only the Normal.Dot template. (Normal.Dot
shows up under the General tab as "Blank Document.") You can add your own
templates to any of the template folders, and any folders you create under the
default template folder appear as tabs on the New dialog box if they contain at
least one .Dot file.

For more information about how the New dialog box works with templates,
refer to Chapter 4.

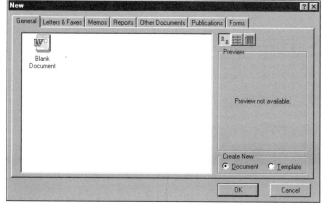

Figure 27-3:
The
improved
File⇨New
command
uses tabs to
organizes
templates.

File Properties

The File⇨Summary info command in Word 6 enabled you to record information about a document, including the document's title, subject, author, keywords, and comments. In Word 7, this useful command has been replaced by a more general File⇨Properties command, which lets you store even more information about your document.

Figure 27-4 shows the dialog box that appears when you call up the File⇨Properties command. As you can see, it groups information about the document under the following tabs:

- ✔ **General:** Displays the Windows 95 file properties for the document file (the filename, type, creation date, size in bytes, attributes, and so on).

- ✔ **Summary:** Includes the same summary information available in the Word 6 File⇨Properties command.

- ✔ **Statistics:** Includes statistical information such as the number of characters, words, lines, and paragraphs in the document.

- ✔ **Contents:** Displays, as you might expect, the contents of the document.

- ✔ **Custom:** Enables you to add any information to the document that you wish.

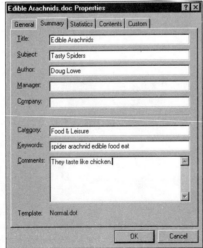

Figure 27-4:
The File⇨
Properties
command
records
useful
information
about your
documents.

Animation

In the Gee Whiz department, Word 7 now sports a flashy animation feature that scrolls text up the screen. It's difficult to describe in a book, but you'll see what I mean the moment your typing reaches the bottom of the page and Word scrolls your text up to accommodate another line.

Unfortunately, there is no way to disable this animation feature. So if your computer isn't fast enough to display the animation effect without a noticeable slowdown, you're out of luck. (Don't yell at me; I'm only the messenger.)

The Highlighter

One of the highly-touted new Word 7 features is the Highlighter, which lets you mark portions of your document quickly, much as you would mark a printed page with a colored highlighter pen. The highlighter tool lets you highlight text using any of four colors: blue, green, pink, and yellow.

To highlight text, click the Highlighter tool in the formatting toolbar and then drag over the text you want highlighted. You can also highlight a single word by double-clicking anywhere in the word, and you can highlight an entire paragraph by triple-clicking anywhere in the paragraph. To remove highlighting, simply drag the Highlighter tool over the text again or click to remove highlighting from individual words or paragraphs.

Find and Replace All Word Forms

In Word 7, the Find and Replace commands have been improved. Both now sport a new option — Fin<u>d</u> All Word Forms — that enables you to search not only for specific words, but also for different forms of the same word. For example, if you search for the word stink and select the Fin<u>d</u> All Word Forms option, Word 7 will find the word stink — and also stank, stunk, and stinking.

If you use the Fin<u>d</u> All Word Forms option in the Replace command, Word 7 will find various word forms *and* replace them with the correct form of the replacement word. For example, if you instruct Word to replace stink with smell, it will also replace stank and stunk with smelled and stinking with smelling.

This feature can be very useful, but it is also potentially error prone. You shouldn't use the Replace All option when replacing words using the Fin<u>d</u> All Word Forms option. Instead, you should manually confirm each replacement to ensure that Word matches the word forms properly.

The Tip Wizard

The Tip Wizard tells you when you're working inefficiently. Think of it as a quiet computer expert sitting patiently behind you, looking over your shoulder as you work. If the Tip Wizard sees you doing something in an awkward way, it jumps up and points out the error of your ways, suggesting a more efficient way to accomplish the same thing.

To activate the Tip Wizard, click the Tip Wizard button in the standard toolbar. The Tip Wizard appears in its own toolbar. The Tip Wizard's tips are brief and to the point. If you don't understand a tip, click the Show Me button for a more detailed explanation.

New Help Button

The Help buttons in many of Word 6's dialog boxes have been replaced with a standard Help button in the title bar, next to the close button. Look back over the figures presented so far in this chapter and you'll see it, near the top-right corner of each dialog box. Click this button to change the mouse pointer to a help pointer (a question mark with an arrow running through it). Then click the help pointer on the portion of the dialog box that is causing you trouble to display help information.

On-the-Fly Spell Checker

Word's new Automatic Spell Checking feature automatically checks your spelling as you type. You'd think this feature would slow Word down considerably, but the effect is barely noticeable, even on relatively slow computers. (I've used it on a 33 MHz 486 without any noticeable delay.) The benefits of on-the-fly spell checking are substantial, not the least of which is that you'll quickly become both a better speller and a better typist due to the reinforcement provided by immediate detection and correction of your spelling errors.

When Automatic Spell Checking detects a misspelled word, it underlines it with a wavy red line. To correct the word, right-click it with the mouse. A list of suggested spellings appears.

Using the Internet Assistant

Internet Assistant is an add-on program that lets you create documents that can be displayed on the World Wide Web. If you don't know what the Internet and the World Wide Web are, run out and pick up a copy of *The Internet For Dummies*

(Levine & Baroudi). Then, when you've become an Internet convert, come back to this section to learn how Internet Assistant can transform Word into a powerful program for creating Web pages.

Although Internet Assistant is available free from Microsoft, it doesn't actually come with Word (or Office, for that matter). The only way to get it is to connect to Microsoft's Internet home page (http://www.microsoft.com) and download Internet Assistant from Microsoft's computers to yours. After you download Internet Assistant, you can install it by following the instructions that come with it.

Once installed, Internet Assistant allows Word to edit HTML documents. (HTML refers to the special format that is required of documents that can be displayed on the World Wide Web. HTML stands for *HyperText Markup Language*, but that won't be on the test.) Internet Assistant automatically translates Word's formatting features — such as heading styles, numbered and bulleted lists, and tables — to HTML equivalents. As a result, Internet Assistant allows you to easily publish your Word documents on the World Wide Web.

HTLM is far too complicated a subject to discuss in depth here. If you're interested in learning HTML, I suggest you get ahold of *HTML For Dummies*, published by IDG Books Worldwide (who else?).

Converting a Word document to HTML

One of the most common uses of Internet Assistant is converting existing Word documents to HTML format. For example, Figure 27-5 shows an example of a simple Word document that someone might want to publish on the Web.

Converting a Word document such as this one to HTML format is easy once you've installed Internet Assistant. Just follow these steps:

1. **Open the document in Word.**

   Use the File⇨Open command just as you normally would.

2. **Choose the File⇨Save As command.**

   The normal Save As dialog box will appear.

3. **Select HTML Document (.htm) in the Save as type field.**

4. **If desired, choose a new location and name for the file.**

5. **Click the Save button.**

   The file is automatically converted to HTML format and saved.

Note that saving a file in HTML format changes it's appearance, as shown in Figure 27-6.

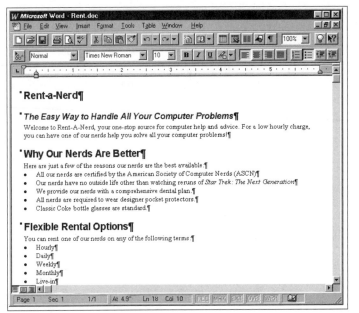

Figure 27-5:
A document
about to be
converted
to HTML
format by
Internet
Assistant.

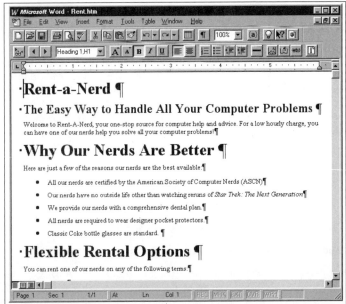

Figure 27-6:
A document
that has
been
converted to
HTML.

Adding HTML elements to a document

Internet Assistant allows you to add many types of HTML elements to your documents. For example, you can add horizontal rules, pictures, or links to other documents. The following sections explain how to add these elements.

Adding a horizontal rule

One of the most commonly used formatting features in HTML documents is the horizontal rule. Horizontal rules are simply lines drawn across the page to visually separate groups of information.

To insert a horizontal rule, follow these steps:

1. **Position the insertion point where you want the horizontal rule to be inserted.**

2. **Choose the Insert⇨Horizontal Rule command.**

   Or click the Horizontal Rule button. Either way, a horizontal rule is inserted.

Figure 27-7 shows a document with several rules inserted. Note that these rules appear differently in Word than they do when viewed on the Internet using a Web browser. For example, Figure 27-8 shows how this same page appears when viewed using Microsoft's Web browser, Internet Explorer.

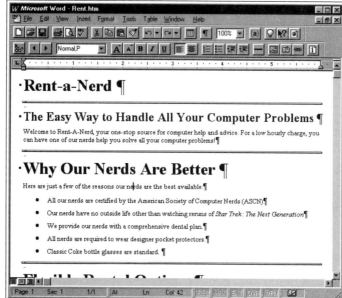

Figure 27-7:
A document with horizontal rules.

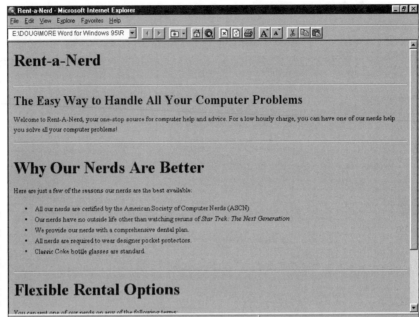

Figure 27-8:
The same
document
viewed in
Internet
Explorer

Inserting a picture

To insert a picture into an HTML document, follow these steps:

1. **Move the insertion point to the position where you want the picture inserted.**

2. **Summon the Insert⇨Picture command.**

   Or click the Picture button. Either way, the Picture dialog box appears, as shown in Figure 27-9.

Figure 27-9:
The Picture
dialog box.

3. **If the picture resides on your hard disk, click the U̲nderline Browse button and locate it. If the picture is on the Internet, type the address of the picture in the I̲mage source field.**

4. **Type a brief description of the picture in the A̲lternate text field.**

This text is displayed when the page is viewed using a browser that does not support pictures or if the Internet user has chosen not to view pictures.

Note: You can ignore the Lin̲k Path button.

5. **Click OK.**

The picture is inserted.

Inserting a hyperlink

A *hyperlink* is a bit of text that, when clicked, causes another page to be displayed. The page can be another page of your own creation, or it can be any other page anywhere on the Internet.

To add a hyperlink to your document, follow these steps:

1. **Highlight the text that you want to make a link.**

For example, to create a link for the Americal Society of Computer Nerds in Figure 27-10, I highlight those words.

2. **Choose the I̲nsert⇨HyperLin̲k command.**

 Or click the Hyperlink button. Either way, the Hyperlink dialog box appears, as shown in Figure 27-10.

Figure 27-10: The Hyperlink dialog box.

Hyperlink	☒
T̲ext to Display:	OK
American Society of Computer Nerds	Cancel
F̲ile or URL:	He̲lp
	U̲nlink
Browse... · Link P̲ath...	
Bookmark L̲ocation in File:	

3. **Type the address of the Web page you want the link to refer to in the F̲ile or URL field.**

If you want the link to refer to a file on your hard disk instead, click the U̲nderline Browse button and locate the file.

You can safely ignore all of the other buttons on this dialog box.

4. Click OK.

The text you selected is transformed into a link. To indicate that the text is a link, Internet Assistant displays it in blue underlined text.

Learning how to use other Internet Assistant features

In this section, I've presented only a few of Internet Assistant's many features. Fortunately, Internet Assistant comes with its own Help files, which you can access by conjuring up Help⇨Internet Assistant for Microsoft Word.

Another way to learn more about using Internet Assistant is to take the Internet Assistant, tutorial, which is available online at Microsoft's Web page, http://www.microsoft.com. This tutorial shows you how to use Internet Assistant's features, plus it allows you to view samples of actual pages created with Internet Assistant.

Chapter 28

The Goody Box

- -

In This Chapter

▶ Using the spell checker to cheat at crossword puzzles
▶ Cheating at Jumble and Scrabble games
▶ MindBender

- -

*R*emember going to the dentist when you were a kid, where, even if you screamed your head off the whole time, yelling "Blood-thirsty ax murderer!" the dentist told you what a good little boy or girl you were and asked if you wanted to pick a prize from the Goody Box?

That's kind of what this chapter is like. Even if you've been screaming your head off at me throughout this whole book, I still think you've been a good little boy or girl. Wouldn't you like to pick a prize from the Goody Box?

The prizes you'll find in this chapter are a hodgepodge of interesting, sometimes useful, sometimes fun things to do with WinWord.

Using the Spell Checker to Solve Crossword Puzzles

Hmm. A nine-letter word meaning "loss" whose first letter is *D*, fourth letter is *R*, and last two letters are *NT*.

Been stuck on that one for hours? No problem. WinWord's spell checker can find the word for you. All you have to do is substitute a question mark for each letter that you don't know, and WinWord finds every word in its dictionary whose spelling matches the pattern.

For example, to find all the nine-letter words whose first letter is *D*, fourth letter is *R*, and last two letter are *NT*, use the spell checker to look up *d??r???nt*. It finds two words: *decrement* and *detriment*.

To look up words using the spell checker, follow these steps:

1. **Call up the spell checker.**

   Click the Spell button on the Standard toolbar, use the <u>T</u>ools⇨<u>S</u>pelling command, or press F7. Don't worry about the position of the cursor.

2. **In the Change <u>T</u>o field, type the word you want to look up, using question marks to fill in for any letter you don't know.**

   Make sure you account for all the missing letters with question marks.

3. **Click the <u>S</u>uggest button.**

   WinWord finds all the words in its dictionary that match the pattern.

The question mark represents one character. You can also use an asterisk to represent any number of characters. For example, to find all the words that start with *pro* and end with *ent*, no matter how many characters are in between, look up *pro*ent*. You'll find *procurement, proficient, prominent, pronouncement, proponent,* and *provident.*

A Nifty Little Macro for Cheating at Jumble Games

WinWord's built-in spelling checker has a nifty ability to take a jumbled-up collection of letters and put them back in the right order. For example, give it the letters *rmtoucpe,* and it spews forth *computer.* Give it *dnre,* and it emits *nerd* and *rend.*

Unfortunately, Microsoft decided that the people who publish those Jumble puzzles in newspapers may sue them if they made this feature available to just anybody, so they hid it deep within the bowels of WinWord, where only the high priests of WordBasic may enter. To use the Jumble feature, you have to write a macro.

Roll up your sleeves, put on your pocket protector, and follow these steps:

1. **Call up the <u>T</u>ools⇨<u>M</u>acro command.**

   The Macro dialog box appears.

2. **Type UnJumbler in the <u>M</u>acro Name field.**

3. Click the Create button.

A macro window opens.

4. Type the following macro exactly as shown.

Yes, it's a lot of typing. But if you like those Jumble games, it's worth it. Here it is:

```
Sub MAIN
Dim Matches$(20)
Begin Dialog UserDialog 396, 200, "The UnJumbler", .UnJumbler
  Text 9, 12, 145, 13, "Word to UnJumble:", .Text1
  Text 9, 31, 71, 13, "Matches:", .Text2
  TextBox 166, 10, 213, 18, .Word
  ListBox 11, 54, 192, 120, Matches$(), .Matches
  PushButton 245, 49, 134, 21, "UnJumble", .UnJumble
  PushButton 291, 81, 88, 21, "Done", .Done
End Dialog
Dim dlg As UserDialog
Dialog dlg
End Sub


Function UnJumbler(id$, action, suppval)
Dim Matches$(20)
If action = 2 Then
  If id$ = "UnJumble" Then
    On Error Resume Next
    Word$ = DlgText$("Word")
    ToolsGetSpelling Matches$(), Word$, "", "", 2
    DlgListBoxArray "Matches", Matches$()
    UnJumbler = - 1
    DlgFocus "Word"
  End If
End If
End Function
```

5. Use the File⇨Save Template command.

This saves the Unjumbler macro in the NORMAL.DOT template.

6. Use the File⇨Close command to close the macro editing window.

7. To run the macro, call up the Tools⇨Macro command and double-click UnJumbler in the list of available macros.

When you run the UnJumbler macro, the dialog box shown in Figure 28-1 appears. Type the scrambled word in the Word to UnJumble field and then click the UnJumble button. The macro unscrambles the word and displays the results in the Matches list. You can unscramble as many words as you want before clicking the Done button to end the macro.

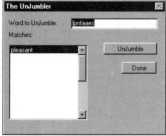

Figure 28-1:
Cheaters
never
prosper.

✔ You've got to type in the macro exactly as shown and check carefully for typographical errors. If you get a weird error message when you run the macro, call up the Tools⇨Macro command, select the UnJumbler macro, and click the Edit button. Then carefully review the macro for typos.

✔ The UnJumbler can't deal with multiple words. If you type two or more words in the Word to Unjumble field, the UnJumbler ignores them. And you're on your own if the letters represent two or more scrambled-up words.

Try the UnJumbler on Scrabble puzzles, too. It only works when there is a solution that uses all seven letters, which occurs quite frequently. I tried it on this morning's puzzle, with the following results:

l-e-t-a-y-h-h (second letter double)	healthy (17 points)
b-d-r-e-m-a-l (triple word score)	marbled (36 points)
g-v-s-n-i-k-i	Vikings (15 points)
e-a-n-r-d-t-g	granted (9 points)

With a 50 point bonus for each seven-letter word, that's a score of 277. Not bad for someone whose editor says he doesn't no how to spel.

You can get the Unjumbler to find six-letter words from a seven-letter Scrabble rack with a little work. Type in just six of the seven letters and click the UnJumble Button. Try it seven times, leaving out a different letter each time, to find the best word.

MindBender: The Secret WinWord Game

Windows itself comes with two games: Solitaire and MineSweeper. Did you know that Word for Windows also comes with a game? It's a variation of the old Concentration card game, where you flip over pairs of cards looking for matches. It's called MindBender, and it's hidden in a document template named MACRO60.DOT.

Here's the procedure for calling up MindBender:

1. **Call up the File⇨Open command.**

   The Open dialog box appears.

2. **Change the List Files of Type field to Document Templates (*.DOT).**

3. **Navigate to the \MSOffice/Winword/Macros directory and select the MACROS7.DOT template.**

4. **Click OK to open the template.**

5. **Call up the Tools⇨Macro command.**

6. **Find MindBender in the list of macros and double-click it.**

The MindBender game starts. Click the Start Game button to reveal the game board that's shown in Figure 28-2 and begin a game.

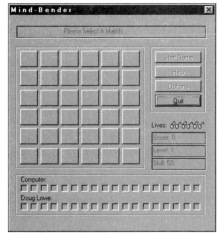

Figure 28-2:
The
MindBender
game.

Here are some tips when playing MindBender:

✔ To play the game, click two squares. MindBender briefly reveals the pictures hidden behind those two squares and covers them up again if they don't match. Then the computer takes its turn. Pay attention.

✔ If the computer plays too fast for you, click the Options button and change the computer speed to Slow.

✔ If you can't find the MACROS7.DOT template, you may have to retrieve it from the installation diskettes. See Chapter 31 for the procedure.

✔ Most programmers just can't resist the urge to throw in a secret way to cheat at games, and the programmer who wrote MindBender is no exception. Immediately after you click the Start Game button, hold down the following six keys simultaneously: Shift, Ctrl, Alt, M, J, and W. In a moment, the screen will reveal the position of all the hidden pictures, but only for ten seconds. This is enough time for you to memorize the locations of at least a few of them. (By the way, M, J, and W are apparently the initials of the programmer who wrote MindBender.)

Chapter 29
Weird Places You Can Click

· ·

In This Chapter

▶ Using the right mouse button

▶ Saving time by double-clicking the mouse

▶ Using the mouse to select text

▶ Dragon droppings

· ·

*W*ordPerfect is often criticized for its confusing *Ctrl+Alt+Shift+whatever function key* assignments. Well, we Word for Windows users will have none of that. We've gladly traded confusing function key assignments for confusing mouse click shortcuts, like *double-click here* or *right-click there*. Hmph.

This chapter is about the weird places you can click the WinWord screen.

Fun with the Right Mouse Button

We Windows users have one stunning advantage over Macintosh users: we have more buttons on our mice than they do. Most of us have two mouse buttons, and some of us even have three. Lowly Macintosh users have but one mouse button.

For years, these extra mouse buttons were fun to brag about at parties but offered few real benefits. Now, though, with Word for Windows 6, you can at long last use the right mouse button constructively: click the right mouse button, and a *shortcut menu* pops up that's loaded with commands that are relevant to whatever you right-clicked. For example, right-click some plain text and you get the text shortcut menu, shown in Figure 29-1. Right-click a numbered list and you get the numbered list shortcut menu, shown in Figure 29-2.

Figure 29-1:
The shortcut
menu for
regular text.

Figure 29-2:
The shortcut
menu for a
numbered
list.

Notice that the menu for the numbered list contains additional commands that are relevant only to numbered lists.

In all, there are 25 different shortcut menus that pop up, depending on where you right-click. There's a special shortcut menu for right-clicking a frame, a picture, a heading paragraph, a field, a drop cap, a drawn object, a table or a table cell, and more. There's even a special shortcut menu for right-clicking a toolbar.

✔ If you're interested, you can see a complete listing of all 25 shortcut menus by calling up the Tools➪Customize command, clicking the Menus tab, and scrolling through the Change What Menu drop-down list. After the menus that appear on the menu bar (File, Edit, View, and so on) you'll see all 25 shortcut menus.

✔ If you discover that your favorite command doesn't appear in a shortcut menu, use the Tools➪Customize command to add the command to the shortcut menu. See Chapter 16 for a refresher on creating custom menus.

✔ Right-clicking plays an important role in the new on-the-fly spell checker. If you right-click a word that has been marked as misspelled, a list of suggested spellings appears in the shortcut menu.

Surprising Places You Can Double-Click

Double-clicking is the art of clicking the mouse button twice, really fast. Depending on what the mouse is pointing at when you double-click, various things happen:

✔ Double-click a word to select that word. (More interesting ways to select text with the mouse are found in the next section, "Selecting Text with the Mouse.")

✔ Double-click a toolbar to change the toolbar to a floater. Double-click it again to send it back to its fixed location. (This works only if you double-click the toolbar somewhere outside the buttons. In other words, it doesn't work if you double-click one of the toolbar's buttons.)

✔ Double-click an open carton of milk in the refrigerator to remove floaters.

Interesting things can happen when you double-click various parts of the status bar at the bottom of the WinWord window:

✔ Double-click the letters REC on the status bar to pop up the Record Macro dialog box and record a macro. See Chapter 17 for more information about macros.

✔ Double-click the letters MRK in the status bar to pop up the Revisions dialog box to control revision tracking. See Chapter 23 for more information about tracking revisions.

✔ Double-click the letters EXT to change WinWord into Extend mode, where every move causes WinWord to extend the highlight to select more and more text. This will drive you crazy, and you'll want to double-click EXT again to make it stop.

✔ Double-click the letters OVR to throw WinWord into overtype mode, where any text you type clobbers the text already on the screen. Double-click again to revert to regular insert-text-as-you-type mode. (Double-clicking OVR is hardly easier than pressing Insert, which accomplishes the same thing.)

✔ Double-click the letters WPH to pop up the WordPerfect Help dialog box.

✔ To cancel printing when you print a document, double-click the dancing printer icon that appears in the status bar.

✔ Double-click anywhere else on the status bar to pop up the Go To dialog box.

Sometimes it's fun to double-click in the ruler:

✔ Double-click a tab stop in the ruler to pop up the Tabs dialog box.

✔ Double-click the indentation sliders in the ruler to pop up the Paragraph (Indents and Spacing) dialog box.

✔ In a table, double-click the portion of the ruler that appears between cells to pop up the Cell Height and Width dialog box.

✔ If you have two or more columns, double click the portion of the ruler that appears between the columns to pop up the Columns dialog box.

✔ Double-click elsewhere on the ruler to pop up the Page Setup dialog box.

Selecting Text with the Mouse

There are several ways to select text with the mouse, most of which you probably know about already, but a few of which may be new:

- ✔ To select a block of text with the mouse, hold down the left mouse button while dragging the mouse to highlight the text.

- ✔ Another way to select a block of text with the mouse is to click at the start of the block, hold down Shift, and then click at the end of the block. Everything inbetween will be selected.

- ✔ To select a single word, double-click the mouse anywhere on the word. Click-click.

- ✔ To select an entire paragraph, triple-click the mouse anywhere on the paragraph. Click-click-click.

- ✔ To select an entire sentence, hold down Ctrl and click the mouse anywhere in the sentence.

- ✔ To select a column of text, hold down Alt, press and hold the left mouse button, and drag. Drag the mouse left or right to increase or decrease the width of the column selected, and drag the mouse up or down to extend the column up or down. (This technique is most useful after you've arranged text into columns using tabs and you want to rearrange the columns.)

Some of the mouse selection techniques require you to click the *selection bar*, that invisible but ever-present narrow band to the left of the text:

- ✔ Click the selection bar once to select an entire line of text. Click.

- ✔ Double-click the selection bar to select an entire paragraph. Click-click.

- ✔ Triple-click the selection bar to select the entire document. Click-click-click.

- ✔ To select several paragraphs, double-click the selection bar to select the first paragraph and hold the mouse button down after the second click. Then drag the mouse up or down the selection bar to select additional paragraphs.

In a table, you can select individual cells, columns, or rows:

- ✔ To select a cell, click the mouse on the cell. To select several cells, hold down the left mouse button and drag the mouse across the cells you want to select.

- ✔ To select an entire column, click the top gridline of the column. The mouse pointer changes to a down-arrow when it's in the right position to select the column. You can select several columns by dragging the mouse in this position.

✔ To select an entire row, click the selection bar to the left of the row. To select several rows, drag the mouse in the selection bar.

Dragon Droppings

One of the more unusual features of Word for Windows 95 is the capability to drag text with the mouse and drop it in a new location. This feature is politely referred to as *dragon dropping*.

To dragon drop text, follow these steps:

1. **Select the text you want to relocate.**

2. **Press and hold the mouse button anywhere in the selection.**

 3. **Move the mouse to the new location. The mouse pointer changes to a funny shape to indicate that you are about to step in a dragon dropping.**

4. **Release the mouse button and the text is relocated.**

Before you step in the dragon dropping, consider the following:

✔ If you don't like this feature — and you may well find that you don't — you can disable it via the Tools➪Options command. Select the Edit tab and then uncheck the Drag-and-Drop Text Editing check box.

✔ On the other hand, if you can't get the dragon drop technique to work, check the Tools➪Options command Edit settings to make sure that the Drag-and-Drop Text Editing check box is checked.

✔ Dragon dropping even works between separate documents. To dragon drop from one document to another, open both documents and then use the Window➪Arrange All command. Doing so lines up the currently open document windows so you can see them all at once. Next, select the text or graphics you want to move and then drag it right over the window borders into the second document. When you release the mouse button, the text moves to the second document.

✔ Hold down the Ctrl key while dragon dropping to copy text rather than move it.

Chapter 30

Leftover Tips That Just Didn't Fit Anyplace Else

*L*ike a good mechanic, I always end up with a few parts left over after I finish a book. I hate to throw good tips away, so I decided to give them their own chapter. The only thing these tips have in common is that none of them belong anywhere else.

Making Word Start All by Itself

If you use Word every day, you're probably bored by now with performing the menial task of clicking on the Start button, pointing to the Program menu, and clicking on the Microsoft Word icon. Wouldn't it be nice if Word would just start all by itself whenever you turn on your computer? Yes, it would, and yes, you can set up Word to do just that. In fact, it's a pretty easy trick. All you have to do is add a shortcut to Word to a special folder called the StartUp folder. (Pocket protectors are not required.)

Follow these easy steps to make Word start automatically whenever you start or restart your computer:

1. **Click on the Start button and point to the Settings command. When the menu appears, click Taskbar.**

   The Taskbar Properties dialog box appears.

2. **Click the Start Menu Programs tab in the Taskbar Properties dialog box.**

   The Taskbar Properties dialog box changes to show controls that let you configure the Start Menu. See Figure 30-1.

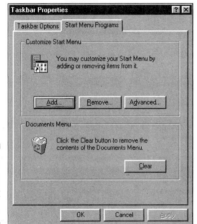

Figure 30-1:
Configuring
the Start
Menu.

3. **Click on Add.**

   The Create Shortcut dialog box appears.

4. **Click on Browse.**

   The Browse dialog box appears, which resembles a standard Open dialog box.

5. **Locate the winword.exe program file in the \MSoffice\Winword folder and double-click it.**

   If you don't have an \MSoffice\Winword folder, look in \Winword instead.

6. **When the Create Shortcut window reappears, click Next.**

   A list of the folders and programs that are already in the Start⇨Programs menu appears.

7. **Double-click the StartUp folder.**

   You'll probably have to scroll down the list to find it. The list is presented in alphabetical order.

8. Click on Finish and then click on OK to close the Taskbar Properties window.

You're done! The next time you start your computer, Word will load automatically.

If you decide you no longer want Word to start automatically, you can delete Word from the StartUp folder. Repeat the first two steps of the preceding procedure, but then click Remove instead of Add. A list of programs and folders in the Start⇨Programs menu appears. Double-click on the StartUp folder to reveal the programs in the StartUp folder, and then click on Microsoft Word and click the Remove button. Click Close to return to the Taskbar Properties dialog box, and then click OK.

Unraveling WinWord's Command-Line Parameters

Huh? Wait just a minute! I thought command-line parameters vanished 250 gazillion years ago at the end of the Paleo-DOS era of computing. Alas, not so. Even the slickest Windows programs still use command-line parameters. Word's are summarized in Table 30-1.

Table 30-1	Word's Command-Line Switches
Command	*What It Does*
winword *filename*	Automatically opens a file.
winword /n	Starts Word without loading an initial empty document.
winword /a	Starts Word without loading any templates. Default settings are used for options.
winword /m*macro*	Starts Word and automatically runs a macro.
winword /m	Prevents any AutoExec macro from running.
winword /t *template*	Starts Word and creates a new document based on the specified template.

To use these switches, you must start Word from a shortcut. To create a shortcut that has one of these switches, follow these steps:

1. Double-click on the My Computer icon on your desktop and then locate the \MSoffice\Winword folder in your C drive.

2. **Point to the winword.exe icon; then press and hold the right mouse button and drag the winword.exe icon from the My Computer window to your desktop.**

   When you release the right mouse button, a pop-up menu appears.

3. **Select Create Shortcut.**

   Word creates a shortcut icon on your desktop.

4. **Right-click the new shortcut icon and select the Properties command.**

   The Properties dialog box appears.

5. **Click the Shortcut tab and edit the command that appears in the <u>T</u>arget field to include the switch you want to use.**

   For example:

   ```
   c:\msoffice\winword\winword.exe /m
   ```

6. **Click OK.**

Shrinking Text to Fit the Page

Have you ever been frustrated by a document with a last page that contains only a line or two of text? Of course you have. There's no shame in admitting it. Fortunately, WinWord provides relief in the form of a feature called *Shrink-to-fit*. This nifty little feature nips and tucks your document in a bold effort to eliminate that last short page. Sometimes it works; sometimes it doesn't. But if you want to get rid of that silly-looking one-line page, it's at least worth a try.

Here's the entire "make-it-fit-better" procedure in a nutshell:

1. **Choose the <u>F</u>ile⇨Print Pre<u>v</u>iew command.**

   Shrink-to-fit is available only in Print Preview mode.

2. **Click the Shrink-to-fit button in the Print Preview toolbar.**

   Word tries like mad to shorten the document by a page. If the procedure works, you see the document reformatted so that it's one page shorter. (You may have to scroll through the document to verify that the short page is really gone.) If it doesn't, you instead see an apologetic tail-between-the-legs dialog box telling you that it didn't work.

   ✔ You may not be happy with the results of WinWord's reformatting efforts. It may do something really crazy, such as change the text font size from nicely legible 10-point to eye-squinting 8-point. If so, press Ctrl+Z to undo the damage.

✔ If Shrink-to-fit doesn't work, you can always try manually shortening the document. Adjust the margins, point sizes, line spacing, space between paragraphs, and so on. You may also try rewriting your prose to be a wee bit more concise, rather than long and verbose in a rambling sort of way, an obvious victim of the three cardinal sins of succinct writing, these being, of course, repetition, redundancy, and reiteration, which can leave your readers understandably wondering if you were voted "most talkative" in high school and — gee, where did the time go? — will this sentence ever *end?*

✔ If Shrink-to-fit doesn't give satisfactory results and manually shortening the document doesn't seem to work either, consider doing just the opposite: Instead of shortening the document to get rid of that last one- or two-line page, try rewriting or reformatting to make the document longer so that the last page isn't quite so embarrassingly short. Add a few points of extra space between paragraphs, increase the margins, or do whatever else has to be done to lengthen that annoying final page.

Using the Spike

You can't get very far in Word without learning how to use the basic cut-and-paste keys: Ctrl+X to cut text to the Clipboard, Ctrl+C to copy text to the Clipboard, and Ctrl+V to paste text into your document from the Clipboard. These keys are great as far as they go, but at times you really need a more powerful cut-and-paste feature.

Suppose, for example, that you want to create a new document by moving information from a half-dozen existing documents. Using regular cut-and-paste, you would employ a procedure something like the following:

1. **Create a new document.**

2. **Open a document containing something you need to move.**

3. **Cut the text you need to the Clipboard.**

4. **Switch back to the new document.**

5. **Paste the text from the Clipboard into the new document.**

6. **Repeat Steps 2 through 5 until the new document is assembled.**

This procedure works, but it involves a great deal of unnecessary switching back and forth between documents. What if you could just cut text to the Clipboard without obliterating the Clipboard's existing contents? Then you could simply cut the text you need from one document, open another document and cut some more text, and so on until you've cut all the text you need. Then you switch to the new document and paste in all that text with one swift keystroke.

Word enables you to do precisely that by using an obscure little feature known as *the Spike*. The Spike has nothing to do with volleyball, punk rock hairstyles, or Snoopy's little cousin. Rather, the Spike is a kind of super clipboard, which accumulates bits and pieces of text, graphics, or whatever else you place on it. Then, with a single keystroke, it inserts its entire contents into a document. Follow this procedure to use the Spike:

1. **Select the text, graphics, or whatever else you want to move from the initial document and place on the Spike.**

2. **Press Ctrl+F3.**

   Ctrl+F3 is the magic "Cut-to-Spike" key. The selected text or graphics is deleted from the document and added to the Spike.

3. **Perform Steps 1 and 2 again for other bits of text and graphics you want accumulated on the Spike.**

   You can open other files to collect information from several documents to put on the Spike.

4. **After you've gathered up all the text and graphics you need, position the cursor at the point in the target document where you want everything inserted.**

5. **Press Ctrl+Shift+F3.**

   Ctrl+Shift+F3 is the magic "Put-the-Spike-Here" key. All the text and graphics on the Spike is inserted into the target document.

The Spike is kind of a peculiar gadget. Keep the following thoughts in mind while using it:

- ✔ You cannot place anything on the Spike without simultaneously deleting it from the document's text. (Too bad. WinWord really should have a "Copy-to-Spike" key to complement its "Cut-to-Spike" key. But it doesn't.)

- ✔ One way around the problem of not being able to copy text to the Spike is to use the following sequence of keys: Ctrl+C, Ctrl+F3, Ctrl+V. This procedure copies the selection to the Clipboard, cuts the selection to the Spike, and then inserts the copy of the selection from the Clipboard back into the document at its original location. This leaves a copy of the text in the Spike, which you can later paste into a document by pressing Ctrl+Shift+F3. (If you're really adventurous, record this key sequence as a macro and assign it to the keyboard combination Ctrl+Alt+F3 — your very own "Copy-to-Spike" command.)

- ✔ The Spike is actually a special AutoText entry. Choose the Edit⇨AutoText command to summon a dialog box that displays the contents of the Spike.

Inserting Special Characters

You probably already know about the Insert⇨Symbol command. Did you know that several of the special symbols accessible from this command are assigned keyboard shortcuts? Table 30-2 lists the more useful of these symbols and their shortcuts.

Table 30-2   Keyboard Shortcuts for Special Symbols

Symbol	Name	Keyboard Shortcut
©	Copyright	Alt+Ctrl+C
®	Registered mark	Alt+Ctrl+R
™	Trademark	Alt+Ctrl+T
—	Em dash	Alt+Ctrl+ – (minus sign on the numeric keypad)
–	En dash	Ctrl+ – (minus sign on the numeric keypad)
. . .	Ellipsis	Alt+Ctrl+. (period)

✔ If you can't remember the keyboard shortcuts for these symbols, choose the Insert⇨Symbol command and click the Special Characters tab in the dialog box that appears. A list of these characters appears, along with their keyboard shortcuts. The list also includes a few characters for which no keyboard shortcuts exist.

✔ You can add a keyboard shortcut to any special character by choosing the Insert⇨Symbol command, clicking the Symbols tab or the Special Characters tab in the Symbol dialog box that appears, and choosing the Shortcut Key button.

✔ An *em dash* is a dash that is the width of the letter M. An *en dash* is as wide as a letter N. If using a dash as a punctuation mark — like this — you should use an em dash instead of two hyphens. The old double-hyphen treatment is a carryover from the days of manual typewriters.

✔ The minus sign required for the em dash and en dash shortcuts is the minus sign on the numeric keypad, way off to the far-right side of the keyboard. (This would probably be Rush Limbaugh's favorite key if he used a PC, but he's a Mac fanatic.) The shortcut won't work if you use the hyphen that's between the 0 and the equal sign (=) at the top of the keyboard.

Using the Microsoft Toolbar

If you use other Microsoft programs and you'd like to access them from within WinWord, consider activating the Microsoft toolbar. To do so, choose the View⇨Toolbars command to summon the Toolbars dialog box and check the Microsoft toolbar. Then click OK.

Table 30-3 lists the buttons available on the Microsoft toolbar.

Table 30-3	Buttons in the Microsoft Toolbar
Button	*Microsoft Program*
	Excel
	PowerPoint
	Mail
	Access
	FoxPro
	Project
	Schedule+
	Publisher

✔ Each button on the Microsoft toolbar activates another Microsoft program. If the program is already running, clicking its button simply switches to the program. It the program is not running, clicking its button runs it.

✔ You can easily remove buttons for programs you don't use. Just hold down the Alt key and drag the unwanted tool off the toolbar. Poof! The button magically vanishes. (You can get it back by using the Tools⇨Customize command, as explained in Chapter 16.)

✔ For more information about toolbars, see Chapter 16.

Chapter 31

Word for Windows Setup Revisited

. . . .

In This Chapter

▶ Adding WinWord features you originally left out

▶ Removing WinWord features you realize you don't really need

▶ Reinstalling WinWord to fix bizarre behavior

▶ Getting rid of WinWord when you've finally had enough

. . . .

*W*hy would anyone in his or her right mind want to revisit the Word for Windows Setup program? I thought that Setup's sole purpose in life was to copy WinWord from a bunch of floppy disks or a CD-ROM onto your hard disk. You mean there's more?

Yup. There are several reasons why you might want to run WinWord's Setup program after you've installed Word.

When you first install Word, you are asked how much of WinWord to install: all of it (*complete installation*), as little of it as possible (*minimum installation*), or a custom combination of features (*custom installation*).

If you picked the minimum installation option, you may later realize that some really important WinWord features — like the MindBender game that comes in the MACROS7.DOT template — got left out. Never fear! You can run Word Setup to install the missing feature.

On the other hand, you may have opted for a complete installation, but now you're running low on disk space and you realize that you never use paltry clip art. By running Word Setup to remove the clip art, you can free up about 5MB of disk space. You can free up more disk space by removing other parts of Word.

Running Word Setup

Note: Word is distributed in several packages, by itself or in combination with other products. For example, Microsoft Office bundles Word with Excel and PowerPoint; Microsoft Office Professional adds the database program Access. To further confuse things, Word is available on diskettes as well as on CD-ROM. To simplify this chapter, I assume you obtained Word as a part of Office or Office Pro on CD-ROM. Fear not because the procedures for running Word's setup program are similar.

To run the Microsoft Office Setup program to add or remove optional features, follow these steps:

1. **Quit Word and all other Office programs.**

   You can't run the Office Setup program while any of the Office programs are running.

2. **Find the Office CD-ROM disc and insert it in the CD-ROM drive.**

   Or, if you purchased Word by itself or in some other bundle, find the appropriate CD-ROM. If you purchased Word on diskettes, clear off a place on one end of your desk where you can stack the diskettes.

3. **Click the Start button; then select Settings⇨Control Panel.**

   The Control Panel will appear.

4. **Double-click the Add/Remove Programs icon.**

   The Add/Remove Programs Properties dialog box appears, as shown in Figure 31-1.

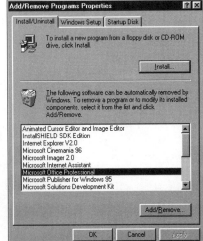

Figure 31-1:
The Add/
Remove
Programs
Properties
dialog box.

5. Select Microsoft Word.

If Microsoft Word doesn't appear in the list, look for the package that you purchased that included Word. For example, in Figure 31-1, I've selected Microsoft Office Professional.

6. Click Add/Remove.

The Setup program starts, displaying a screen similar to the one in Figure 31-2. (The screen will vary a bit depending on which package you obtained Word with.)

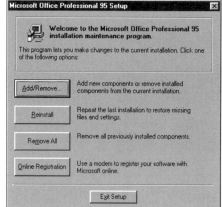

Figure 31-2: The Setup program.

7. Click the Add/Remove button.

Setup displays the Maintenance dialog box, shown in Figure 31-3. Each major program option is listed in the Options list.

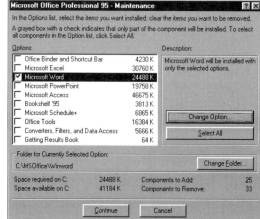

Figure 31-3: The Maintenance dialog box.

8. **To add or remove an option, click it's check box.**

9. **To add or remove some but not all of an option's features, click the option and then click the Change Option button.**

   A dialog box appears listing the individual settings for the option you chose. For example, Figure 31-4 shows the dialog box that appears when you select Microsoft Word and click the Change Option button.

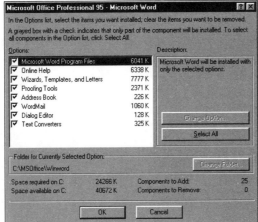

Figure 31-4:
Changing
Word's
setup
options.

10. **Check or uncheck the options you want to add or remove; then click OK.**

11. **Click the Continue button to add or remove the selected options.**

   Setup will follow with several annoying prompts asking if you're sure you know what you're doing.

If you dare run Setup, keep the following important points in mind:

   ✔ If you're using floppy disks, you'll be asked to insert specific disks as they are needed. Do what you're told, and no one will get hurt.

   ✔ Always keep your original installation disks in a safe location. If you need to return to the Setup program — and eventually you will (trust me) — you'll need the installation disks.

   ✔ As you check or uncheck various options, you can monitor the amount of additional disk space required or the amount of disk space to be freed up.

   ✔ If WinWord is acting strangely, it's remotely possible that one of its files has been accidentally deleted. Running Setup and clicking the Reinstall button can fix this problem.

Chapter 32

Beware the Dreaded Document Virus

• •

In This Chapter

▶ What a document virus is

▶ How to tell if you have one

▶ How to get rid of the darn thing

• •

*L*ast summer, as I was finishing up another book for IDG Books Worldwide, I began to notice something strange about the way Word for Windows was behaving. I couldn't change the template attached to my documents, and I couldn't save my documents under a different format. I soon realized that many of my documents had somehow been switched from normal Word document format to template format. In other words, even though my documents all had filenames that ended with .doc, they were actually templates rather than documents.

An old Word for Windows trick is to create a template and then rename it to a filename that has a DOC extension. The templates will then appear to be documents, with just a few restrictions: You won't be able to attach a template to the document because the document already *is* a template; and you won't be able to use the Save As command to change the file format.

Why go to all this trouble? Because template files have several capabilities that normal document files do not, most notably the capability to carry macros. In particular, the template-documents can carry an AutoOpen macro which runs automatically when the template-document is opened.

Computer virus experts have known for years that application programs such as Microsoft Word, which support AutoOpen macros, are wide open targets for virus infections. All one has to do is create a template-document with an AutoOpen macro that contains the instructions necessary to "infect" other documents — that is, to copy the AutoOpen macro itself into other documents. In fact, the programming required to create such a virus is pretty trivial. Any competent programmer can create such a virus in a matter of hours.

A support engineer from Microsoft suggested that I might have such a virus. He advised me to look for the following macros in my Normal.dot template:

- ✔ AAAZAO
- ✔ AAAZFS
- ✔ AutoOpen
- ✔ FileSaveAs
- ✔ Payload

Sure enough, all five of these macros were present in my Normal.dot. My computer had been infected by a new virus, now known as "Winword.Concept Virus" or the "Prank Macro," as Microsoft prefers to call it.

After your Normal.dot template has been infected by Winword.Concept, any document you subsequently save is stored in template format and carries the macros necessary to infect other systems. As a result, this virus can be spread merely by sharing Word documents. If you save a Word document and then pass the document to a friend, whether over a network or via diskettes, your friend's system will be infected when he or she opens the document. The old adage that viruses can only be transmitted via executable programs no longer applies.

Fortunately, the Winword.Concept virus is pretty benign. It does manage to convert your document files to template format, which is definitely a major inconvenience. But other than that, it doesn't do any real damage to your computer. The Winword.Concept virus was apparently created just to prove the point that a virus could be spread in this way.

However, the macro does provide the mechanism of delivering a "payload," perhaps to demonstrate that the virus writer could just as easily have done some major damage. Take a look at the Payload macro which is copied to Normal.dot by the Winword.Concept virus:

```
Sub MAIN
    REM That's enough to prove my point
End Sub
```

The Payload macro is merely an ominous comment statement that doesn't do anything. It could just as easily consist of statements that delete files from your hard disk. So even though the Winword.Concept virus isn't malicious, other such viruses can be.

Is it a virus or a prank?

Microsoft insists that Winword.Concept is not a virus. They refer to it instead as a "prank macro." Their rationale for this is that Winword.Concept isn't a true virus, in that it doesn't spread by attaching itself to executable program files.

I disagree. The technical definition of a virus is any program that is (1) self-replicating and (2) spreads by means of attaching itself to an executable program that serves as a "host." Winword.Concept easily meets these two criteria: It is self-replicating (it can create copies of

itself), and it is spread by attaching itself to a document file that serves as a host. For all intents and purposes, Word templates (and templates masquerading as documents) *are* a type executable program file, in that they can contain executable programs in the form of macros.

Calling this virus a "prank macro" is kind of like congress referring to a tax increase as "revenue enhancement." As they say, if it walks like a duck and quacks like a duck, it's a duck.

Determining Whether You Have the Winword.Concept Virus

When the Winword.Concept virus first strikes, it displays the dialog box shown in Figure 32-1.

Figure 32-1:
The dialog box shows up when the Winword. Concept virus infects your computer.

If you ever see this dialog box immediately after opening a document, drop everything, reread this chapter, and remove the virus before the infection spreads.

If for some reason this dialog box slips by unnoticed (amazingly, it does — even I didn't notice it), you can find out if you have been infected by the virus by choosing the Tools⇨Macro command and looking for macros with the following names:

- ✔ AAAZAO
- ✔ AAAZFS
- ✔ AutoOpen
- ✔ FileSaveAs
- ✔ Payload

If your Normal.dot template contains these macros, you have been infected.

Removing the Infection

You can easily remove the virus from your Normal.dot template by deleting the five macros listed in the previous section. To remove the virus from an infected document, delete the macros and then use the Save As command to save the document in document format rather than in template format.

Microsoft has created a file called Scanprot.dot, which removes the virus infection for you. If you have access to the Internet, you can obtain a copy of this file from the Microsoft Word Home Page located at http://www.microsoft.com/msoffice/msword. You can also obtain it from CompuServe, AmericaOnline, and The Microsoft Network.

Preventing Document Virus Infections

The Scanprot.dot file installs macros in your Normal.dot template to prevent your Normal.dot from being infected. This file works pretty well against the Winword.Concept virus, but it won't be long before more robust document viruses start to appear. A simple change to the Winword.Concept macro, which any experienced WordBasic programmer can make, will circumvent Scanprot.dot's method of preventing infection.

The root cause of the problem is the very existence of AutoOpen macros. Any time you open a document, you need to realize that that document may actually be a template that contains an AutoOpen macro. The solution is to disable AutoOpen macros. You can take this action by creating a macro named AutoExec in your Normal.dot template. Follow these steps:

1. **Choose the Tools⇨Macro command.**

2. **Choose Normal.dot (Global Template) in the Macros Available In list box.**

3. **Type AutoExec in the Macro Name field.**

4. Click **C**reate.

5. Type in this macro exactly as follows:

```
Sub MAIN
   DisableAutoMacros
   MsgBox "Auto Macros are disabled to prevent virus infec-
          tions!"
End Sub
```

6. Choose the **F**ile⇨**C**lose command. When asked if you want to keep the changes to the macro, click **Y**es.

7. Exit Word and then restart Word.

If you routinely use documents that contain legitimate AutoOpen, AutoNew, or AutoClose macros, you need a different approach. Rather than disable all Auto macros, you can bypass the AutoOpen and AutoClose macros on a document-by-document basis when you open and close documents. Here's how:

✔ To bypass the AutoOpen macro, hold down the Shift key while opening the document.

✔ To bypass the AutoClose macro, hold down the Shift key while closing the document.

As a precaution, I recommend that you get into the habit of holding down the Shift key whenever you open or close a document.

Chapter 33

The Easter Egg

*A*rtists sign their paintings. Authors get their names on the covers of their books. Journalists have their bylines.

What about lowly programmers?

You won't find the names of the programmers who created the software that you know and love on the outside of the box, in the manuals, or on the backs of the floppy disks or CDs. Not wanting to be left out, programmers started the tradition of leaving their mark on their work long ago.

The earliest programmers carved their initials on the back of Neolithic counting pebbles using primitive stone tools. Today's programmers usually bury their signatures deep inside the program, forcing you to follow an elaborate sequence of unlikely commands to find their hidden treasures. These signatures are sometimes called *Easter eggs*.

Word's Easter Egg

The programmers who wrote Word for Windows 95 are no exception, of course. To reveal the hidden credits screen in Word, follow these steps if you can:

1. **Click the Underline New button to create a new document based on the Normal template.**

2. **Type the word "Blue" in the new document.**

3. **Highlight the text you just typed and press Ctrl+B to make it boldface.**

4. **Summon the Format⇨Font command and set the Color setting to Blue.**

5. **Press the End key to move the insertion point to the end of the line; then press the Enter key.**

6. **Summon the Help⇨About command**

   The About Microsoft Word dialog box appears, as shown in Figure 33-1. This is normal; nothing unusual yet.

Figure 33-1:
The About
Microsoft
Word dialog
box.

7. **Click the Word icon on the left side of the dialog box.**

   The hidden credits window appears.

Wait for a moment. Soon the credits screen will begin to scroll through a complete list of the Word development team.

   ✔ My, a lot of people worked on Word.

   ✔ If you get bored, press Esc to dismiss the credits screen.

   ✔ Try to be patient. Wait until the end and you'll see some interesting credits. You may even recognize one of the names.

   ✔ Try clicking the credits display as it scrolls.

Index

• E •

● *T* ●

☐ # YES!

Please keep me informed about IDG's World of Computer Knowledge.
Send me the latest IDG Books catalog.